Socio-economic Impact Study with Concurrent Evaluation on Agricultural/Horticulture based Schemes

Socio-economic Impact Study with Concurrent Evaluation on Agricultural/Horticulture based Schemes

Subhrabaran Das
Professor & Head
Department of Economics
Tripura University (A Central University)
Suryamaninagar, Tripura (W), Tripura

ALLIED PUBLISHERS PVT. LTD.
Noida • Mumbai • Kolkata • Chennai • Bangalore

ALLIED PUBLISHERS PRIVATE LIMITED

D-5, Sector-2, **Noida**–201 301
Ph. Nos.: 0120-4320295/2542557/4352866 • E-mail: delhi.books@alliedpublishers.com

17 Chittaranjan Avenue, **Kolkata**–700072
Ph.: 033-22129618 • E-mail: cal.books@alliedpublishers.com

15 J.N. Heredia Marg, Ballard Estate, **Mumbai**–400001
Ph.: 022-42126969 • E-mail: mumbai.books@alliedpublishers.com

No. 25/10, Commander-in-Chief Road, Ethiraj Lane (Next to Post Office)
Egmore, **Chennai**–600008
Ph.: 044-28223938 • E-mail: chennai.books@alliedpublishers.com

P.B. No. 9932, No. 15, 3rd Floor (Next to Vijaya Bank), 5th Cross, Gandhinagar, Karnataka,
Bangalore–560009, Ph.: 080-41530285 / 22386239
E-mail: bngl.journals@alliedpublishers.com / apsabng@airtelmail.in

Website: www.alliedpublishers.com

ISBN: 978-93-90951-62-8

Published by Sunil Sachdev and printed by Ravi Sachdev at Allied Publishers Pvt. Ltd.,
D-5, Sector-2, Noida–201 301

Preface

Agriculture is the primary base of Indian economy though there is a vast diversity in land pattern due to diverse topographic region. But the growth rate of agricultural sector is not impressive; it is below four per cent in India which is lowest in comparison to secondary sector and tertiary sector. The agricultural farmers are fighting for their survival mainly due to high cost of production, agricultural credit at a higher rate of interest from the private loan provider and marketing problem due to non-availability of minimum support price. Apart from that sometimes adverse weather and climatic condition farmers are facing huge loss in agriculture. If loss occurs in agriculture then achieving sustainable development goals (SDGs) especially Goal 1 and Goal 2 will be affected. Goal 1 envisages end of poverty in all its forms everywhere and Goal 2 envisages zero hunger and Achieve food security and improved nutrition and promote sustainable agriculture. In order to achieve the sustainable development goals, Govt. of India has launched different agricultural and horticultural scheme to protect the loss of farmers. These schemes are implemented in the states of India with the initiatives of the state governments. Different schemes have different objectives such as to strengthen research—extension—farmer linkages, to provide timely and adequate credit to farmers to meet their production credit needs, to increase production of rice, wheat, pulses, coarse cereals (Maize and Barley) and nutritious cereals through area expansion and productivity enhancement, to supplement the financial needs of all landholding farmers' families, to provide insurance coverage, to stabilise the income of farmers to ensure their continuance in farming, to create required agro-infrastructure, etc. Though different schemes have different objectives, but the basic objective is same to improve the livelihood condition of the farmers.

The study titled "Socio-economic impact study with concurrent evaluation on Agriculture/Horticulture based Schemes" is undertaken for the impact assessment of the Agricultural/Horticultural based schemes given to the tribal beneficiaries belong to the State of Tripura for the improvement of their livelihood. The project is an impact assessment project sponsored by the Tribal Welfare Department, Govt. of Tripura. There are different chemeson agriculture/horticulture launched by the Central Govt. time to time which are implemented by the state government in order to improve the livelihood condition of the tribal. The basic objective of this project is to assess whether the tribal farmers are benefitted or not from the different schemes implemented by the government and to assess the impact of these schemes in order to improve the socio-economic condition of the tribal farmers.

The study is based on the primary data which is collected from the six districts out of eight districts in Tripura. From these six districts, fourteen blocks has been selected. From these blocks, a total of 500 beneficiaries have been selected randomly. On the basis of their response, a final outcome of the project is arrived and finally a conclusion has been done. This study would be beneficial to the government for taking the appropriate policy decisions further and it would be a bench mark to the researchers who will work on the tribal agriculture.

This study would not be possible until the full support of Tribal Welfare Department, Govt. of Tripura. So, I would like to thank Shri L.T. Darlong, Director, Tribal Welfare Department, Govt. of Tripura, Shri A.H. Jamatia, Addl. Director, Tribal Welfare Department, Govt. of Tripura, and Shri Saswata Sen, Former Joint Director, and Shri Sukanta Paul, Senior Research Officer, Tribal Welfare Department, Govt. of Tripura and also to other staffs of Tribal Welfare Department who are associated with this project and provide their kind help for the project. I am also thankful to my research scholar Ariful Hoque and Kiran Bhowmik for their active help. I am thankful to my field staffs specially Badal Debnath, Swarup Chandan Roy, Sukanti Roy, Shankar, Kaushik, Pradip, Sushanta, Birakta for their active help to complete the study.

Finally, I am thankful to my father, father-in-law, mother-in-law, wife Susmita and my beloved son Somsubhra for encouraging me and help to complete the work.

Subhrabaran Das

Contents

List of Tables

List of Figures

List of Abbreviations

Abbreviations	*Full Form*
AAI	Average Annual Income
ACP	Agriculture Commerce Policy
AEI	Average Expenditure Index
AII	Agricultural Income Index
APEDA	Agricultural and Processed Food Products Export Development Authority
APL	Above Poverty Level
ATMA	Agricultural Technology Management Agency
AYUSH	Ayurveda, Yoga and Naturopathy, Unani, Siddha and Homeopathy
BPL	Below Poverty Level
CDI	Consumer Durable goods Index
CHC	Community Health Centre
CLI	Cultivated Land Index
eNAM	National Agriculture Market
EPI	Economic Profile Index
GDP	Gross Domestic Product
GPI	Gender Parity Index
HII	Horticultural Income Index
HMNEH	Horticulture Mission for North East &Himalayan States
HMNEH	Horticulture Mission for North East and Himalayan States
IS	Inorganic Sugarcane
IWMP	Integrated Watershed Management Programmes
KCC	Kisan Credit Card
MGNREGA	Mahatma Gandhi National Rural Employment Guarantee Act
MIDH	Mission for Integrated Development of Horticulture
MSP	Minimum Support Price

Abbreviations	*Full Form*
NABARD	National Bank for Agricultural and Rural Development
NFSM	National Food Security Mission
NHB	National Horticultural Board
NHM	National Horticulture Mission
NMMI	National Mission on Micro Irrigation
NMSA	National Mission For Sustainable Agriculture
NRLM	National Rural Livelihood Mission
NSSO	National Sample Survey Organization
NTFP	Non-Timber Forest Produce
OS	Organic Sugarcane
PHC	Primary Health Centre
PKVY	Paramparagat Krishi Vikas Yojana
PMFVY	Pradhan Mantri Fasal Vikas Yojana
PM-KISAN	Pradhan Mantri Kisan Samadhan Nidhi
PMKSY	Pradhan Mantri Krishi Sinchayee Yojana
PM-KUSUM	Pradhan Mantri Kishan Urja Surakshaevam Utthaan Mahabhiyan
PNB	Punjab National Bank
PSE	Producers' Subsidy Equivalent
PVTGs	Particularly Vulnerable Tribal Groups
RKVY	Rashtriya Krishi Vikas Yojana
SCA	Special Central Assistance
SDGs	Sustainable Development Goals
SHM	State Horticulture Mission
SLCCCI	State Level Co-ordination Committee on Crop Insurance
TADI	Tribal Agricultural Development Index
TSP	Tribal Sub Plan
TSS	Tribal Sub-Scheme
TTAADC	Tripura Tribal Areas Autonomous District Council
WPRI	Work Participation Rate Index

Executive Summary

1. Introduction

Agriculture is the backbone of Indian economy because more than 70 per cent of the rural households depend on agriculture. Though there is a huge diversity in India in terms of different topographic region and different land pattern, but agriculture contributes about 17 per cent to the total GDP and provides employment to over 60 per cent of the population. Presently, the growth rate of agricultural sector is not impressive; it is below four per cent in India which is lowest in comparison to secondary sector and tertiary sector. The agricultural farmers are fighting for their survival mainly due to high cost of production, agricultural credit at a higher rate of interest from the private loan provider, marketing problem due to non-availability of minimum support price and of course adverse as well as highly volatile weather and climatic condition. In order to make the sustainable development in the agricultural sector as well as to improve the farmers' livelihood condition Government of India has implemented different schemes time to time. Most of these schemes are centrally sponsored scheme with a ratio of state liability 90:10. The basic objective of all schemes implemented by the government is to improve the agricultural sector and farmers' standard of living so that SDGs Goal 1 and 2 can be achieved. These schemes are also useful to provide supportive services to the farmers at reasonable prices including supply of seeds, fertilizer, irrigation, machinery and equipment and loans. It is also useful to provide appropriate pricing policy such as minimum support price (MSP) to increase the income of the farmers. It is also useful to strengthen the biological protection of the crops, creation of storage facilities, and to provide the appropriate risk management measures such as crop insurance to the farmers for providing timely compensation. But, a large section of marginal farmers are not aware about these schemes, and as a result of this, a significant portion of farmers especially the marginal farmers do not avail the benefits of these schemes.

More emphasis on agriculture can provide also the employment opportunity to rural agricultural and non-agricultural labourers. Increase in production of agricultural and horticultural products can fulfill not only the domestic demand but also increase the exports of it. However, poor performance of agriculture can also hamper the industrial performance because lesser agricultural production will increase the agricultural price and as a result terms of trade will go against the industrial sector which will affect the economy finally.

2. Necessity of the Study

Tripura is one of the small and poor states among the North-eastern states belonging in a remote corner of the country. Topographically, the state can be divided into seven distinguishable features viz; hill range, hillock (tillas), valley, lunga (low lying areas between the hillocks), flat land, river, and lake. Out of the total area, about 60 per cent consists of hills, hillocks, and hilly terrains. About one-third of people are belonging to 19 indigenous tribal communities. To understand the backwardness, it is necessary to explore the condition of these vulnerable endogenous groups in this state. As per the 2011 census, there is approximately 31.8 per cent tribes belong to Tripura; of which Tripuri is a major tribal group that consists of approximately 50 per cent population of the total tribal population. The state faces some specific challenges in pursuit of the Sustainable Development Goals (SDGs) due to geographical isolation, communication bottleneck, lack of proper marketing infrastructures, limited plain land for agriculture, and adverse climatic condition, and as a result process of development is seriously hampered. The economy of the state is based on agriculture with low capital formation, low per-capita income, high rate of unemployment, high incidence of poverty, and high central dependency. The Tribal Welfare Department, Govt. of Tripura has taken some measures through different schemes and programme to promote the socio-economic development of the tribal though these are not sufficient. As the tribal economy is based on agriculture and horticulture, the Central Govt. has also taken different agricultural and horticultural development programme for the income generation of the tribal community. To materialise the scheme Govt. has selected some beneficiaries to facilitate these agricultural schemes and programme. This study attempts to evaluate these schemes or programmes and to examine the impact of these schemes on their socio-economic life.

3. Objective of the Study

The study is focused mainly on two aspects viz; evaluation of the agriculture and horticulture based schemes and impact of the schemes on their socio-economic life. The following objectives can be framed based on these aspects.

- To investigate the socio-economic problems that the rural tribal people are facing in Tripura.
- To examine the socio-economic status of rural tribal people across different tribal community.
- To examine the productivity of different agriculture/horticulture production who have got the benefits of the govt. scheme.
- To examine the impact and concurrent evaluation on Agriculture/ Horticulture based schemes taken by the government on income and employment generation of the beneficiaries.

The study investigates the status of tribal people and also investigates what problem they are facing regularly. The government has taken a policy of income and employment generation through agriculture/horticulture based scheme for the tribal who belongs to vulnerable sections of the society. The study also focuses whether the productivity increases or not and the benefits are percolated to the stakeholders properly or not. In this regard the proposed study focuses on impact and concurrent evaluation of the agriculture/ horticulture based scheme and impact of this scheme on the socio-economic livelihoods of the beneficiary stakeholders.

4. Research Methodology

The methodology for this study is divided into two parts viz; methodology for data collection and methodology for data analysis. The study is based on both secondary and primary data. The list of total beneficiaries has been collected from the scheme provider (secondary source). Secondary information regarding different types of agricultural beneficiaries and list of beneficiaries over last five years is taken from different Govt. Office such as Tribal Welfare Department, TTAADC, Zonal Offices under TTAADC, etc.

The list of total beneficiaries has been collected from the scheme provider (secondary source).

Primary data has been collected through using three stages Purposive Random Sampling method. In Tripura, there are eight districts. Out of these districts, six districts (75 percent) have been selected in the first stage. In the second stage, two blocks have been selected from Gomati (viz; Killa and Matabari), West Tripura (viz; Jirania and Mandai), Sepahijala (viz; Jampuijala and Nalchar) and Khowai district (viz; Kalyanpur and Teliamura); however three blocks have been selected from Dhalai (viz; Ambassa, Manu and Salema) and South Tripura district (viz; B.C. Nagar, Rajnagar, and Rupaichhari). A total of 14 blocks have been selected from six districts. Finally, sample beneficiaries have been selected at random from the selected blocks. The selection of beneficiaries in the final stage is taken from the list of beneficiaries under the Tribal Sub Plan (TSP) collected from secondary sources. Out of these surveyed six districts, 100 sample households have been collected from the Dhalai, South Tripura, Gomati and West Tripura district; however, 50 sample households' data have been collected from Khowai and Sepahijala districts of Tripura. A total of 500 beneficiaries have been selected from the total beneficiaries of the different schemes and from different tribal community under Tribal Sub Plan of the 14 blocks.

For data analysis advanced statistical and econometric techniques have been used. To investigate the proper implementation process of the schemes, tabular and graphical presentation can be done by collecting the information from secondary sources and that a cross verification can be done from primary sources. To examine the socio-economic status of the tribal people a comprehensive area-wise and community-wise socio-economic index have been constructed by using Dimension index.

The formula for the dimension index is already mentioned in the earlier.

$$DI = \frac{\text{Actual} - \text{Minimum}}{\text{Maximum} - \text{Minimum}}$$

A composite Socio-economic Index (SEI) is calculated be taking a weighted average of two dimensions viz; social dimension and economic dimension. The social dimension consists with eight indicators viz; level of education, housing type, sanitation type, gas connection, area of bastu, housing space, water source and distance of water source from their house. The formula for Social Index (SI) is given in the following equation.

$$SI = \frac{\sum_{i=1}^{8} X_i}{8}$$

where, *X*'s are index value of different social indicators.

The economic dimension consists with eight indicators viz; annual average income, economic profile, work participation rate, availability of consumer durable goods, average expenditure, cultivated land, horticultural income and agricultural income. The formula for Economic Index is given in the following equation.

$$EI = \frac{\sum_{i=1}^{8} Y_i}{8}$$

where, *Y*'s are index value of different economic indicators.

From these two equations a composite Socio-economic Index (SEI) can be constructed in the following.

$$SEI_i = \frac{SI_i + EI_i}{2}$$

In order to check the impact of agricultural schemes for improving their average annual income, paired t-test is used.

5. Findings of the Study

The Tripura Tribal Areas Autonomous District Council was constituted under the Seventh Schedule to the Constitution of India. The Tripura Tribal Areas Autonomous District Council Bill, 1979 was unanimously passed by the Tripura Legislative Assembly on March 23, 1979. The Tripura Tribal Areas Autonomous District Council was constituted in January 15, 1982 through voting by secret ballot and the elected members were sworn in on January 18, 1982. Subsequently, the Constitution of India had been amended by a Bill and it was passed in the Indian Parliament on August 23, 1984 for introduction of the Sixth Schedule of the Constitution in India. The total area of the TTAADC is 7,132.56 sq. km. which covers about 68 per cent area of the state. The TTAADC is governed by a council which has 30 members. Out of 30 members, 28 members are elected through adult suffrage, while 2 members are nominated by the Governor of Tripura. Out of 28 elected seats, 25 are reserved for Scheduled Tribes and 3 for other categories. There are 23 rural development blocks in ADC area. Out of 23 blocks, eight blocks are in West Tripura, four are in North Tripura, seven are in Dhalai and rest four blocks are in the South Tripura district. The development programme of the Council is presently implemented by the four Zonal Development Offices and 33 Sub-zonal Development Offices within the TTDDAC areas. At grassroots level, there are 587 Village committees functioning as primary units as institutions of local self-governance similar to Gram Panchayats in Non- ADC areas.

From the secondary information, it is observed that health infrastructure is very poor in the TTAADC area as there are only two hospital and one health sub-centre which is not sufficient for the area of 7132.56 square km. However, the educational infrastructure is relatively better than health infrastructure.

From the primary survey, it is found that male population is much higher than the female percentage of population. The sex ratio among these selected 14 blocks of Tripura is found very poor in B.C. Nagar block and Rajnagar block of South Tripura district. It is observed that 64.20 percent of the sample households are Hindu, followed by 20.60 Christian households and remaining 15.20 percent households are the believers of Buddhist religion. Buddhist believers are mainly found in Manu and Rupaichhari block.

From the primary survey, it is found that respondents' level of education is very poor. 37.80 per cent of them are illiterate, 28.60 per cent have only primary level of education. After secondary education, the enrolment rate in higher classes is found to be very poor. As the survey data indicates, 4.40 per cent of the respondents have completed higher secondary level of education and a mere 0.40 per cent is found to have studied up to graduate level.

It is found that housing condition of the beneficiary farmers is very poor. More than 76 per cent households are living in kaccha houses and only 16 per cent live in pucca houses and rest are in semi-pucca houses. Most of the houses have only two rooms and they are living in very small area of house and their average area of bastu is in only around one kani of land. Though most of them are living in kaccha house, but their sanitation condition is improved. It is found that 68.6 per cent households are using semi-pucca sanitation facilities and only 17 per cent households have kaccha sanitation facilities.

It is also observed that out of the 500 sample households, 29.2 per cent of the households are living under the above poverty line (APL) category, 35.2 per cent are living under the below poverty line (BPL) category and only 19 per cent are Ad-hoc families. The rest of the households belong to either Antyodaya (15.6 per cent) or Arnapurna (one per cent) category.

Majority (79.2 per cent) of the sample households having the access to supply water for their drinking and only 11.4 per cent of the households collect their drinking water from tube wells. It is worth mentioning that 5.6 per cent of the total sample households still depend on unsafe sources of drinking water such as pond. 1.6 per cent of the respondents have reported that they rely on other sources like hand pump, use of motor in house etc. for their drinking water.

It is important to note that houses of all beneficiaries are electrified and 86.4 per cent households have Ujjala gas connection. It is observed that out of the total sample households, 75.2 per cent have reported to possess television, 97.6 per cent possess smart phone and 69.8 per cent of the households have reported to possess bicycle.

Most of the beneficiary farmers are marginal farmers (29 per cent) and they have only up to one kani of land. 26.2 per cent farmers have only 1–2 kani of own land, 19 per cent respondents have 2–3 kani of own agricultural land, 12.6 per cent have 3–4 kani own agricultural land and very few (only 0.60 per cent) have own land of above five kani agricultural land.

Most of the farmers have livestock for their both own consumption as well as additional supportive income for the family. It is observed that poultry, piggery, cow, goat, duck and broiler are the common livestock almost in all blocks. Rearing of Buffalo and sheep are very rare in the study area.

It is found that out of the total production of rice, the maximum 45 per cent rice is produced by the small farmers, which is under the production limit of 1000–2000 Kg. The next highest 31 per cent rice is produced by the marginal farmers which are under the lowest production limit of (up to 1000 Kg.) which is followed by the production limit of 2000–3000 Kg. (22 per cent) and only 1.80 per cent production belongs to the production group of above 3000 Kg.

It is found that out of the total sample beneficiaries only small percentage beneficiaries are doing horticultural practices and mainly they are doing rubber plantation, banana and betel nut. It is observed that only 14.40 per cent households have rubber plantation, 1.80 per cent households have betel nut and only 0.40 per cent households are doing banana. It is observed that a sizable amount of production and income is found from the rubber plantation. A total of 47159 kg of rubber production (rubber sheet) comes out annually from 72 beneficiaries and they earned total revenue Rs. 59,62,050.00 per annum. A total of 168 kg betel nut is produced annually by nine sample beneficiaries and they have earned revenue of Rs. 56,400.00 per annum.

It is found that most of the beneficiary farmers earn up to Rs. 10000 income and between Rs. 10000–20000 income group from their agriculture. 29.4 per cent sample beneficiary farmers earn up to Rs. 10000 income by selling their agricultural product and 29.6 per cent sample beneficiary farmers earn Rs. 10000–20000 income, 17.6 per cent farmers earn Rs. 20000–30000 income and 13.4 per cent farmers earn Rs. 30000–40000 income by selling their agricultural products. Only very negligible percentage of farmers earns more than Rs. 50000 income by selling their agricultural products.

It is found that monthly average household expenditure on food is Rs. 3186.55, which is followed by average expenditure on gas (Rs. 784.25), average educational expenditure (Rs. 568.60), average mobile expenditure (Rs. 391.35), average electricity expenditure (Rs. 245.24) etc.

The socio-economic status of B.C. Nagar block of South Tripura district is best compare to other selected blocks which is followed Jirania block (0.625) of West Tripura which is followed by Matabari block (0.605) of Gomati district, Jampuijala block (0.575) of Sepahijala district, Kalyanpur block (0.504) of Khowai district etc. However, the worst socio-economic condition is found in Mandai block (0.330) of West Tripura district. The socio-economic condition is also poor in Rupaichhari block (0.349) which is ranked 13th, Ambassa is ranked 12th and Manu is ranked 11th.

Out of the total operational holdings in Tripura, 87.95 per cent holding belong to 'marginal' farmers, holding less than one hectare of land, and they operate 52.80 per cent of the total operated area.

Rice is the principal staple food in Tripura and is cultivated in 54.54 per cent of the total cropped area. It is grown in both hilly and valley regions of the state. Jhum or shifting cultivation is practiced in the hill region and settled farming in the plains.

Maize is the second most important food grain grown in Tripura. It is used both for direct consumption and as well as feed ingredient for pig and poultry farming of the state. The area under maize production has increased from 2150 hectares in 2005–06 to 14635 hectares in 2019–20 with a growth rate of 18.68 per cent.

The total production of oilseeds in Tripura is found to increase significantly along with increase in area. Groundnut, sesamum and rape/mustard are the major important oilseed crops grown in Tripura. The area under groundnut cultivation is found to increase from 379 hectares in 2005–06 to 2367 hectares in 2019–20. The highest oilseed production has been recorded in 2019–20.

The suitable agro-climatic conditions of Tripura also favour the cultivation of different types of non-food grain crops like jute, mesta, cotton and sugarcane in the state. It is observed that there is a gradual decline in the area coverage of jute while production is showing an increasing trend.

Cotton is another important fibre crop being cultivated in Tripura. It is found that there is a continuous decline in both area and production of this crop. The decline in area under cotton cultivation seems due to switching over to other remunerative short duration crops like maize, sesamum etc.

Sugarcane is another important agricultural crop grown in Tripura but over the years its production has declined along with decline in area.

The good agro-climatic conditions, deep fertile soils, subtropical humid climate with abundance of rainfall offer tremendous scope for the development of horticulture in Tripura. Among the important horticultural crops, pineapple grown in Tripura is widely acclaimed as the best in the country.

There is a huge potential of growing fruits and plantation crops like litchi, mango, pineapple, orange, guava, jackfruit, banana, lemon, cashew nut, coconut and areca nut commercially, which may cater to the needs of other North Eastern States and neighbouring country like Bangladesh as well. Recent development in Indo-Bangla relationship has also opened up new avenues for export possibilities.

The trend of production of mango is found to increase along with increase in area. Among the different tropical and sub-tropical fruits, pineapple grown in Tripura is widely known for its excellent quality. Since 2018 pineapple is being exported to many other countries.

Orange is another important fruit which is significant in terms of increase in area and production. Jackfruit is another important fruit grown in Tripura. The agro-climatic conditions, fertile and acidic soil with abundant rainfall favour the cultivation of jackfruits in Tripura. It is one of the major commercial fruit crops in Tripura and has high local demand. However, the area under jackfruit cultivation is found to decline from 8645 hectares in 2005–06 to 5487 hectares in 2019–20 with a negative growth of 2.11 per cent.

Cashew nut is a commercially important plantation crop being cultivated in Tripura, which offers considerable scope for enhancing the state economy by generating more income and employment potential. The state has nearly 5,000 registered cashew nut growers, out of which 3,000 are from Rajnagar alone.

There are a large number of indigenous fruits such as mosambi, berry, palm, jamun, bael etc. being cultivated in Tripura.

Tripura occupies a pivotal position in India's rubber map in terms of relative shares in area, production as well as potential area identified for natural rubber cultivation.

The Govt. of India has launched the several agricultural and horticultural schemes throughout the nation to improve the agricultural scenario of the nation as well as to improve the economic condition. But only few of these schemes are successfully implemented especially in Tripura. PM-Kishan is most important scheme in Tripura and which is successfully implemented in the state. Pradhan Mantri

Krishi Sinchayee Yojana (PMKSY) is another successful scheme implemented in Tripura and through this scheme irrigation has been developed in the state. Rashtriya Krishi Vikas Yojana (RKVY) scheme is also another important scheme through which the agro-infra-structure has been developed in the state. The farmers are benefited from this scheme; however there is a huge gap between allocation of fund and release of fund. There a high potential to develop the agro-infrastructure if the overtime gap between allocation of fund and release of fund reduces. The more release of fund under this scheme would develop the storage facilities and market facilities such as more mandi can be constructed and as a result farmers can be benefited. National Food Security Mission is also another important scheme implemented in Tripura.

From the field survey, it is found that the farmers are received the benefit mainly from three schemes viz; PM-Kishan, RKVY and NFSM. It is observed that maximum average benefit of the RKVY scheme is received by the beneficiary households from Matabari block, followed by Killa block, B.C. Nagar block, Taliamura, Kalyanpur etc. whereas the minimum average amount of money is received by the beneficiary households from the Nalchar block. In case of NFSM scheme, the beneficiaries from Kalyanpur block of Khowai district have received the highest amount of benefit which is followed by Teliamura block, Rupaichhari block, B.C. Nagar block, Jirania block etc.

Finally, it is also concluded that agricultural schemes have positive impact on change in agricultural income of the beneficiary households in the study area. The impact is also positive and significant on change in households' income. However, beneficiary farmers are facing some serious problems in producing agricultural/horticultural products such as irrigation problem as they belong to tilla land, problem of getting credit at normal rate of interest, poor road connectivity, high transport charge, lack of vehicles, lack of proper and complete market information, lack of marketing facilities and lack of awareness about different govt. agricultural/horticultural schemes etc.

6. Major Findings at a Glance

- Out of total 500 sample beneficiaries, 64.20 per cent beneficiaries belong to the Hindu community which is followed by Christian (20.60 percent), and Buddhist (15.20 percent).
- Out of the total population of the sample households, 48.7 percent are female and sex ratio is 950 per 1000 male population.
- Level of education among the beneficiaries is very poor. 37.80 per cent of them are illiterate, 28.60 per cent have only primary level of education. The enrolment rate in higher classes is found to be very poor.
- Housing condition of the beneficiary farmers is very poor. More than 76 per cent households are living in kaccha houses and only 16 per cent live in pucca houses and rest are in semi-pucca houses. Their average area of bastu is in only around one kani of land.
- Sanitation condition of the beneficiary household is better. It is found that 68.6 per cent households are using semi-pucca sanitation facilities and only 17 per cent households have kaccha sanitation facilities.
- Out of the total sample households, 29.2 per cent of the households are living under the above poverty line (APL) category, 35.2 per cent are living under the below poverty line (BPL) category and only 19 per cent are Ad-hoc families.
- 79.2 per cent sample households having the access to supply water for their drinking and only 11.4 per cent of the households collect their drinking water from tube wells. It is worth mentioning that still 5.6 per cent households are using unsafe sources of drinking water such as pond.
- It is observed that out of the total sample households, 75.2 per cent have reported to possess television and 97.6 per cent possess smart phone.
- Most of the beneficiary farmers are marginal farmers (29 per cent) and they have only up to one kani of land. 26.2 per cent farmers have only 1–2 kani of own land,19 per cent respondents have 2–3 kani of own agricultural land, 12.6 per cent have 3–4 kani own agricultural land.
- It is found that out of the total production of rice, the maximum 45 per cent rice is produced by the small farmers, which is under

the production limit of 1000–2000 Kg. The next highest 31 per cent rice is produced by the marginal farmers which are under the lowest production limit of (up to 1000 Kg.) and 22 per cent produces within the production limit of 2000–3000 Kg.

- A small percentage of beneficiary is doing horticultural practices and mainly they are doing rubber plantation, banana and betel nut. It is observed that only 14.40 per cent households have rubber plantation, 1.80 per cent households have betel nut and only 0.40 per cent households are doing banana.
- 29.4 per cent sample beneficiary farmers earn up to Rs. 10000 income by selling their agricultural product and 29.6 per cent sample beneficiary farmers earn Rs. 10000–20000 income, 17.6 per cent farmers earn Rs. 20000–30000 income and 13.4 per cent farmers earn Rs. 30000–40000 income.
- The socio-economic status of B.C. Nagar block is best compare to other selected blocks and worst socio-economic condition is found poor in Mandai block of West Tripura district.
- Out of the total operational holdings in Tripura, 87.95 percent holding belong to 'marginal' farmers, holding less than one hectare of land, and they operate 52.80 percent of the total operated area.
- Rice is the principal staple food in Tripura and is cultivated in 54.54 percent of the total cropped area. Maize is the second most important food grain grown in Tripura. The area under maize production has increased from 2150 hectares in 2005–06 to 14635 hectares in 2019–20 with a growth rate of 18.68 per cent.
- Natural rubber cultivation is mostly cultivated horticulture. Apart from that some fruits such as pineapple, jackfruit, mosambi, orange are produced in Tripura and these are also exported from the state.
- Pradhan Mantri Krishi Sinchayee Yojana (PMKSY), Rashtriya Krishi Vikas Yojana (RKVY), National Food Security Mission (NFSM) and Kishan Credit Card (KCC) are the most important schemes implemented in Tripura.
- From the field survey, it is found that the farmers are received the benefit mainly from three schemes viz; PM-Kishan, RKVY and NFSM.
- From the statistical analysis it is concluded that agricultural schemes have positive impact on change in agricultural income of

the beneficiary households in the study area. The impact is also positive and significant on change in households' income.

- However, the beneficiary farmers are facing some major problems such as irrigation, transportation, marketing and lack of awareness about different govt. agricultural/horticultural schemes.

7. Conclusions

The study is an impact assessment study for the agricultural and horticultural schemes in Tripura based on the primary survey. From the findings it is concluded that the tribal farmers in Tripura are mostly marginal farmers and they depend on the agriculture and horticulture for their livelihoods. They are producing mainly foodgrains such as rice, maize, oilseeds etc. Apart from the agricultural products they are also producing horticultural products such as rubber, pineapple, jackfruits, banana, orange and these are also commercially viable. They are also producing non-foodgrains items such as jute, mesta, cotton etc.

PM Kishan, RKVY and NFSM are the most successful schemes implemented in Tripura and tribal beneficiaries are getting more benefits from these schemes.

Finally, it is also concluded that agricultural schemes have positive impact on change in agricultural income of the beneficiary households in the study area. The impact is also positive and significant on change in households' income.

8. Suggestive Measures

Based on the findings of the study, some suggestive measures can be taken for the betterment of its Impact and in order to achieve SDGs 1 and 2. These suggestions are mentioned in the following:

- Rashtriya Krishi Vikas Yojana (RKVY) scheme is an important scheme implemented in the state through which the agro-infrastructure can be developed. Though the farmers are benefited from this scheme, but there is a huge gap between allocation of fund and release of fund from this scheme. There a high potential to develop the agro-infrastructure if the overtime gap between allocation of fund and release of fund reduces. The increase in release of fund under this scheme would develop the storage facilities and market facilities. At least one mandi should be constructed at the block level so that the farmers can get more marketing benefit to improve their economic condition.

- Marketing is a major issue to the beneficiary farmers in Tripura. No Kishan Mandi is found in the study area. As a result of this farmers are facing serious marketing issue. In order to solve the problem of the farmers Kishan Mandi should be constructed. The fund can be taken from different sponsoring agency like NABARD, APEDA etc.
- There is lack of sufficient of warehouse and storage facilities in Tripura. The small and marginal farmers unable to store it after post harvesting. As a result they are bound to sale immediate after post-harvesting at the lower price to the middleman. The problem can be solved with proper initiatives by the concerned department. Some sponsoring agencies like APEDA, NABARD etc. are providing support to construct the warehouse and cold storage.
- Irrigation is a major problem in tribal cultivated land. Water conservation (rain water) is need in the tilla land and that can be done under the MGNREGA. Installation of standalone solar agricultural pumps can be constructed in Tripura under PM-KUSUM scheme. This is useful for both deep irrigation and water conservation also.
- To improve the marketing issue Kishan Mandi can be constructed at the block level; so that farmer can sale their product to Kishan Mandi directly not to the middleman.
- Awareness about the govt. schemes is needed to familiarize the several govt. schemes. An official initiative is required in this regard and makes them aware what types of benefits are available and how to get these through these schemes.
- Soil testing for fertility of land, quality of seed testing should be a mandatory task before cultivation of land. In this regard, a necessary step should be taken towards this direction with the help of Indian Council of Agricultural Research, Lembuchhera.

Finally, in order to achieve the SDGs 1 and 2, a model is constructed and recommended which is given in the following:

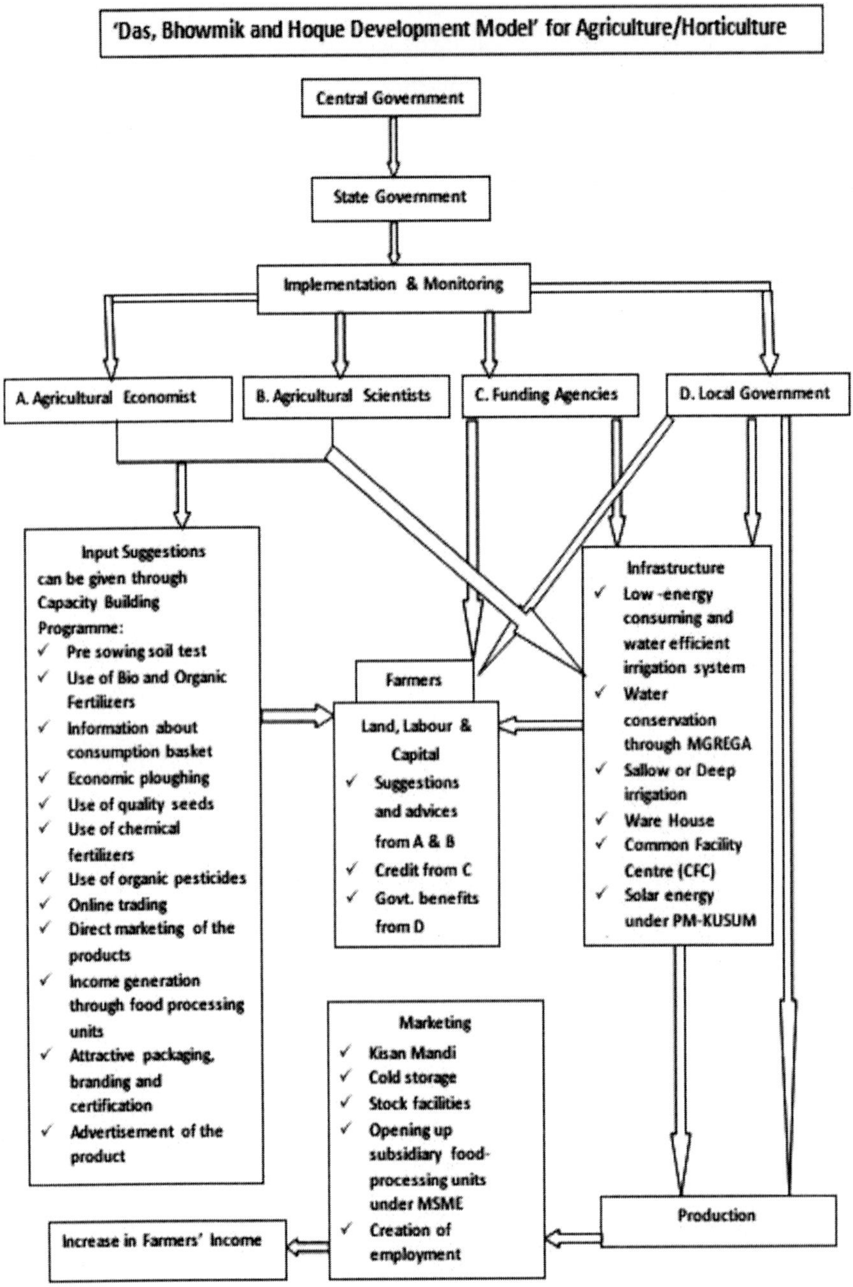

CHAPTER 1

Introduction

Agricultural growth and rural development have significant potential to achieve inclusive growth among Asian countries. Agricultural growth is necessary for reduction of poverty and inclusive growth (Bolt, 2004). Inclusive growth approach came into force since the 11th five year plan and is going to stay as a critical aspect determining the sustainability of future agricultural growth in India. Inclusive growth is essential to develop agriculture in a sustainable manner, by reducing disguised unemployment in the farm sector by shifting labour to non-farm sector and increasing productivity and incomes (Sharma and Singh, 2010). Agricultural development is an important component of inclusive growth approach, as agriculture is a backbone of the country. Approximately 60 per cent rural households in India depend on agriculture and horticultures for their livelihoods. Agriculture and horticulture serves as a source of income for a substantial portion of the population in less developed and developing countries—as suppliers of food, raw materials, and foreign exchange to the country (Das, 2022).

The study is conducted in the state Tripura focusing on the tribal farmers. Tripura is one of the small and poor states among the North-eastern states belonging in remote corner of the country. Tripura is one of the state among the seven sisters' states in the North-eastern part of India located between 22°56″ and 24°32″ North latitude and between 90°09″ and 92°20″ East latitude. It is bounded on the North, West, South and South-east by Bangladesh whereas in the east it has a common boundary with Assam and Mizoram. Topographically, the state can be divided into seven distinguishable features viz; hill range, hillock (tillas), valley, lunga (low lying areas between the hillocks), flat land, river and lake. Out of total area about 60 per cent consists of hills, hillocks and hilly terrains. About one-third people are belonging to 19 indigenous tribal communities. There are major 19 tribes viz; Tripuri, Reang, Chakma, Halam, Garo, Lusai,

Darlong, Mog, Jamatia, Debbarma etc. belonging in Tripura. Tribals of the Tripura are categorized into three types viz; Tripuris, Reangs, Jamatias, Noatias, Koloi, Rupini, and Murasing are indigenous to the state; in the second category Lushai, Kuri, Halam, Mogs, Chakmas, Garo, Khasis, Lepchas and Bhutias are the tribes who have a major presence in the neighbouring states of Tripura; and in the third category Munda, Santhal, Orang and Bhils are belonging who have come from main land India.[1]

There are 23 Agricultural Sub-Divisions in eight districts of Tripura. A total of 2,80,000 hectares of land is cultivated in Tripura and out of that 1,27,000 hectares land have irrigation potential. As per the Agricultural Census Report 2010–11, out of this total cultivable land, 82 per cent cultivable land is under the marginal holding, 13 per cent is under the small holding and only five per cent is under the control of medium and large holding.

For a comprehensive development of the nation no section of the society should be excluded from the process of development. Social exclusion is defined as a social process that involves denial of equal rights which other enjoy, resulting in the inability of individuals from excluded groups to participate in the basic political, economic and social functioning of the society that in turn, resulting in high human deprivation among them. Sen (2000) has brought more clarity in general concept of social exclusion; he has drawn a distinctions between unfair exclusion and unfair inclusion. Theoretically, it is reasonable to assume that only those exclusions that exclude people of certain social groups from having access and entitlements or rights, where such exclusion violates the recognized and acceptable principles, rules, and norms and practices of fairness may be considered as unfair exclusion. Sen's concept of unfair inclusion is similar to the concept of discrimination that is used in social science literature, especially in the discipline of economics, as a form of market discrimination. In the exclusion of a social group, variables associated with social and cultural identities, such as caste, ethnicity, religion, gender, colour and race become important and result in exclusion of all persons belonging to specific social groups.

---

[1] Ministry of Development of North Eastern Region (2011): 'North East Rural Livelihood Project', pp. 142.

The study is fully concentrated on the tribal farmers belong to the state Tripura. From the ancient period the tribal community is identified as the aboriginal inhabitants of our country; and they are socially excluded. For centuries, they have been living a simple life based on the natural environment and have developed cultural patterns congenial to their physical and social environment. Scheduled Tribes (STs) are indigenous, have their own distinctive culture, are geographically isolated and are low in socio-economic conditions. For centuries, the tribal groups have remained outside the realm of the general development process due to their habitation in forests and hilly tracts (Jaykumar *et al.,* 2016).

1.1 Statement of the Problems

Presently, Indian agriculture has been facing a severe crisis since last few years. Farmers are struggling for their livelihoods. Till now, the agricultural sector could not achieve the target rate of growth of four per cent. The problem is persisted and grown significantly. The problem arises due to several reasons such as volatile weather condition, accessibility of informal credit at a higher rate of interest, use of traditional technology in the production process, poor storage and warehousing facilities, lack of proper market information, and lack of awareness and information about the consumer's preference etc. The gravity of the problem in agricultural sector increases day by day especially for farmers working in small and medium size farms. As a result, a large number of farmers protested against the agricultural policy through a long march toward the capital (Das, 2022). Though finally, the Govt. has withdrawn this agricultural policy for the benefit of the small and marginal farmers.

During pandemic situation due to Covid-19, the situation was worsen, because jobless people came back to their home and engaged in agricultural activity; as a result marginal productivity decreases due to excess supply of labour. The Economic Survey noted that the agriculture and allied sector is the largest employer of workforce as it accounted for a sizeable 18.8 per cent (2021–22) in Gross Value Added (GVA) of the country. Agriculture and the allied sector proved to be the most resilient to the Covid-19 shock as it registered a growth of 3.6 per cent in 2020–21 and improved to 3.9 per cent in 2021–22.[2]

Though the Constitution of India is based on the principle of liberty, fraternity, equality and justice to all citizens but, unfortunately these affirmations are only in the Constitution. The fruits of development are not being properly shared among the tribal people on any front. They are still lagged behind the mainstream of the society not because that they are incapable but they have been denied the opportunity to prove their capability.

Available research studies point out that these problems are more severe in rural tribal community because they are belonging in a literary backward community due to poor and dilapidated socio-economic condition and due to poor educational status, malnutrition, infectious diseases and they got meager facilities from the Government as the government schemes etc. The economic problems need special attention in the context of tribal communities of India. The economic problems also arise due to poor knowledge in technology, lack of awareness for their self development and unskilled attempt in production process. As a result of this there is low productivity. They depend mainly on the agriculture/horticulture for their livelihoods. A support programme based on agriculture/horticulture is needed to sort out these problems and to increase the production for which more income can be generated; so that productivity, efficiency and human capital can be improved. Without this development of human capital, their socio-economic position could not be improved and that can hamper the process of inclusive and comprehensive development.

1.2 Necessity of the Study

The purpose of the study is to focus on the impact of the agricultural and horticultural based schemes for improving the socio-economic status of the rural farmers and to reduce the extent of inequality or to reduce the development gap between the poorer section and richer section of the society.

---

[2] *Source:* Business Standard, dated January 31, 2022.

The United Nations has formulated 17 SDGs (Sustainable Development Goals) in order to achieve the sustainable development across the world. Out of these 17 SDGs, first three goals are highlighted on eradication of poverty, elimination of hunger, and ensuring good health and well-being. Goal 1 focuses on the eradication of poverty which implies end of poverty in all forms everywhere and no person should be below the poverty line (BPL). Goal 2 focuses on the zero hunger which includes achieving food security, improving nutrition and promotion of sustainable agriculture; it also includes the distribution of food among the various segment of population in the country. Goal 3 focuses on the good health and well-being which can ensure the healthy lives. Achieving goal 3 depends on achievements of first two goals. In order to achieve these SDGs, the Govt. has launched some schemes on agriculture and horticulture such as Pradhan Mantri Krishi Sinchai Yojana (PMKSY), PM Kishan Samman Nidhi, Paramparagat Krishi Vikas Yojana (PKVY), National Food Security Mission (NFSM), electronic National Agricultural Market (e-NAM), Rashtriya Krishi Vikas Yojana (RKVY) etc. to improve the growth of the agricultural sector and improve the income of the farmers; so that they can upgrade and maintain their livelihood.

The study is focused on the tribal people of the state Tripura. As per 2011 census, there are approximately 31.8 per cent tribes are belonging in Tripura; of which Tripuri is major tribal group which consists approximately 50 per cent population of total tribal population. Tribal Welfare department, Govt. of Tripura has taken some measures through different schemes to promote the economic development of the tribal though these are not sufficient. Central Govt. has also taken several agriculture and horticulture based schemes for the income generation of the farmers. This study attempts to evaluate the agriculture and horticulture based schemes and to examine the impact of these schemes on their socio-economic life of the tribal farmers.

1.3 Area of Study

For this project the study area has been taken from the TTAADC area. In Tripura there are presently eight districts and out of that six districts have been selected based on the tribal demographic concentration. These districts are viz; Dhalai, Gomati, South Tripura, West Tripura, Khowai and Sepahijala.

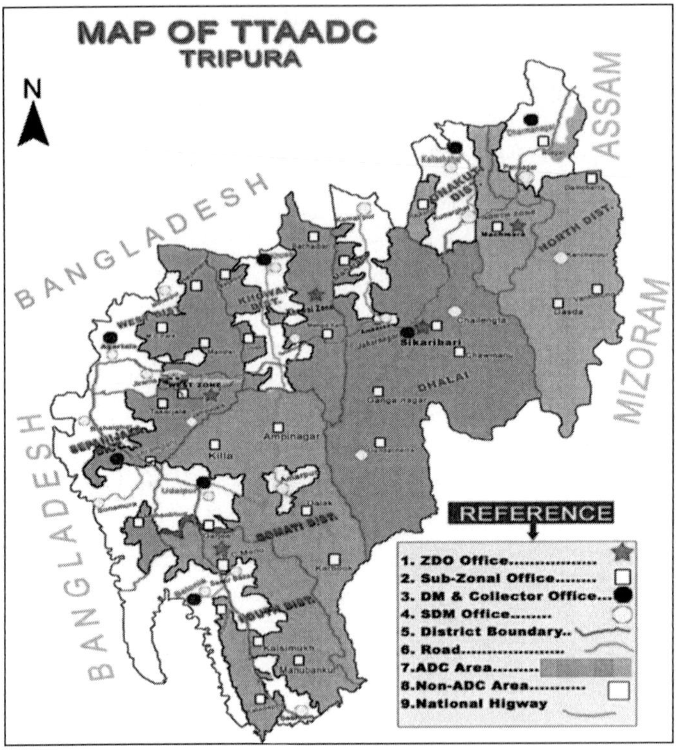

Figure 1.1: Map of TTAADC, Tripura

1.4 Objectives of the Study

The study is focused mainly on two aspects viz; evaluation of the agriculture and horticulture based schemes and impact of the schemes on their socio-economic life. The following objectives can be framed based on these aspects.

- To investigate the socio-economic problems that the rural tribal people are facing in Tripura.
- To examine the socio-economic status of rural tribal people across different tribal community.
- To examine the productivity of different agriculture/horticulture production who have got the benefits of the govt. scheme.

- To examine the impact and concurrent evaluation on Agriculture/ Horticulture based schemes taken by the government on income and employment generation of the beneficiaries.

1.5 Research Questions

On the basis of above mentioned objectives, some research questions can be framed in the following:

1. What are the socio-economic problems that tribal people are facing in Tripura?
2. What is the socio-economic status of rural tribal across different community in Tripura?
3. Are the productivity increases of different agriculture / horticulture production of the beneficiaries?
4. How far this scheme taken by the government has proven successful in generating income and employment through the productivity of tribal in Tripura?

1.6 Nature and Scope of the Study

The study investigates the status of tribal people and also investigates what problem they are facing regularly. The government has taken a policy of income and employment generation through agriculture/ horticulture based scheme for the tribal who are belonging to vulnerable sections of the society. The proposed study is focused on whether the productivity increases or not and the benefits are percolated to the stakeholders properly or not. In this regard the study is focused on impact and concurrent evaluation of the agriculture/horticulture based scheme and impact of this scheme on the socio-economic livelihoods of the beneficiary stakeholders.

1.7 Research Methodology

The methodology for this study is divided into two parts viz; methodology for data collection and methodology for data analysis. The study is based on both secondary and primary data. The list of total beneficiaries has been collected from the scheme provider (secondary source). Secondary information regarding different types of agricultural beneficiaries and list of beneficiaries over last five years is taken from different Govt. Office such as Tribal Welfare Department, TTAADC, Zonal Offices under TTAADC, etc.

Methodology for Primary Data Collection

Primary data have been collected through using three stages Purposive Random Sampling method. In Tripura, there are eight districts. Out of these districts, six districts (75 percent) have been selected in the first stage. In the second stage, two blocks have been selected from Gomati (viz; Killa and Matabari), West Tripura (viz; Jirania and Mandai), Sepahijala (viz; Jampuijala and Nalchar) and Khowai district (viz; Kalyanpur and Teliamura); however three blocks have been selected from Dhalai (viz; Ambassa, Manu and Salema) and South Tripura district (viz; B.C. Nagar, Rajnagar, and Rupaichhari). A total of 14 blocks have been selected from six districts. Finally, sample beneficiaries have been selected at random from the selected blocks. The selection of beneficiaries in the final stage is taken from the list of beneficiaries under the Tribal Sub Plan (TSP) collected from secondary sources. Out of these surveyed six districts, 100 sample households have been collected from the Dhalai, South Tripura, Gomati and West Tripura district; however, 50 sample households' data have been collected from Khowai and Sepahijala districts of Tripura. A total of 500 beneficiaries have been selected from the total beneficiaries of the different schemes and from different tribal community under Tribal Sub Plan of the 14 blocks. The household data have been collected from the beneficiaries of this scheme through structured schedule. Schedule consists with four sections containing with General Information (Profile), Social Information, Economic Information and Impact of Agricultural and Horticultural schemes. Total sampling design is presented in the Table 1.1.

In order to investigate the impact apart from the field survey, a focus group discussion has been done at the Gandachara sub-division of Dhalai during October 2022. The reason for selection of Gandachara sub-division as the Gandacharra is tribal dominated area which is also under the aspirational district Dhalai in Tripura. The survey team has visited Gandachara sub-division and taken the focus group discussion at Purba kalajhari village under the Gandachara sub-division of the Dhalai district.

Table 1.1: Sampling Design from Population with Demographic Size

Districts	*Blocks*	*No. of Respondents*
Dhalai (Population 205637)	Ambassa	17
	Manu	46
	Salema	37
Sub Total		***100***
Gomati (Population 184007)	Killa	60
	Matabari	40
Sub Total		***100***
South Tripura (Population 151329)	B.C Nagar	31
	Rajnagar	42
	Rupaichhari	27
Sub Total		***100***
West Tripura (Population 149847)	Jirania	49
	Mandai	51
Sub Total		***100***
Khowai (Population 138104)	Kalyanpur	22
	Teliamura	28
Sub Total		***50***
Sepahijala (Population 118385)	Jampuijala	32
	Nalchar	18
Sub Total		***50***
Total		**500**

Source: Census 2011.

Methodology for Data Analysis

For data analysis advanced statistical and econometric techniques have been used. To investigate the proper implementation process of the schemes, tabular and graphical presentation can be done by collecting the information from secondary sources and that a cross verification can be done from primary sources. To examine the socio-economic status of the tribal people a comprehensive area-wise and community-wise socio-economic index have been constructed by using Dimension index.

The formula for the dimension index is already mentioned in the earlier.

$$DI = \frac{\text{Actual} - \text{Minimum}}{\text{Maximum} - \text{Minimum}}$$

A composite Socio-economic Index (SEI) is calculated be taking a weighted average of two dimensions viz; social dimension and economic dimension. The social dimension consists with eight indicators viz; level of education, housing type, sanitation type, gas connection, area of bastu, housing space, water source and distance of water source from their house. The formula for Social Index (SI) is given in the following equation.

$$SI = \frac{\sum_{i=1}^{8} X_i}{8}$$

where X's are index value of different social indicators.

The economic dimension consists with eight indicators viz; annual average income, economic profile, and work participation rate, availability of consumer durable goods, average expenditure, cultivated land, horticultural income and agricultural income. The formula for Economic Index is given in the following equation.

$$EI = \frac{\sum_{i=1}^{8} Y_i}{8}$$

where, Y's are index value of different economic indicators.

From these two equations a composite Socio-economic Index (SEI) can be constructed in the following.

$$SEI_i = \frac{SI_i + EI_i}{2}$$

In order to check the impact of agricultural schemes for improving their average annual income, paired t-test is used. For this test the hypotheses are constructed in the following:

- **Null Hypothesis:** H_0: $\mu_1 - \mu_2 = 0$ (i.e.; there is no difference in their average annual household's income parameters before and after getting the benefit of agricultural scheme.)
- **Alternative Hypothesis:** H_1: $\mu_1 - \mu_2 \neq 0$ (i.e.; there is a difference in their average annual household's income parameters before and after getting the benefit of agricultural scheme.)

Where, μ_1 and μ_2 are the average annual household's income before and after getting benefits from different agricultural schemes. The test statistic is written in the following:

$$t = \frac{(\overline{X_1} - \overline{X_2}) - (\mu_1 - \mu_2)}{\sqrt{\frac{s_1^2}{n} + \frac{s_2^2}{n}}} \sim t_{(n-1)+(n-1)}$$

Where; $\overline{X_1}$ and $\overline{X_2}$ are the average sample parameter of average annual household's income of the beneficiaries before getting and after getting benefits from different agricultural schemes in the concerned block; n is the number of beneficiaries in the village and s_1^2 and s_2^2 are the sample variance of average annual household's income before and after getting benefits from different agricultural schemes.

$$s_j^2 = \frac{\sum_{i=1}^{n}\left(X_i - \bar{X}_j\right)^2}{(n-1)}$$

for all j = 1 and 2 (for two sample) and for all i = 1, 2, 3,.., n.

If the observed value of paired t-test exceeds the table value of t-distribution with (2n-2) degrees of freedom, then null hypothesis is rejected ie; test is significant which means there is a difference in average annual household's income before and after getting benefits from different agricultural schemes. If the observed value is less than table value of t-distribution with (2n-2) degrees of freedom, then null hypothesis is accepted and test is insignificant.

Variables used in the Study and its Justification

For the study several dependent and independent variables are taken which are mentioned in the following with its justification.

For measuring Social Status Index some variables or indicators are already mentioned earlier viz; Literacy, level of education, health, housing condition, household accessories, period of stay, marital status, family size, land holding. The justifications of these variables are mentioned in the following:

- *Literacy:* Literacy is an important variable which combat against poverty through getting employment opportunities. It improves health through creation of awareness and promotes self-development as well as societal development (Sahoo, 2011). For measuring Human Development Index, UNDP has also taken it as an important indicator.

- ***Level of Education:*** Level of education is a major factor in economic and social development (Sahoo, 2011; Dung and Pattnaik, 2013). Higher level of education reflects the higher social status and it is also often associated with better economic opportunities as well as the expansion of social resources (American Physiological Association, 2007). Education conveys information regarding earning potential across the lifespan (Shavers 2007).
- ***Housing Condition:*** Housing condition is an important indicator for showing social status of a family (Dung and Pattnaik, 2013). Housing is the third basic needs of the human beings. Poor housing condition reflects poor socio-economic status of the family.
- ***Household Accessories:*** Household accessories are also an important indicator of socio-economic status. A small accessory reflects poor socio-economic status (Bofah and Hannula, 2017).
- ***Marital Status:*** Marital status of an individual is another important indicator of the socio-economic status. It can improve the quality of life and indicates the better social status because the persons who can take the family burden and responsibility go to marry in the society.
- ***Family Size:*** Family size and household composition are required to calculate poverty (American Physiological Association, 2007). It also helps to calculate per-capita income and per-capita expenditure and that information indicates the actual economic position of the family.
- ***Size of Land Holding:*** Size of land holding is another important indicator of socio-economic status. Large land holding size shows the better status of the house. Several authors have taken this variable as an indicator of socio-economic status (Sharma, 2018; MART, 2011; Agarwal, 1998).

For measuring Economic status, the variables or indicators viz; occupation, monthly income, savings, indebtedness, expenditure, other economic accessibility, other financial benefits available from the Govt. programmes are considered.

- ***Occupation:*** American Physiological Association (2007) has mentioned that occupation can be assessed by asking participants about their current or most recent occupation or job title. Occupation, irrespective of salary, is a traditional indicator of socio-economic status because it is believed to convey information regarding an individual's power, income, and educational requirements associated with various positions in the occupational structure. Occupation can provide the financial benefits and can assess the person's mental health in terms of satisfaction.
- ***Income:*** Income is related to the economic position of the family (Pandey, 2009). Lack of income has been found to be related to poorer health, mainly due to reduced access to goods and services (such as health care) that can be beneficial to health (American Physiological Association, 2007).
- ***Expenditure:*** Household expenditure is one of the important determinants of socio-economic status of the family. This variable is taken as an essential expenditure to maintain the basic needs in their daily livelihoods.

1.8 Outline of the Rest of the Chapters

Introductory chapter is followed by

- Chapter 2 which contains Review of Literature.
- Chapter 3 is focussed on Socio-economic Status of Rural Tribal in Tripura.
- Chapter 4 is discussed on Development of Agricultural and Horticultural Production in Tripura.
- Chapter 5 is discussed on the Impact of Agricultural & Horticultural Schemes on the Tribal Livelihoods.
- Chapter 6 discusses Summary, Conclusions and Suggestions.

Finally, the study ends with Bibliography.

CHAPTER 2

Review of Literature

There are many literatures which are reviewed on socio-economic status. Some of these literatures are reviewed in the following in a chronological order.

Das (2022) attempts to examine how far the state Tripura has developed toward to achieving its SDGs so that state can reduce its central dependency. He has also examined the impact of globalization on its sustainable development and explores the possibility of development in different sectors of the economy toward fulfilling the SDGs through globalization. The agricultural and horticultural production in the state has increased over time. But, it is also found that agricultural farmers' income is very low due to an increase in loss in the production process. The state is in the take-off stage; it needs to go long way to make it developed. The state has lot of potentialities for its sustainable development.

Das (2021) has developed a theoretical modeling in determining the optimum size of government intervention on agricultural farmer those who are fighting for their survival mainly due to high cost of production, agricultural credit at a higher rate of interest from the private loan provider and marketing problem due to non-availability of minimum support price. Especially the small and medium size agricultural farmers are facing serious problems such as lack of awareness and information about change in consumers' preference, problem of agricultural credit, use of traditional technology in production process, poor storage and warehousing facilities, lack of organized agricultural market, uncertainty about environment etc. Due to this adversity, the small and medium scale farmers are facing huge loss and fall into the debt trap and as a result of this they are committing suicide. Some farmers also do not get any motivation further to produce agricultural crops. To control the situation, govt. intervention in agricultural sector can be effective for the agricultural farmers who are making loss through producers' subsidy equivalent (PSE). PSE is an indicator of the annual monetary value of gross transfers from the govt. to support agricultural producers through policy measures.

Thangjam (2020) evaluates the performance of Tribal Sub Plan (TSP) with respect to the livelihood security and socio economic status of the beneficiary farmers in Meghalaya. The study is based on the collection of primary data and a total of 270 and 120 beneficiary farmers have been selected from Ri-bhoi and West Garo Hills districts of Meghalaya, making a total of 390 respondents. Based on the inputs received, the beneficiary farmers have been divided into 6 domains viz., Crop, Birds, Fishery, Livestock, Farm Equipment, and Multiple inputs. A Tribal Agricultural Development Index (TADI) has been developed to evaluate the performance of Tribal Sub Plan. The study finds that 70.77 per cent of the respondents are in the range of 0.4–0.7 of TADI values, 28.46 percent respondents have scored between 0.1–0.4 and few (0.77 percent) respondents have scored above 0.7. The study thus infers that Tribal Sub Plan has moderately benefitted the tribal beneficiary farmers.

Kumar (2019) has examined the compound growth rate and trend in rice production and productivity across Indian states. Rice is the staple food for more than 50 per cent of the population across the globe. As a labour-intensive crop, the rice cultivation provides livelihood and employment to millions of people. About 90 per cent of the rice produced in India is used for domestic consumption. The compound growth rate (CGR) of rice is only 0.369 per cent per annum. The paper reveals that there are regional differences in area under rice across regions. Among the southern states, except Tamil Nadu, Andhra Pradesh and Karnataka have registered positive growth in terms of area though the growth rate is lower. It is also found that increase in temperature in India could reduce farm net revenues by 9–25 per cent. The climate challenge facing by the Indian agriculture needs to be addressed in a proper way. It is evident that the annual mean rainfall and also that during monsoon periods decline over the years and the variability in rainfall is also increasing. He has also focused on another threatening issue which is an increase in temperature that adversely affects agriculture. The changes in temperature, radiation, rainfall andCO_2 levels can affect the yield of rice through their direct effect as well as indirect effects such as higher incidence of pests and diseases, and availability of water for irrigation.

Palaniswami (2019) has focused on climate change which is a continuous phenomenon, and its variability is a complex phenomenon. He has used time series data analysis and found projected temperature and precipitation changes in India during 2070–2099. A multi-level assessment and high resolution data analysis are required to map future climate scenarios and their impacts with reduced uncertainty. This includes both natural and social science-related data, including climate and weather, soils, water availability, cropping patterns, productivity and socio-economic variables which are necessary for impact assessment. The study shows that a rise in temperature during the last few years has caused an overall loss in the crop production in the country.

Gozgor (2019) has pointed out that the level of economic integration is negatively related with the agricultural commodity price volatility and the food price volatility. The prices of agricultural commodities are very important by means of production and international trade and it has significant effects on the aggregate economic activity and the level of integration at the world level. The stability of export revenues depend on the investments in infrastructure in case of developing countries. International market is very much difficult for poor and developing economies because the poor and developing economies are not competitive in the international market. As the poverty rates in developing countries depend on agricultural price fluctuations and the people in the developing countries send most of their income on food products, the institutional quality can also be an important determinant for the benefit of comparative advantage between the countries.

Vamsi *et al.* (2019) analyses the impact of Rashtriya Krishi Vikas Yojana (RKVY) on income distribution pattern of sheep rearers in Chittoor district of Andhra Pradesh. A total number of 38 beneficiaries have been selected as sample for the study for a period of three years from 2010–11 to 2012–13. The Gini concentration ratios in respect to the incomes of the beneficiaries are found to be 0.576, 0.545, and 0.498 in the 1st, 2nd and 3rd years, respectively. The study thus brings out that the RKVY scheme has a positive impact on the income levels of the sheep rearers thereby reducing the inequality with regard to income levels as time progressed. The study concludes that sheep farming with technical intervention in the form of superior inputs could lead to reducing the income inequality.

Hamsini and Rashmi (2019) review the currently available crop insurance schemes and their effectiveness in Chikmagalur district of Karnataka. The study is based on primary data collected from a sample of 348 farmers through a well-structured questionnaire. The study finds that crop insurances have helped the farmers in stabilizing their income and in repayment of their loans. It also reveals that Pradhan Mantri Fasal Bima Yojana (PMFBY) provides more benefits compared to any other schemes and majority of the farmers were satisfied with the currently available crop insurance schemes.

Patil and Hosamani (2018) investigate the impact of National Horticulture Mission (NHM) on horticulture development in Karnataka. The study is based on both primary and secondary sources of information. The primary data has been collected through intensive survey of the sample farmers through structured questionnaire by personal interviews. Three horticultural crops namely, grapes, mango and pomegranate in three districts (Vijayapura, Dharwad and Koppal) of Karnataka have been selected for the study. The sample respondents for each fruit crop are 90 and the total sample size is 270. Secondary data on area, production and productivity of selected crops has been collected from the Directorate of Horticulture, Bangalore, for the period 1998–99 to 2013–14. The study finds that out of total physical achievement (2.10 lakh ha) of horticultural crops under NHM, the highest area of about 60.82 per cent has been covered under fruit crops followed by flowers (12.88 percent), plantation crops (12.36 percent), spices (11.24 percent) and least is medicinal and aromatic plants (2.69 percent). Further, it is observed that the instability in area, production and productivity of horticulture crops has been reduced after the implementation of NHM in the study area which shows better performance of NHM in horticulture development. The study concludes that even though NHM has made lot of efforts to increase the income and employment opportunities to the beneficiaries but still the beneficiaries are facing some major constraints like, insufficient subsidy amount, incidence of pest and disease and delay in getting the subsidy.

Aditya *et al.* (2018) examine the impact of crop insurance on farm income, production expenses and productive investments in agriculture and identify the factors that influence farmers' decision to buy crop insurance. For the purpose, the study employs data from Situational Assessment Survey of Farmers conducted by the NSSO in 2012–2013 which includes a sample of 35,200 households spread across 4,529 villages of the states and union territories of India. The data has been collected for two major agricultural seasons, namely Kharif (2012) and Rabi (2012–13). The study brings out that the adoption of crop insurance by farmers is very poor with only 4.80 per cent and 3.17 per cent of the sample farmers insuring their crops in Kharif and Rabi season, respectively. This is mainly due to lack of awareness about insurance products. The study also reveals that educated farmers with better extension contact are more likely to insure their crops. Land holding size and subsidy on premium is also found to increase the probability of farmers to adopt crop insurance. Moreover, factors like lower social status, tenant farming and exposure to deficit-rainfall in the previous year are found to be negatively associated with farmers' decision to insure.

Chaturvedi (2018) evaluates the effectiveness of Rashtriya Krishi VikasYojana (RKVY) in seven districts of Meghalaya state. The primary data has been collected through intensive sample survey of 493 beneficiaries under RKVY across seven districts through structured questionnaire by personal interviews and focus group discussion. The study covers the period from 2007–08 to 2012–13. The study results indicate that out of the total sampled beneficiaries in seven districts, 60 percent of them reported that they have benefitted with the irrigation check dams constructed under RKVY. The maximum numbers of irrigation check dams were constructed in Jaintia Hills while the least are in South Garo Hills district. The overall impact of watershed projects under the RKVY has been found positive. With regard to horticultural schemes under RKVY, it is found that about 65 per cent of respondents are satisfied with these schemes.

Amarender (2018) examines the impact of Paramparagath Krishi Vikas Yojna (PKVY) on area expansion, productivity, profitability and sustainability of organic farming in India. The study is based on the collection of both primary and secondary level data. Primary data has been collected from a sample of 490 clusters spread across 15 states for the period 2015–16 to 2016–17. The study also includes a control group of farmers who are practicing conventional farming to compare the cost and benefits of organic farming with conventional farming. The study shows that the PKVY is picking up in Sikkim, Tamil Nadu, Chhattisgarh, Karnataka, Kerala and Maharashtra, while in other states, the scheme is lagging behind. The study also finds that mostly commercial crops (such as chillies and cotton) were grown in a conventional way, whereas pulses and oilseeds were grown in an organic way. As regards farmers' perception, 46 percent of the beneficiaries mentioned that they adopted organic farming to reduce cost, followed by getting health benefit (43 percent). Moreover, 57 percent of the sampled farmers reported lack of certification as the reason for them not shifting to organic farming. The study concludes that the overall impact of PKVY is quite impressive in the study region.

Kumari and Devadas (2017) has suggested that there is an important role of agricultural productivity in the process of industrialization and agricultural production related or linkage between increase in agricultural production and poverty reduction and it has admitted the role of agriculture in economic development and the economic development can be achieved by means of ensuring the sustainable agricultural growth. The region Patna, India is considered for the study in order to judge the set of policy guidelines for the sustainable economic development of the area and recommendations for the economic development of Patna region.

Clements and Jiawei (2017) analyze the interrelationships between Engel's law, the diversity of food consumption and its quality by using an index-number approach. For the purpose, the study employs unpublished data from the World Bank's International Comparison Program for 31 items of food in more than 150 countries. The study results indicate that diets of rich countries are substantially more diverse than those of the poor. The diets of rich countries are about three-and-one half times more diverse than the poor's and diet diversity increases with income with an elasticity of 0.3. Using a weighted covariance between income elasticities and consumption to measure the quality of food consumption, the study finds considerable differences between pairs of countries. Higher incomes bring higher quality food, but the overall elasticity is small. Furthermore, better-quality food comes at a higher price, but interestingly, this cost, relative to lower-quality food, is low in richer countries. The study thus concludes that there is a modest tendency for the structure of prices to be regressive in its impact on the global distribution of real income.

Ramesh *et al.* (2017) examine the impact of National Horticulture Mission (NHM) scheme on the beneficiaries of horticultural farmers in Karnataka. The study is based on primary data, collected from 240 beneficiaries and 90 non-beneficiaries of NHM scheme in four districts of Karnataka. The study results indicate that the distribution of land holding among beneficiaries is highest with 3.16 hectares per household per year in comparison with non-beneficiaries with 2.3 hectares per household per annum. It is also observed that the implementation of NHM scheme has generated more employment among beneficiaries with 217 man-days per household per year in comparison with non-beneficiaries with 176 man-days per household per year. The study concludes that the implementation of NHM scheme in Karnataka has brought about medium level impact among 67.68 per cent of the beneficiaries while it has a low and high level of impact among 16.67 per cent and 15.00 per cent of the beneficiaries respectively.

Manjunatha *et al.* (2017) examine the effectiveness of the National Horticulture Mission (NHM)/Horticulture Mission for North East and Himalayan States (HMNEH) in meeting the objectives for which the scheme has been conceptualized. The study is based on both primary and secondary sources of information. Primary data has been collected from 4033 beneficiaries spread across 29 states and 2 UTs for the period 2012–13 to 2015–16. The study results indicate that the overall achievement ratio in terms of reaching the target is 0.89 and Maharashtra, Andhra Pradesh, Chhattisgarh, Assam, Himachal Pradesh, Tripura, Manipur and Mizoram have recorded the best achievement ratio of more than one. The overall average increment in area under horticultural crops is found to be around 17 per cent. The maximum increase in area has been noted among flowers, followed by vegetable and fruits. The study concludes that the interventions of NHM/HMNEH have been successful in terms of augmenting area, production, productivity and gross value of the horticultural output.

Awotide *et al.* (2016) have concentrated and mentioned that the agriculture has a dominant and strategic role in the development and the intensity to adopt the improved rice varieties and the effect of market participation on farmers' welfare in Nigeria. The formation of associations among the rural farmers should be encouraged and the prioritites should be given on the head of the household in this type of association. The technological development and higher adoption of improved rice varieties would lead to an increase in rice yield. The higher production helps the farmers and helps to get marketable surplus. It would lead to an increase the household income. The farmer's association and programme that would improve contact extension with the agents in compliance with the increase market participation and generate improvement in the welfare of rural households.

Simtowe *et al.* (2016) has stated that the technology in agriculture production for particular varieties of agricultural product may help to increase seed availability to farmers as well as need for improved access to credit. Technology adoption studies are mainly concentrated on estimating adoption rates and understanding the relation between technology adoption and its relevance for socio-economic condition and policy variables. The author also argues that importance of improving farmers is the access to their financial markets. It is important to improve the farmers' access to credit services; so that they can easily acquire credit to purchase improved seeds. The women participation would significantly increase in case of cultivation of improved verities of agricultural product if the policy implementation will particularly support for credit.

Sharma (2016) evaluates the impact of Pradhan Mantri Irrigation (Watershed Development) Project on land use and cropping pattern in different categories of farms in Madhya Pradesh. The study is based on both primary and secondary data. Primary data has been collected from 1285 beneficiary farmers across 33 Integrated Watershed Management Programmes (IWMPs) of 32 districts of the State for the agriculture year 2015–16. It has been observed that over all progress of the IWMP with respect to change in irrigation potential, land use pattern, cropping pattern, production and productivity of crop are noteworthy. A remarkable progress in area under irrigation, production and productivity has not only been observed in the area under study but it has been found across various sizes of holdings which show the inclusiveness in implementation of the programme. Furthermore, land use pattern indicates that the net cultivated area and operational holdings of farmers have increased and cropping pattern is found to be shifted from less to more remunerative crops.

Kc and Adhikari (2015) has found that most of the women in the region are illiterate, and many never attended schools. Even though girls are going to school, they drop out of school by the age of 13–14 years. The villages do not have access to the healthcare service providers within the villages. The majority of tribal populations residing in rural areas are directly or indirectly dependent upon primitive agricultural practices and forests for their livelihoods. At the same time, they make income from labour jobs in an unorganized market. The current practices of agriculture in the tribal region are not economically sustainable, particularly because the yields for many agricultural commodities are low compared to developed nations. Tribal households are not engaged in non-farm enterprises, possibly because the inhabitants have limited access to alternative sources of capital, impeding any opportunity to diversify their enterprises. Women perceive SHGs solely as a financial intermediary, and thus some women, who perceive they cannot save, opt not to be part of SHGs. This raises a concern if SHGs are missing their purpose of providing a community platform where women can come together to address social or community issues.

Behera (2015) has examined the GDP growth performance of the state Gujarat and others Indian states. In the context of industry he has analyzed the source of agricultural growth performance of Gujrat from the year 2000. The policies of government for the agriculture growth and rural development are being focused in the study. It has the central focus that the link of agricultural development and inclusive growth. Through farmer sector growth rural development is possible. The study concludes with the point that there is a positive relation between agricultural growth and economic growth. The effective agricultural policy relating to irrigation, electrification, research, extension, subsidies and fertilizer consumption etc has taken by the Gujrat government. The paper also reveals that agriculture contribution of the state GDP has increased the economic growth of the state.

Kumar (2015) examines the impact of Rashtriya Krishi Vikas Yojana (RKVY) on input use, production, income and employment among the beneficiary farmers in Gujarat. The study is based on both primary and secondary sources of information. Primary data has been collected from 449 selected beneficiary farmer households using a well-structured questionnaire from eight RKVY districts of Gujrat for the period 2007–08 to 2012–13. The study results indicate that more than 78 per cent of farmers have benefited from agriculture mechanization and crop development activities under RKVY. Around 14 per cent of the total sample farmers benefited from horticulture and micro/minor irrigation projects. Farmers benefited under animal husbandry constituted about 3.3 per cent. It is also observed that about a quarter of the total sample households received benefits on various inputs like seeds, fertilizers, plant protection chemicals etc. However, about 61 per cent of the sample farmers reported problems in accessing subsidy under RKVY. The study highlights that there is a strong need for building capacity of farmers in using new technology through field visits and training programmes.

Nag *et al.* (2015) examine the impact of Participatory Seed Production Programme of RKVY on the adoption behaviour of paddy seed producers of Kalahandi district of Odisha. The study is based on primary data, collected from 120 respondents (60 beneficiaries and 60 non beneficiaries) from 6 villages of Kalahandi district. The study is carried out using ex-post facto research design for the year 2013–14. The study finds that beneficiaries have greater level of cognitive and motivational factors viz., attitudes, knowledge, risk bearing, innovativeness etc. than non-beneficiaries. Further, they have more favorable attitudes towards agricultural technology than non-beneficiaries. The level of knowledge of beneficiaries about various aspects of seed production technology is higher whereas, non-beneficiaries are ignorant about some aspects of the seed production technology. The study also reveals that the adoption behavior of beneficiaries is greater than that of non- beneficiaries.

Hoda and Terway (2015) evaluate the policies of the central government and the Reserve Bank of India to enhance institutional credit flows to agriculture and analyze the cost and benefits of subsidies for agricultural credit and generalized debt waivers in India. For the purpose, the study employs secondary sources of information for the period 1951 to 2013. The study reveals that though there has been an impressive growth in institutional credit since 1951, the dependence of farmers on non-institutional sources for agricultural credit remains as high as 36 per cent in 2013. It also finds that the steps taken to enhance institutional credit such as the opening of a large number of rural branches of commercial banks, priority sector lending, Kisan Credit Cards and the financial inclusion initiative have really been instrumental in the impressive rise in agricultural credit. On generalized debt waivers, the study finds that they create expectations of similar waivers in future and disincentives farmers from repaying loans. As a result, there is a contraction of credit available to farmers as the lenders tend to reduce the size of their lending operations. The study, therefore, strongly argues against generalized debt waivers in future.

Lavanya *et al.* (2015) evaluates the impact of Rashtriya Krishi Vikas Yojana (RKVY) on income distribution of piggery beneficiaries in Andra Pradesh. A total number of 38 beneficiaries who have completed three years of pig rearing have been selected as sample for the study. The study is conducted in four districts of Andhra Pradesh, namely Chittoor, Kadapa, Kurnool and Nellore. The Gini concentration ratios in respect to the incomes of the beneficiaries are found to be 0.698, 0.535, and 0.445 in the 1st, 2nd and 3rd years, respectively. The study thus reveals that the RKVY scheme is able to help the piggery beneficiaries to have an improved standard of living by reducing the inequality with regard to income levels. The study concludes that the RKVY programme has brought in substantial improvement in the income and savings of the piggery beneficiaries.

Roy *et al.* (2015) estimate the growth performance of agriculture in the North Eastern states of India by using time series data on area, production and productivity of food grains for the period 1972–73 to 2011–12. The methods used in the study include estimation of compound growth rate, acceleration, deceleration or stagnation of growth and instability analysis. The study results indicate that during the overall study period, among the states, Nagaland registered the highest significant growth in area, production and yield, followed by Arunachal Pradesh and Mizoram. All the North Eastern states have shown positive growth rates in area, production and yield increase.

The decomposition analysis of growth shows that sources of output growth were almost same in all the periods. During the period 1982–83 to 2001–02, the major contributor to food security of the region has been found of area effect. However, during the period 2002–03 to 2011–12, yield effect was the major contributing factor to food security of the region. The study identifies non-availability of adequate quantity of quality seeds and lack of use of inputs like fertilizers, weed control and disease and pests protection chemicals as the major constraints in food grain production in the region.

Das and Das (2014) have explained the status of shifting cultivation in the state Tripura though the state Government of Tripura has banned the shifting cultivation in Tripura. The possible alternative of the shifting cultivation is settled agriculture which may be acceptable by the Tribal people of Tripura, as the tribal are depending on agriculture. It is observed that there is lack of floodplains for settled agriculture and due to that the tribal populations of hilly Tripura are still continued to depend on shifting cultivation for their subsistence livelihood. The livelihood of tribal people of Tripura are bound to worsen with time as they don't have any alternative to manage their food and they are engaged in shifting cultivation, though the shifting cultivation is still continuing in its present of land degradation, ecological balance and other issues related with environment.

Ragasa *et al* (2014) have noted that the success depends on organization and human capital strengthening, financial sustainability, effective participation of the civil society and demonstrated impact of the participation. The decentralization platforms for policy dialogues have the potential to improve the local level participation. So, it is important to decentralize the policy to improve their capacity to articulate their demands for rural service. Appropriate institutional and policy reforms are being required with an eye to achieving food security for all in developing countries and it is important to allow local policy makers to solve their problems in their own context.

Patnaik (2014) examines the impact of National Mission on Micro Irrigation (NMMI) in terms of water saving, increase in area, production and productivity of major crops in 13 selected states of India. The study is carried out in 64 districts of the selected states and primary data has been collected through participatory discussion and structural interviews of more than 7400 beneficiaries and non-beneficiaries. The study reveals that the NMMI has benefitted the farmers in term of enhanced productivity and reduced cost on electricity and fertilizers. The average productivity of fruits and vegetables has increased about 42.30 per cent and 52.80 percent respectively. Besides, the scheme has also succeeded in reducing the irrigation cost reduced by 20–50 percent. Use of micro irrigation system has also helped the farmers in cutting down the electrical consumption about 31 percent. Successful implementation of the scheme has also led to average reduction in fertilizer usage with average reduction of about 28 percent in total fertilizer consumption in the surveyed states. All the surveyed states reported increase in farmer's income in the range of 20 to 68 per cent with an average increase of 48.5 per cent. The study concludes that the NMMI has helped to widen the food basket of the country by bringing more area under irrigation and with judicious use of water.

Roy (2014) has attempted to investigate the pattern of food consumption and its impact on nutritional status of rural Indian population. The study employs data from National Sample Survey, 66th (2009–10) along with 61st (2004–05) and 50th (1993–94), for the period 1993–94 to 2009–10. Consumption of major food items like cereals and cereal substitutes, pulses and pulse products, milk and products, egg, fish & meat, edible oil are calculated across decile classes for detailed analysis. The study finds that cereals, cereal substitutes and pulses consumption have declined substantially and consistently for every states and for all decile classes of consumers including the poorest. The extent of decline is being more for higher expenditure classes. The study also reveals that all the states have experienced a noteworthy increase in intake of edible oil. However, there has been negligible change in the protein rich animal products and dairy products during the study period. The study concludes that states with well-functioning public distribution system (PDS) are experiencing improvement in nutritional status.

Agrawal (2014) evaluates the impact of National Food Security Mission (NFSM) on the production of wheat, rice and pulses in the State of Madhya Pradesh. The study is conducted in six districts of Madhya Pradesh and a total of 1200 individual beneficiaries have been selected for the study from 120 villages. The study reveals that there has been only 15 percent women farmer participation in the agricultural activity under this scheme. Further, the participation of the marginal farmer under NFSM is also very less (21 percent) and they are engaged in subsistence farming and grow low value crops. The study also reveals that at the state level 65 per cent beneficiaries were supported by the scheme in the wheat production, 26 per cent beneficiaries were provided support in rice production and 56 per cent beneficiaries were rendered help in pulses production. As regards impact of the NFSM on crop production, it is observed that due to the inputs under the scheme, there is an increase in the crop production ranging from 25 per cent to 41 per cent. Furthermore, majority of the respondents reported that their income has increased due to this scheme.

Saheb *et al.* (2013) have examined the impact of the skills such as vocational skills, life skills and technical knowledge to raise their efficiency and increase their productive ability of the socio-economically backward and educationally disadvantaged groups belonging to Kerala, Tamil Nadu, Karnataka and Andhra Pradesh. They have found that majority of the trainees are from weaker sections and within this women outnumber the men. 21.53 per cent of the total population of the respondents' families is illiterate and majority of them have come from lower income group. Nearly, half of the beneficiaries are satisfied with the training programme. Overwhelming majority of the beneficiaries benefited from this programme in terms of self-employment and wage employment. Majority of the self-employed invested their own capital towards income generating activity; the role of banks in extending credit for investment is negligible. Standard of living of the majority of the beneficiaries has improved in terms of household consumption, health care, children's education etc.

Kumar (2013) assesses the impact of National Horticulture Mission (NHM) in terms of area, production and productivity of identified horticultural crops covered under NHM in seven states of India for the period 2000–01 to 2009–10. The study is based on both primary and secondary sources of information. The primary data has been collected through intensive sample survey of 1112 beneficiary farmers across seven states through structured questionnaire by visits and personal interviews. The study finds that, at the aggregate, NHM seems to have overall positive effect on the horticultural crops. The area under fruits increased from four million hectares in 2001–02 to more than 6 million hectares by the end of the 2009–10. Area under vegetables increased from 6.2 million hectares in 2001–02 to eight million hectares in 2009–10. Area under floriculture and aromatic plants also experienced some increase during the study period. Area under all horticultural crops increased from 16.6 million hectares in 2001–02 to 20.9 million hectares in 2009–10. Production of all horticultural crops increased from 146 million tons in 2001–02 to 223 million tons in 2009–10. Among the selected beneficiary households, area under selected crops increased among almost all farm size holdings. However, there were wide fluctuations in the yield rate in the selected crops among the beneficiary farmers. Majority of the households indicated that their income has increased after shifting to horticultural crops. The study highlights that NHM has failed completely in making provision of processing facility, providing market for the end product through procurement and building capacity by proper training.

Sharma (2012) has pointed out that there is a disparity between urban and rural income increases due to serious agrarian crisis. The neglect of agriculture and rapid growth of non-agricultural sector is one the important reason this disparity increases. There are many factors for slowdown in agricultural growth. The author suggests that the some policies have to be taken for the development of agriculture to get agricultural back for the broader development; so that there could be substantial increase in investment in agricultural research and agricultural development. The study further suggests that in case of agriculture, it is very important to follow multi-dimensional model of organization and management and it is important to do integration of agricultural-input, agricultural-production and agro-processing and marketing part of the value chain.

Sivagnanam (2012) examines the impact of National Horticulture Mission (NHM) scheme in terms of increase in area, production and productivity of two selected horticultural crops viz., pineapple and peeper in Kerala. The study is based on primary data collected through a sample survey of 98 farmers from two districts of Kerala, namely Ernakulam and Wayanad, for the period 2004–05 to 2009–10. While analyzing the impact of NHM on area, the study finds that there has been no change in the area under pepper crop cultivated by the sample respondents and it remained the same over the study period. The average area under pepper crop per household stood at 0.61 acre. In case of pineapple, the average area increased from 1.21 acres in 2004–05 to 2.92 acres during 2009–10. Further, the average yield of pineapple obtained by the sample respondents marginally increased while in case of peeper, the yield decreased marginally during the study period. As regards perception of sample households about NHM, over 74 percent of them reported that the scheme helped them by providing seedlings/nursery. According to 60 percent of the respondents, subsidy provision was a great benefit. About 83 percent of the respondents expressed that NHM increased employment opportunities for the farmers by increasing area under horticultural crops.

Dev and Venkatanarayana (2011) examine the employment and unemployment situation of the youth in India during the last two-and-half decades (1983 to 2007–08) and analyze the trends in labour force and workforce participation rates, unemployment, joblessness, working poor, growth and employment elasticities etc. The study is based on the secondary data from the published as well as unit record data related to NSS employment and unemployment survey for the analysis. The study finds that labour force and work participation rates have fluctuated between 40 to 44 percent during the last three and half decades. The number of youth unemployed in India increased from 6.5 million in 1993–94 to 9.5 million in 2004–05. Out of this, 61 percent are in rural areas while 70 per cent of them are males. Further, India has 459 million workers in 2004–05. Out of this, 423 million (92 percent) are unorganized workers. The study also reveals that literacy and educational levels are increasing for Indian youth. However, about 89 per cent of the youth have not taken any kind of vocational training. The study thus highlights the issues and problems of youth population by looking at trends in youth labour market and population outside the labor force.

Kalyani *et al.* (2011) analyze the performance of tribal women in terms of work participation rate and contribution to family income in agriculture and allied sector of Andhra Pradesh. A sample of 100 tribal farm women, 25 each from four panchayats in East Godavari District of Andhra Pradesh has been selected for the study based on stratified random sampling procedure. A 15 point scale is used to test the performance of tribal women. The study reveals that the sample tribal women work for about 12 to 15 hours per day in agriculture and allied activities. They collect minor forest product and sell these products in the nearby sandy and exchange the produce for their daily requirements through barter system. The study thus brings out that the work participation rate and performance of tribal women in majority of agricultural activities is high in comparison to their male counterparts and they contribute lion's share to the family income. The study concludes that lower the socio-economic status of the sample households, the higher is the contribution of women towards their family income.

Chattopadhayay and Roy (2011) evaluate the impact of National Horticulture Mission (NHM) in terms of increase in area, production and productivity of two selected horticultural crops viz., pineapple and mandarin oranges in West Bengal. The study is mainly based on primary data collected through an intensive sample survey of 100 beneficiary households from two districts of West Bengal, viz; Jalpaiguri and Darjeeling. The study results indicate that both area and yield rate of mandarin oranges have increased significantly during the period 2004–05 to 2009–10 and there has been a marginal increase in area and yield rate of pineapple over the period. At the same time, there has been a gradual increase in the coverage under certified inputs indicating a gradual shift of production technology with certified inputs in place of traditional inputs. In case of marketing of output, the study finds that there has been a complete absence of formal marketing channels like government agencies or cooperative bodies for the beneficiary pineapple and mandarin orange growers in the study region. The study also reveals the subsidy provided under the NHM forms only a negligible amount of the total investment required. The study concludes that the NHM performed well by providing financial assistance to the farmers. However, there has been an aspiration for enhancement of subsidy among the beneficiary farmers, while at the same time they appeal for development of proper marketing facilities, enhancement of institutional credit and improvement of extension and capacity-building services under NHM.

Singh and Grover (2011) examine the productivity and profitability of organic and inorganic wheat cultivation in Punjab by collecting primary data from a total sample of 160 farmers (85 organic growers and 75 inorganic growers) spread across 30 villages in the districts of Patiala and Faridkot for the period 2008–09. The area under organic farming has been found about 27 per cent of the total operational area in Kharif as well as Rabi seasons for the sample organic growers. The major share of organic area has been found under wheat and paddy crops, each of which accounted for about 15 per cent of the total operational area of sample organic growers. The total variable cost on per acre for the cultivation of organic wheat has been found less as compared to inorganic wheat. The regression analysis reveals that with one per cent increase in expenditure on farmyard manure, biodynamic and machine labour, the organic wheat productivity would increase by 0.114 per cent, 0.703 per cent and 0.556 per cent, respectively, showing significant impact on value productivity. The study clearly brings out that though, the organic wheat cultivation has been found more profitable for the growers in the study area, and the significant reduction in its productivity level poses a serious challenge in terms of food security of the nation.

Tuteja (2011) examines the impact of National Horticulture Mission (NHM) on the beneficiary farmers in Haryana. For the purpose, primary data has been collected through a field survey of 150 beneficiaries in the selected three districts (Rohtak, Hissar and Sirsa) of Haryana for the year 2008–09. The study results indicate that the status of horticultural crops in terms of area devoted is poor in Haryana as these crops cover only 1.4 per cent of the gross cultivated area. However, area and production of horticultural crops especially fruits and vegetables grow at a healthy rate. The study also finds that the net returns from cultivation of garlic followed by aonla is higher than traditional crops and selected horticultural crops generated greater employment as compared to cereals and several traditional crops. With regard to household income, majority of the beneficiary farmers reported increase in household income after the implementation of NHM, but the major beneficiaries of the Mission are large farmers. The study concludes that though NHM has completed initial phase of its implementation in Haryana but its impact on area, production and yield of selected horticultural crops is limited due to low coverage of farmers.

Ayaz and Hussain (2011) investigate the impact of institutional credit on technical efficiency of agricultural production in Pakistan. The study is based on primary data collected through a farm level survey of 300 rural farmers (150 credit users and 150 non-users of credit) from Faisalabad district in the Punjab province of Pakistan for the year 2009. The study employs Stochastic Frontier Production Function Approach to measure technical efficiency. The study reveals that the overall mean efficiency score is 0.84 indicating that 16 percent of the sample farmers are technically inefficient. It also finds that farming experience, education, access to farming credit, herd size and number of cultivation practices have constructive and significant impact on farmer's technical efficiency. Among the variables considered for inefficiency analysis, the variable 'access to farming credit' is found to have the highest coefficient value (–0.14) indicating the importance of agricultural credit thereby showing that availability of credit to farmers is much more important than any other factor to improve the resource use efficiency in agriculture sector. The household size of the sample farmers, area operated and the dummy variable for plant protection measures are all the factors negatively affecting the efficiency of farmers. The study highlights that shortage of credit availability or capital constraint faced by the farmer is one of the major problems in the adoption of modern technologies and efficiency improvement in the agricultural sector of Pakistan.

Reddy and Kumar (2010) delineate the situation of the Scheduled Tribes of Andhra Pradesh in the background of various policies of the state during the successive plan periods, and its impact on their socio-economic mobility. Politically, this community is the most voiceless in the state. Their unsecured livelihood position in terms of lack of legal entitlements of the resources they use, both land and non-timber forest produce, push them into deep economic vulnerability. The present economy of the tribal in the state is a consumption-subsistence economy with its main occupations being settled agriculture, podu (shifting) cultivation and collection of Non-Timber Forest Produce (NTFP), which totally comprise 88 per cent of their occupation status. The types of forest-based livelihoods of the poorest sections of tribal communities are NTFP based (57 percent), fodder for goats and sheep (26 percent), fuel wood sale (12 percent) and wood-based craft making (5 percent). The majority of the hill tribes in Andhra Pradesh suffer from the absence of proper infrastructure and communication facilities. Improper management of schemes and inefficient implementation of suitable programmes in the tribal region create a major problem. The majority of the tribal people are not even aware of the development schemes implemented by government agencies. Without creating awareness among the tribal people, it is difficult to achieve better results.

Sharma and Singh (2010) examines that the inclusive growth is essential to develop agriculture on sustainable manner by reducing disguised unemployment in the farm sector in the way of shifting labour to the non-farm sector and increase average size of land holding resulting marginal productivity of labour and land increases.

Kumar (2010) attempts to examine the performance of agricultural credit flow and tries to identify the factors responsible for increasing the use of institutional credit at the farm household level in India. The study is based on the secondary data compiled from diverse sources. The study reveals that the institutional credit to agriculture in real terms has increased tremendously during the past four decades. Further, the structure of the sources of agricultural credit has witnessed a significant change and commercial banks have emerged as the major source of institutional credit in recent years. It has also been observed that the quantum of institutional credit availed by the farming households is affected by a number of socio-demographic factors which include education, farm size, family size, caste, gender, occupation of household, etc. The study suggests that the procedure for loan disbursement should be made simple so that it may not be difficult for the less-educated and illiterate households to access institutional financing agencies for credit.

Kumar (2009) investigates the impacts of on-going agricultural schemes on the livelihood of the farmers in the tribal areas of agro-climatic regions of Madhya Pradesh. The study is conducted in 200 villages in 12 districts of Madhya Pradesh, covering 4,007 households, 50 focus groups discussions, and interviews with key informant in both state and field level during December 2008 to February 2009. The study results indicate that agriculture is not a very viable economic operation for vast majority of farmers in the study area. About 22.3 percent of the households are landless and small and marginal farmers among tribal are more (63.9 percent) than small and marginal farmers among non-tribal (55.9 percent). The overall picture of utilization of technology and adoption of package of practices in tribal agriculture are found very low. It has also been observed that only 10 to 15 percent of the farmers' households have benefited from the on-going agricultural interventions.

Kshirsagar (2008) assesses the impact of organic sugarcane (OS) farming on input use, costs, yields and returns in relation to conventional inorganic sugarcane (IS) farming by collecting primary data from a total sample of 142 sugarcane-growing farmers (72 growing organic sugarcane and 70 growing inorganic sugarcane) from Jalgaon and Kolhapur districts of Maharashtra for the year 2004–05. The study finds that organic sugar cultivation enhances human labour employment by 16.90 per cent and its cost of cultivation is also lower by 14.24 per cent than inorganic sugar farming. However, the average yield of OS crop has been found to be 96.63 tonnes per hectare as against 103.56 tons per hectare of IS crop showing that OS farmers realized 6.79 per cent lower yield than IS farmers. The yield stability measured by Coefficient of Variation indicates that yields are more stable under organic sugar farming than the inorganic sugar farming. The study also reveals that the OS farming gives 15.63 per cent higher profits and profits are also more stable on OS farms than the IS farms.

Panda (2006) has discussed about the pattern and variation of livelihood among different tribal community of Orissa as there are large number of tribal community. There is a huge diversity and variation in socio-cultural livelihood of 62 tribal communities in Orissa. Among the tribal people, more than half are non-workers. The main workers among them are cultivators and agricultural labourer; only few percentages of people are engaged in secondary sector.

Bolt (2004) has explained that agricultural growth and rural development have significant potential to achieve inclusive growth among the Asian countries. Growth of agriculture sector is the key for poverty reduction and inclusive growth. Agriculture growth will enhance economic growth and reduce rural poor by increasing their productivity and incomes.

Pinder and Wood (2003) analyse the current macroeconomic policy for the commercialization of agriculture and its impact on the rural poor of Zambia. The target group for this study is 830,000 rural households who are poor and dependent on agriculture. The study indicates that at the macro-level, the Agriculture Commerce Policy (ACP) of the govt. of Zambia is likely to increase the contribution of the agricultural sector to foreign exchange earnings. The policy is also likely to increase agriculture's share of GDP and make a modest contribution to poverty reduction. At the micro-level, the ACPs are likely to build new linkages with international markets, develop new farmer-driven institutions, and promote new crop specific single chain marketing systems. At the micro-level, these policies are likely to improve access to credit and inputs for the small proportion of farmers and provide them with guaranteed markets, increased levels of income and promote the development of a competitive agricultural production and marketing system.

Kumar (1998) has also investigated that different tribal groups are engaged in different type of economic activities such as Tripuri, Riang, Halam etc. community are mainly engaged in shifting cultivation; Chik-Baraik, Bondo, Chakma, Nagas etc. in weaving; Baiga, Chenchu and Kamar etc. make bamboo container; some of the tribal communities are involved in haunting and fishing activities, carpentry activities etc. Most of the tribal women are well engaged in the weaving activities.

Aurora (1964) has investigated the economic condition of a tribal village in Madhya Pradesh. He has investigated that they are belonging in a self-sufficient economy. They are closely connected with the self-sufficient subsistence farming. A corollary to the "subsistence economy" is the close dependence of the levels of income and consumption on the vagaries of nature. Unlike the people in the plains the Adivasi farmer and his family do not have a steady level of living. Some seasons are seasons of plenty and the others of abject hunger and poverty. Indebtedness is the greatest scourge of the Adivasi economy. Borrowing is resorted to for various purposes such as purchasing of seed, expenses for ceremonies.

CHAPTER 3

Socio-economic Status of Rural Tribal in Tripura

The term 'Scheduled Tribes' first appeared in the Constitution of India. Article 366(25) defined scheduled tribes as "such tribes or tribal communities or parts of or groups within such tribes or tribal communities as are deemed under Article 342 to be Scheduled Tribes for the purposes of this constitution". Article 342, which is reproduced below, prescribed procedure to be followed in the matter of specification of scheduled tribes. Article 342 provides for specification of tribes or tribal communities or parts of or groups within tribes or tribal communities which are deemed to be for the purposes of the Constitution the Scheduled Tribes in relation to that State or Union Territory. In pursuance of these provisions, the list of Scheduled Tribes are notified for each State or Union Territory and are valid only within the jurisdiction of that State or Union Territory and not outside. The list of Scheduled Tribes is State/UT specific and a community declared as a Scheduled Tribe in a State need not be so in another State. The inclusion of a community as a Scheduled Tribe is an on-going process. The essential characteristics of these communities are following:

- Primitive Traits
- Geographical isolation
- Distinct culture
- Shy of contact with community at large
- Economically backward

Tribal communities belong to various ecological and geo-climatic conditions ranging from plains and forests to hills and inaccessible areas. Tribal groups are at different stages of social, economic and educational development. While some tribal communities have adopted a mainstream way of life, at the other end of the spectrum, there are 75 Scheduled Tribes known as Particularly Vulnerable Tribal Groups (PVTGs), who are characterised by viz; pre-agriculture level of technology, stagnant or declining population, extremely low literacy and subsistence level of economy.

There are notified 705 Scheduled Tribes in 30 States/Union territories in India. As per Census 2011, the tribal population of the country is 10.43 crore, constituting 8.6 percent of the total population. 89.97 percent of them live in rural areas and 10.03 percent in urban areas. The decadal population growth of the tribal's from Census 2001 to 2011 has been 23.66 percent against the 17.69 percent of the total population.

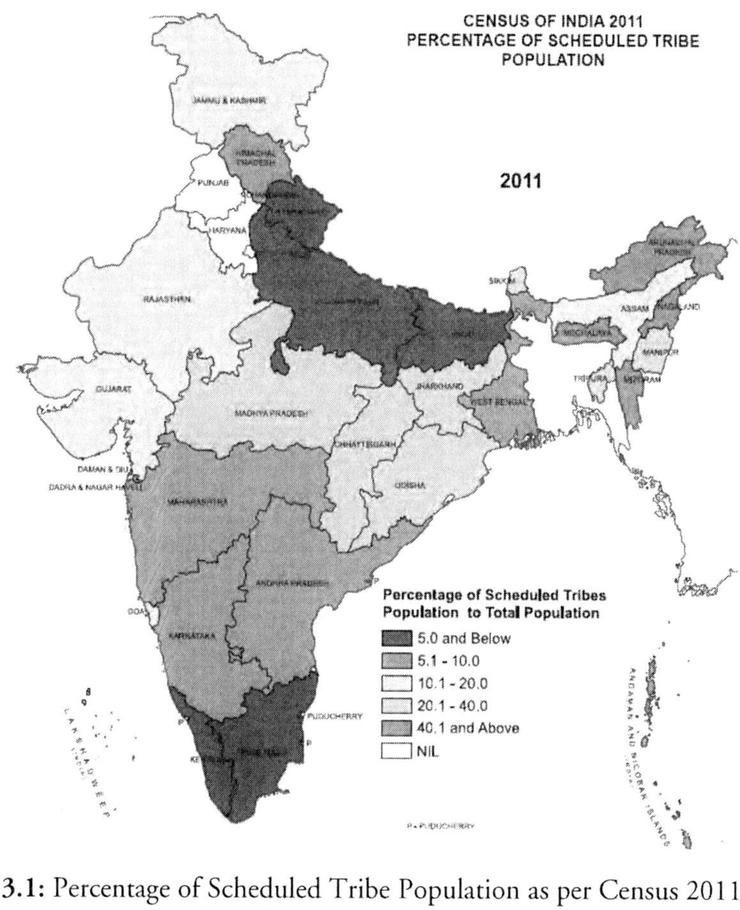

Figure 3.1: Percentage of Scheduled Tribe Population as per Census 2011

Source: Registrar General of India, May 2013.

From the Figure 3.1, it is observed that more than two-third of the ST population is concentrated only in the seven States of the country, viz. Madhya Pradesh, Maharashtra, Orissa, Gujarat, Rajasthan, Jharkhand and Chhattisgarh. Among all States, Mizoram has the highest proportion of Scheduled Tribes (94.43 percent) and Uttar Pradesh has the lowest proportion of Scheduled Tribes (0.57 percent). 17 States and two UTs have higher percentage of ST population than country's average of 8.6 percent. At the district level, 2011 Census reveals that there are 90 districts where ST population is 50 percent or more. As per Census 2001, this number is 75 districts. Out of these 90 districts, 48 districts are in the eight North Eastern States.

Table 3.1 shows the decadal ST population in India. The sex ratio for the overall population is 940 females per 1000 males and that of Scheduled Tribes 990 females per thousand males.

Table 3.1: Decadal Proportion of ST Population in India

Census Year	*Total Population (in Million)*	*ST Population (in Million)*	*Percentage of Total Population*
1961	439.2	30.1	6.9
1971	547.9	38.0	6.9
1981 #	665.3	51.6	7.8
1991 @	838.6	67.8	8.1
2001 $	1028.6	84.3	8.2
2011	1210.8	104.3	8.6

Source: Statistical Profile of STs 2013, https://tribal.nic.in/ST/StatisticalProfileofSTs2013

Note: # Excludes Assam in 1981 @ Excludes Jammu & Kashmir in 1991.

$The figures exclude Mao-Maram, Paomata and Purul sub-divisions of Senapati district of Manipur, census 2001.

Education

Literacy rate (LR) is defined as percentage of literates among the population aged seven years and above. Although literacy levels of STs have improved, but gap in literacy levels both for tribal men and women has not declined significantly. It is increased by 11.86

percentage points from 2001 to 2011 for STs and 8.15 percentage points for total population during the same period (Table 3.2).

Table 3.2: Comparative Literacy Rates of STs and Total Population in India (in percent)

Category/ Census Year	*1961*	*1971*	*1981*	*1991*	*2001*	*2011*
Total Population	28.3	34.45	43.57	52.21	64.84	72.99
Scheduled Tribes	8.53	11.30	16.35	29.60	47.10	58.96
Literacy Gap	19.77	18.15	19.88	22.61	18.28	14.03

Source: Statistical Profile of STs 2013.
https://tribal.nic.in/ST/StatisticalProfileofSTs2013

Gross Enrollment Ratio (GER) for any stage (Different Classes) is defined as percentage of the enrolment in that stage to the estimated child population in the respective age group. The GER has increased from 80.4 percent in 1990–91 to 119.7 in 2010–11 for the STs and from 78.6 percent in 1990–91 to 86.5 percent in 2010–11, for the total population. From 2003–04 to 2010–11, the GER was higher for STs than the SCs and the total population, both for male and female. GER for STs in the elementary stage has improved considerably from 1990–91 to 2010–11. The GER for ST girls improved from 60.2 percent in 1990–91 to 119.8 percent in 2010–11 overall the GER of STs was more pronounced as compared to other social groups.[1]

The Gender Parity Index (GPI) is a socio-economic index usually designed to measure the relative access to education of males and females. In its simplest form, it is calculated as the quotient of the number of females by the number of males enrolled in a given stage of education (primary, secondary, etc.). As per Census 2011, Gender Parity Index (GPI) for STs is seen to be highest in the Classes I–V and lowest in Classes XI-XII. State-wise profile of GPI for STs shows Daman & Diu have the highest GPI in the primary classes, Sikkim has the highest GPI in the upper primary classes while Andaman &Nicobar islands has the highest GPI in the secondary classes. The

[1] *Source:* Statistical Profile of STs 2013.

lowest GPI is noticed in the state of Goa in primary classes with Bihar falling in the category of upper primary and secondary classes.[2]

This chapter mainly focuses on the development aspects on the area where tribal community are belonging in Tripura. For the development of tribal people Tripura Tribal Areas Autonomous District Council (TTAADC) was established. Before discussing the development aspect it is mandatory to discuss about the tribes and the provision for the tribes and their development in Indian Constitution. This chapter is divided into two sections viz; Profile of TTAADC (Section 3.1) and the socio-economic condition of the tribal is discussed in Section 3.2.

3.1 Profile of TTAADC

The princely state of Tripura was an independent kingdom under the Tripuri or Borok dynasty before merging to India dominion on October 15, 1949. The tribal people of Tripura had been asking for autonomy for long years to preserve and promote their distinct ways of life. It was against this background that the state government as well as the central government decided to set up an Autonomous District Council for the areas predominantly having tribal population of the state to introduce internal autonomy in tribal compact areas and thereby protect the social, economic and cultural interests of the tribal population. The objective behind setting up the Autonomous District Council was to hand over certain administrative and legal authority to the Council and in order to devote concerted attention to all aspects of cultural, social and economic improvement of the tribal people. So that people belong to the weaker sections of society and thereby to free them from all kinds of social injustice. There is no doubt that the formation of the District Council under Schedule VI of the Constitution of India had fulfilled the long cherished demand of the tribal people of Tripura for self-government in tribal prone areas. The main objective of forming the District Council under Schedule VI is to remove within a short time the material disparities between the advanced and backward sections of the societies, to strengthen the bonds of unity between the tribal and non-tribal masses, to emancipate

[2] *Source:* Statistical Profile of STs 2013.

not only tribal people but also for all the deprived people from all types of injustice and exploitation. Tripura Tribal Areas Autonomous District Council is a symbol of integrity, harmony and unity of the tribal and non-tribal people of the state. Now it is marching through the concerted efforts of the masses. In the tribal compact areas of the state of Tripura is consisting with 7,132.56 sq. kms. which is almost two-third of the total area of the state.

The Tripura Tribal Areas Autonomous District Council was constituted under the Seventh Schedule to the Constitution of India. The Tripura Tribal Areas Autonomous District Council Bill, 1979 was unanimously passed by the Tripura Legislative Assembly on March 23, 1979. The Tripura Tribal Areas Autonomous District Council was constituted in January 15, 1982 through voting by secret ballot and the elected members were sworn in on January 18, 1982. Subsequently, the Constitution of India had been amended by a Bill and it was passed in the Indian Parliament on August 23, 1984 for introduction of the Sixth Schedule of the Constitution in India. A fresh election under the Sixth Schedule has been held on June 30, 1985 through secret ballot. The headquarter of TTAADC is situated at Khumulwng which is 23 km. away from state capital Agartala.

Table 3.3 shows the details of TTAADC at a glance, Table 3.4 shows the educational infrastructure available and Table 3.5 shows the health infrastructures available in TTAADC area. These are in the following:

From Table 3.3, it is observed that, there are 28 constituencies, and out of that there are 23 ADC blocks and 587 village committees in the TTAADC area. There are six agricultural Sub-Divisions and two horticultural Sub-Divisions in this TTAADC area.

Table 3.3: TTAADC at a Glance

Indicators	*Value*
Total Area of TTAADC (in sq.km.)	7,132.56 sq.km.
No. of TTAADC Constituencies	28
Total members of TTAADC	30* (*Two are nominated by the Governor)
No. of Block in ADC Areas	23
No. of Sub-Zonal Development Offices	33

Indicators	*Value*
No. of Revenue Villages	462
No. of Tahsils	151
No. of Village Committees	587
No. of Police Stations in ADC area	24
No. of Cooperative Banks in ADC area	23
No. of Tripura Gramin Bank in ADC area	46
No. of Range Office	11
No. of Beet Office	40
No. of Agricultural Sub-Divisions	06
No. of Horticultural Sub-Divisions	02

Source: Information collected from TTAADC Office, Khumulwng.

Table 3.4 reveals the educational infrastructure in TTAADC area. From the Table 3.4, it is observed that there are 1466 primary schools, 243 high schools, 69 higher secondary schools, eight degree colleges including technical and professional degree colleges.

Table 3.4: Educational Infrastructures in TTAADC Area

Indicators	*Value*
No. of Primary Schools in ADC area	1466
No. of S.B. Schools in ADC area	212
No. of High Schools in ADC area	243
No. of Higher Secondary Schools in ADC area	69
No. of English Medium Schools in ADC area	24
No. of Colleges (including Technical) in ADC area	08
No. of ITIs in ADC area	03

Source: Information collected from TTAADC Office, Khumulwng.

Table 3.5 reveals the health infrastructure in TTAADC area. From the Table 3.5, it is observed that health infrastructure is very poor in the TTAADC area. There are only two hospitals and one health sub-centre which is not sufficient for the area of 7132.56 square km. However, number of veterinary hospitals and dispensaries for animals are more than the tribal.

Table 3.5: Health Infrastructures in TTAADC Area

Indicators	*Value*
No. of Hospitals	02
No. of Health Sub-Centre	01
No. of Veterinary Hospitals	04
No. of Veterinary Dispensaries	16

Source: Information collected from TTAADC Office, Khumulwng.

Table 3.6: Zone-wise Village Committee and Population of TTAADC Areas (Based on 2005–06

Sl.	*Name of Zone*	*No. of V.C*	*No. of Family*				*Population*			
			ST	*SC*	*UR*	*Total*	*ST*	*SC*	*UR*	*Total*
1.	West Zone	185	72,308	2,436	4,487	79,231	4,02,948	12,423	23,647	4,39,018
2.	South Zone	167	56,260	2,878	7,890	67,028	2,90,153	13,288	37,654	3,41,095
3.	North Zone	79	23,750	2,733	9,865	36,303	1,25,641	13,360	47,486	1,86,487
4.	Dhalai Zone	96	37,158	3,933	5,578	46,669	2,02,818	19,442	27,605	2,49,865
Total		**527**	**1,89,431**	**11,980**	**27,820**	**2,29,231**	**10,21,560**	**58,513**	**1,36,392**	**12,16,465**

Source: Information collected from TTAADC Office, Khumulwng.

Table 3.6 shows zone-wise village committee and demographic profile of the TTAADC area. It is found that most of the tribal families belong to West Zone and South Zone as there is more number of village committee. In West Zone there are 185 village committees and 167 are in South Zone. Comparatively least number of tribal families is found in North Zone as there is only 79 village committee.

3.2 Socio-economic Status of the Surveyed Household Beneficiaries

In order to examine the impact assessment study, the study team has surveyed six districts out of eight districts in Tripura. Out of these surveyed six districts, 100 sample households have been collected from the Dhalai, South Tripura, Gomati and West Tripura district; however, 50 sample households' data have been collected from Khowai and Sepahijala districts of Tripura. This section shows the socio-economic status of the surveyed household beneficiaries in Tripura. The socio-economic status of the tribal households includes social and economic conditions which can be discussed under the following sub-sections.

3.2.1 *Social Status of the Surveyed Household Beneficiaries in the Study Area*

The social status of the surveyed household beneficiaries in the study area can be discussed in the following sub-heads.

Demographic Profile of the Household Beneficiaries in the Study Area

District-wise demographic profiles are explained in the following Table 3.7. Table 3.7 reveals the district-wise and sex-wise demographic distribution of the surveyed beneficiaries.

From Table 3.7, it is observed that data has been collected from a total of 500 sample beneficiary household and out of that 100 beneficiary household have been selected from Dhalai, Gomati, South Tripura and West Tripura district and 50 household have been selected from Khowai and Sepahijala district. Three blocks are selected from both Dhalai and South Tripura district for 100 samples, and two blocks are selected from remaining four districts.

Table 3.7: District-wise and Block-wise Demographic Profile and Sex Ratio of the Sample Beneficiary Households in Tripura

District	*Block*	*Households*	*Total Population*	*Male*	*Female*	*Sex Ratio*
Dhalai	Ambassa	17 (3.40)	81 (3.68)	39 (48.15)	42 (51.85)	1077
	Manu	46 (9.20)	237 (10.76)	122 (51.48)	115 (48.52)	943
	Salema	37 (7.40)	150 (6.81)	77 (51.33)	73 (48.67)	948
Gomati	Killa	60 (12.0)	269 (12.20)	132 (49.07)	137 (50.93)	1038
	Matabari	40 (8.0)	176 (7.99)	92 (52.27)	84 (47.73)	913
Khowai	Kalyanpur	22 (4.40)	97 (4.40)	51 (52.58)	46 (47.42)	902
	Teliamura	28 (5.60)	121 (5.49)	62 (51.24)	59 (48.76)	952
Sepahijala	Jampuijala	32 (6.40)	129 (5.86)	60 (46.51)	69 (53.49)	1150
	Nalchar	18 (3.60)	77 (3.50)	33 (42.86)	44 (57.14)	1333
South Tripura	B.C Nagar	31 (6.20)	142 (6.44)	82 (57.75)	60 (42.25)	732
	Rajnagar	42 (8.40)	179 (8.13)	102 (56.98)	77 (43.02)	755
	Rupaichhari	27 (5.40)	126 (5.72)	64 (50.79)	62 (49.21)	969
West Tripura	Jirania	49 (9.80)	201 (9.12)	105 (52.24)	96 (47.76)	914
	Mandai	51 (10.20)	218 (9.90)	109 (50.0)	109 (50.0)	1000
Total		**500 (100.0)**	**2203 (100.0)**	**1130 (51.3)**	**1073 (48.7)**	**950**

Source: Computed on the basis of Field Survey, December, 2021.

Note: Percentages are given in the parentheses.

So, a total of 14 blocks are analysed in this study. Table 3.7 also reveals that there are total population is 2203 from these 500 household beneficiaries. Out of these populations, 51.3 per cent is male population and 48.7 per cent is female population. The sex ratio per thousand male populations is found 950 in these selected sample households. Most of the populations belong to Killa block (269) of Gomati district which is followed by Manu block (237) under Dhalai district, Mandai (218) and Jirania block (201) under the West Tripura district. It is also observed that the highest sex ratio per thousand male populations is in Nalchar block (1333) of Sepahijala district, which is followed by Jampuijala block (1150) of the same district, Ambassa (1077) of Dhalai district, Killa (1038) of Gomati district, Mandai (1000) of the West Tripura district. The least sex ratio among these selected 14 blocks of Tripura is found in B.C. Nagar block (732) of South Tripura district and the second least sex ratio is found in Rajnagar block (755) in the same district South Tripura.

Table 3.8 reveals the sex-wise and age group-wise distribution among the selected sample blocks. The age group is divided into five categories viz. 0–6 years of age, 7–18 years of age, 19–30 years of age, 31–60 years of age and above 60 years of age group (elderly group). From Table 3.8, it is observed that most of the people belong to the age group of 31–60 years which is followed by the age group of 19–30 years, 7–19 years of age group. Children belong to 0–6 years of age group is least in number. The second least in number is the elderly persons who are above 60 years of age and out of that 60 per cent are elderly male and 40 per cent are elderly female persons. In this sample data set, it is observed that most of the elderly male and female are found in Mandai block of West Tripura district. Most of the people belong to 31–60 years of age group are stay in Killa block of Gomati district. Among the total population, male percentage is 51.3 and female percentage is 48.7.

Table 3.8: Block-wise Demographic Status (Age Group-wise and Sex-wise) of the Sample Beneficiary Households in Tripura

District	Block	0–6 Year		7–18 Year		19–30 Year		31–60 Year		60 Above		Total	
		Male	Female	Male	Female	Male	Female	Male	Female	Male	Female	Male	Female
Dhalai	Ambassa	2	1	9	10	9	13	13	17	6	1	39 (48.15)	42 (51.85)
	Manu	1	5	39	21	23	37	52	48	7	4	122 (51.48)	115 (48.52)
	Salema	0	0	21	14	18	20	30	36	8	3	77 (51.33)	73 (48.67)
Gomati	Killa	3	2	38	44	34	35	52	54	5	2	132 (49.07)	137 (50.93)
	Matabari	2	4	26	22	18	22	41	33	5	3	92 (52.27)	84 (47.73)
Khowai	Kalyanpur	1	1	10	8	12	10	24	23	4	4	51 (52.58)	46 (47.42)
	Teliamura	1	3	18	14	12	9	29	30	2	3	62 (51.24)	59 (48.76)
Sepahijala	Jampuijala	3	1	11	10	11	20	29	30	6	8	60 (46.51)	69 (53.49)
	Nalchar	1	2	8	12	12	11	14	17	1	2	33 (42.86)	44 (57.14)

District	Block	0–6 Year		7–18 Year		19–30 Year		31–60 Year		60 Above		Total	
		Male	Female	Male	Female	Male	Female	Male	Female	Male	Female	Male	Female
South Tripura	B.C Nagar	4	2	23	17	20	19	30	18	5	4	82 (57.75)	60 (42.25)
	Rajnagar	8	9	28	17	28	20	36	30	2	1	102 (56.98)	77 (43.02)
	Rupaichari	4	4	13	18	21	15	24	23	2	2	64 (50.79)	62 (49.21)
West Tripura	Jirania	1	2	19	12	25	25	50	50	10	7	105 (52.24)	96 (47.76)
	Mandai	1	1	16	18	29	32	42	46	21	12	109 (50.0)	109 (50.0)
Total		**32 (46.38)**	**37 (53.62)**	**279 (54.07)**	**237 (45.93)**	**272 (48.57)**	**288 (51.43)**	**466 (50.60)**	**455 (49.40)**	**84 (60.0)**	**56 (40.0)**	**1130 (51.3)**	**1073 (48.7)**

Source: Computed on the basis of Field Survey, December, 2021.

Note: Percentages are given in the parentheses.

Religion-wise distribution of the Household Beneficiaries in the Study Area

District-wise distribution of the religion among the surveyed tribal beneficiaries is given in the following Table 3.9.

Table 3.9: District-wise and Block-wise Religious Profile of the Sample Beneficiary Households in Tripura

District	*Block*	*Hindu*	*Christian*	*Buddhist*	*Total*
Dhalai	Ambassa	11 (64.71)	4 (23.53)	2 (11.76)	17 (100.0)
	Manu	0 (0.00)	1 (2.17)	45 (97.83)	46 (100.0)
	Salema	33 (89.19)	4 (10.81)	0 (0.00)	37 (100.0)
Gomati	Killa	46 (78.67)	14 (23.33)	0 (0.00)	60 (100.0)
	Matabari	29 (72.50)	8 (40.00)	3 (7.50)	40 (100.0)
Khowai	Kalyanpur	19 (86.36)	3 (13.64)	0 (0.00)	22 (100.0)
	Teliamura	18 (64.29)	10 (35.71)	0 (0.00)	28 (100.0)
Sepahijala	Jampuijala	31 (96.88)	1 (3.12)	0 (0.00)	32 (100.0)
	Nalchar	13 (72.22)	5 (27.78)	0 (0.00)	18 (100.0)
South	B.C Nagar	24 (77.42)	7 (22.58)	0 (0.00)	31 (100.0)
	Rajnagar	19 (45.24)	20 (47.62)	3 (7.14)	42 (100.0)
	Rupaichhari	4 (14.81)	0 (0.00)	23 (85.19)	27 (100.0)
West	Jirania	37 (75.51)	12 (24.49)	0 (0.00)	49 (100.0)
	Mandai	37 (72.55)	14 (27.45)	0 (0.00)	51 (100.0)
Total		**321 (64.20)**	**103 (20.60)**	**76 (15.20)**	**500 (100.0)**

Source: Computed on the basis of Field Survey, December, 2021.

Note: Percentages are given in the parentheses.

From Table 3.9, it is observed that 64.20 percentages of the sample households are Hindu, followed by 20.60 percentage Christian households. The remaining 15.20 percentage households are the believers of Buddhist religion. Block-level data shows that Jampuijala block under the Sepahijala district has the highest number of Hindu households (96.88 per cent) followed by Salema block (89.19 per cent) of Dhalai district, Kalyanpur (86.36 per cent) of Khowai district, Killa (78.67 per cent) under the Gomati district etc. Surprisingly, it is found that, none of the sample households belong to Hindu religion.

The number of Christian households is the highest in Rajnagar block (47.62 per cent) of the South Tripura district, which is followed by Matabari block (40 per cent) under the Gomati district, Teliamura block (35.71 per cent) under the Khowai district. Surprisingly, it is also observed that none of the sample beneficiary family under the Rupaichhari block of the South Tripura district belongs to Christian religion. Manu block (97.83 per cent) has the highest number of sample households belong to Buddhist religion which is followed by Rupaichhari block (85.19 per cent) of the South Tripura district. Out of the 14 sample blocks, Buddhist belongs to only five blocks. The following Figure 3.2 also shows religious profile of the beneficiary households.

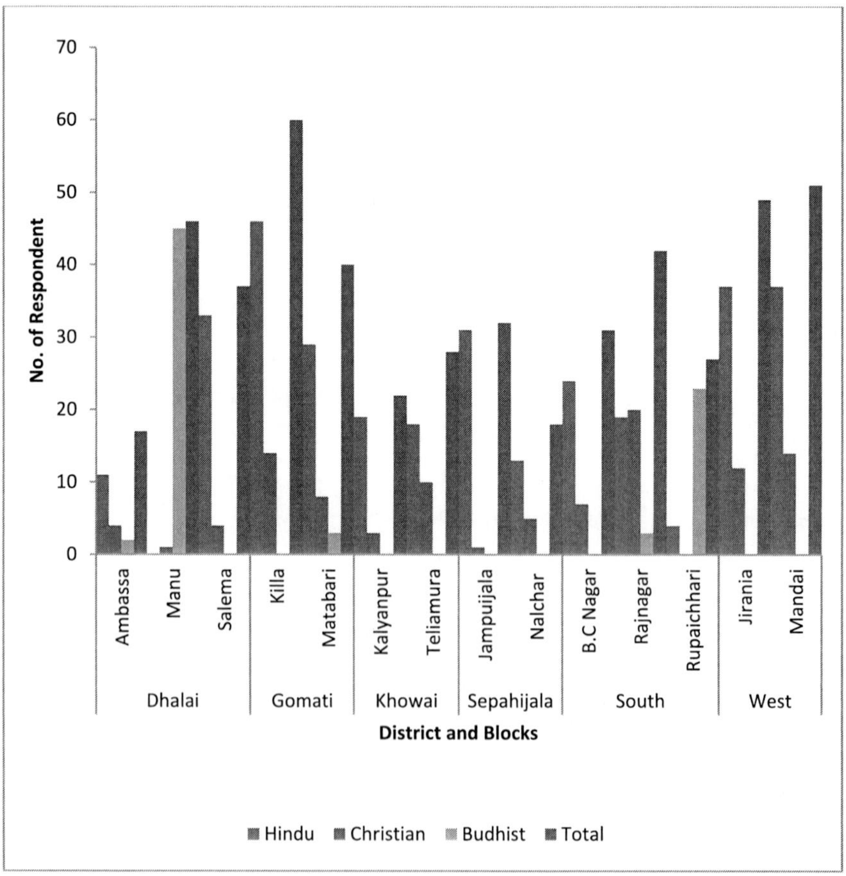

Figure 3.2: Religious Profile of the Sample Beneficiary Households

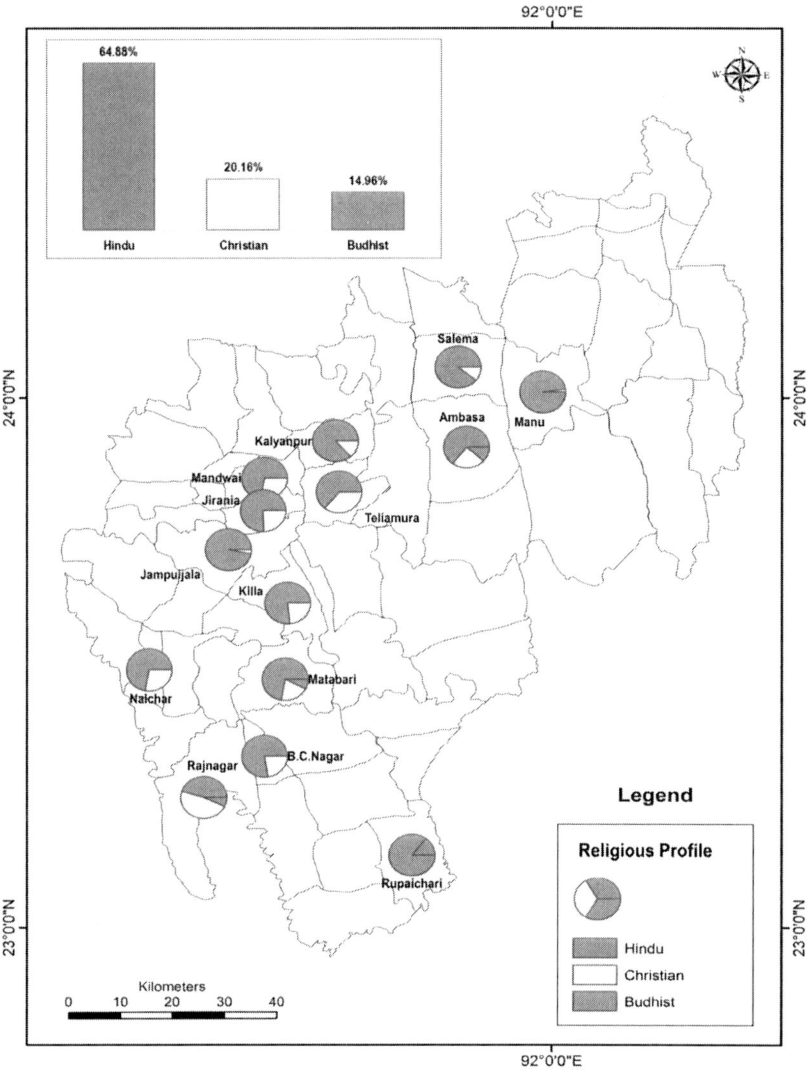

Figure 3.3: Mapping of Blocks with Diverse Religious Profile in the Study Area

Educational Status of the Household Beneficiaries in the Study Area

District-wise educational status among the surveyed tribal household beneficiaries is given in the following Table 3.10. Table 3.10 presents block-wise educational status of the respondents. Out of the total respondents, 37.80 per cent are found illiterate and the rest of them

Table3.10: Block-wise Educational Status of the Respondents in Tripura (in per cent)

District	*Block*	*Illiterate*	*Primary*	*Middle School*	*Secondary*	*Higher Secondary*	*Graduation*
Dhalai	Ambassa	41.18	11.76	11.76	29.41	5.88	0.00
	Manu	39.13	39.13	10.87	10.87	0.00	0.00
	Salema	32.43	32.43	24.32	8.11	2.70	0.00
Gomati	Killa	41.67	36.67	13.33	5.00	3.33	0.00
	Matabari	37.50	27.50	22.50	7.50	5.00	0.00
Khowai	Kalyanpur	54.55	18.18	13.64	4.55	9.09	0.00
	Teliamura	32.14	32.14	17.86	14.29	3.57	0.00
Sepahijala	Jampuijala	56.25	6.25	6.25	28.13	3.13	0.00
	Nalchar	55.56	22.22	5.56	16.67	0.00	0.00
South	B.C Nagar	38.71	29.03	16.13	9.68	3.23	3.23
	Rajnagar	21.43	45.24	23.81	7.14	2.38	0.00
	Rupaichari	37.04	37.04	25.93	0.00	0.00	0.00
West	Jirania	22.45	20.41	26.53	16.33	14.29	0.00
	Mandai	41.18	21.57	11.76	17.65	5.88	1.96
Total		**37.80**	**28.60**	**17.00**	**11.80**	**4.40**	**0.40**

Source: Computed on the basis of Field Survey, December, 2021.

are literate and educated. Out of the total respondents, 28.60 per cent are found to have primary level of education, followed by 17 per cent of the respondents who have completed middle school level of education. 11.80 per cent of the respondents have studied up to secondary level of education. After secondary education, the enrolment rate in higher classes is found to be very poor. As the survey data indicates, 4.40 per cent of the respondents have completed higher secondary level of education and a mere 0.40 per cent is found to have studied up to graduate level.

Block-wise data reveals that the highest percentage of illiterate is found in Jampuijala block (56.25 per cent) followed by Nalchar (55.56 per cent). With regard to primary level of education, Rajnagar block (45.24 per cent) of South Tripura district has the highest percentage of sample respondents who have studied up to primary level, while in case of secondary level of education, the highest percentage is found in Ambassa block (29.41 per cent) of the Dhalai district. Further, Jirania block (14.29 per cent) has the highest percentage of respondents having educational qualification up to higher secondary level. It is surprising that only in two blocks viz; B.C. Nagar block (3.23 per cent) of South Tripura district and Mandai block (1.96 per cent) of West Tripura district, the beneficiary respondents have educational quail-fication up to Graduation level.

Housing and Sanitation Condition of the Household Beneficiaries in the Study Area

Block-wise housing and sanitation condition of the tribal beneficiary households is discussed in the following Table 3.11. Table 3.11 reveals the condition of housing and sanitation type of the beneficiary house-holds.

It is observed that more than 76 per cent of the households reported that they have kaccha houses and 16 per cent live in pucca houses. The rest of the populations (7.8 per cent) live in semi-pucca houses. Block-wise data on the type of houses show that 98 per cent households in Mandai block live in kaccha a house which is followed by Rajnagar block (95.2 per cent), Rupaichhari block (88.9 per cent) of South Tripura district, Ambassa block (82.4 per cent) of the Dhalai district. The least percentage of household beneficiaries having kachha house is in Matabari block of the Gomati district. About 28 percent

Table 3.11: Block-wise House Type and Sanitation Type of the Households (in Percent)

District	*Block*	*House Type*			*Sanitation Type*		
		Kaccha	*Pucca*	*Semi-Pucca*	*Kaccha*	*Pucca*	*Semi-Pucca*
Dhalai	Ambassa	82.4	5.9	11.8	17.6	47.1	35.3
	Manu	58.7	13.0	28.3	37.0	8.7	54.3
	Salema	81.1	13.5	5.4	2.7	54.1	43.2
Gomati	Killa	75.0	18.3	6.7	26.7	5.0	68.3
	Matabari	52.5	32.5	15.0	45.0	7.5	47.5
Khowai	Kalyanpur	63.6	31.8	4.5	0.0	0.0	100.0
	Teliamura	64.3	28.6	7.1	0.0	0.0	100.0
Sepahijala	Jampuijala	71.9	21.9	6.3	12.5	9.4	78.1
	Nalchar	72.2	16.7	11.1	16.7	11.1	72.2
South	B.C Nagar	93.5	6.5	0.0	16.1	6.5	77.4
	Rajnagar	95.2	2.4	2.4	14.3	52.4	33.3
	Rupaichhari	88.9	0.0	11.1	18.5	11.1	70.4
West	Jirania	67.3	30.6	2.0	0.0	0.0	100.0
	Mandai	98.0	2.0	0.0	13.7	3.9	82.4
Total		**76.2**	**16.0**	7.8	**17.0**	**14.4**	**68.6**

Source: Computed on the basis of Field Survey, December, 2021.

of the households in Manu block under the Dhalai district have reported they live in semi-pucca a house which is followed by Matabari block (15 per cent) of the Gomati district. Further, Matabari block has the highest percentage of respondents (32.5 per cent) living in pucca houses followed by Kalyanpur block (31.8 per cent). It is evident from the available data that the condition of housing in the studied area does not suffice the needs of maintaining basic standard of living as more than 75 per cent of the respondents reported to live in kaccha houses. One of the important determinants of hygienic living condition is the availability of proper toilet and sanitation facility at the household level.

Figure 3.4 and Figure 3.5 shows the housing condition and block-wise mapping of the housing condition of the sample beneficiary households in the study area.

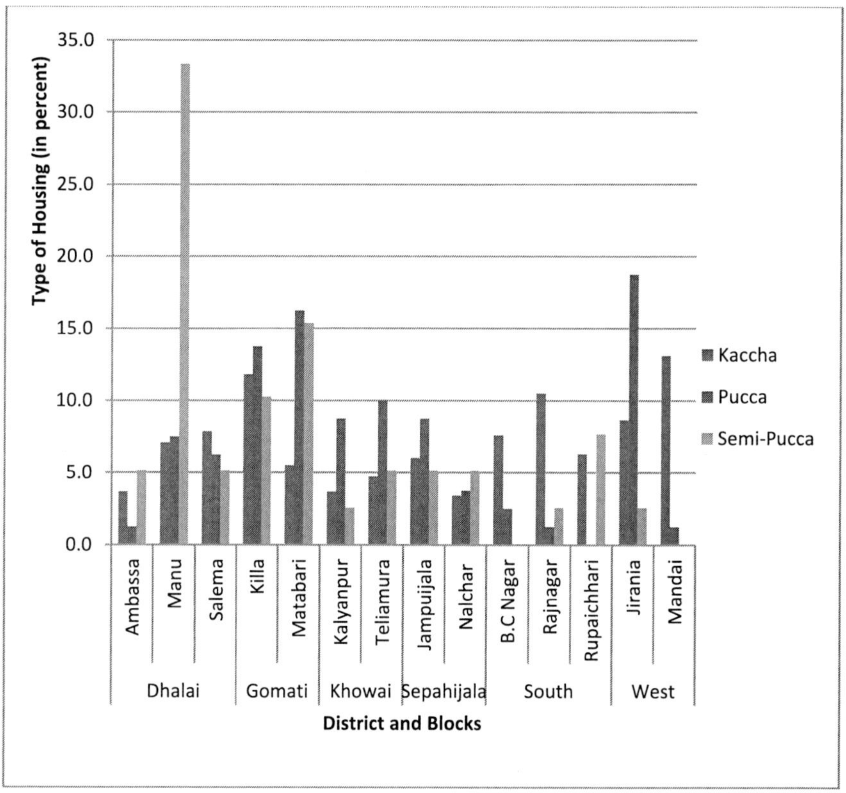

Figure 3.4: Housing Condition of the Beneficiary Households

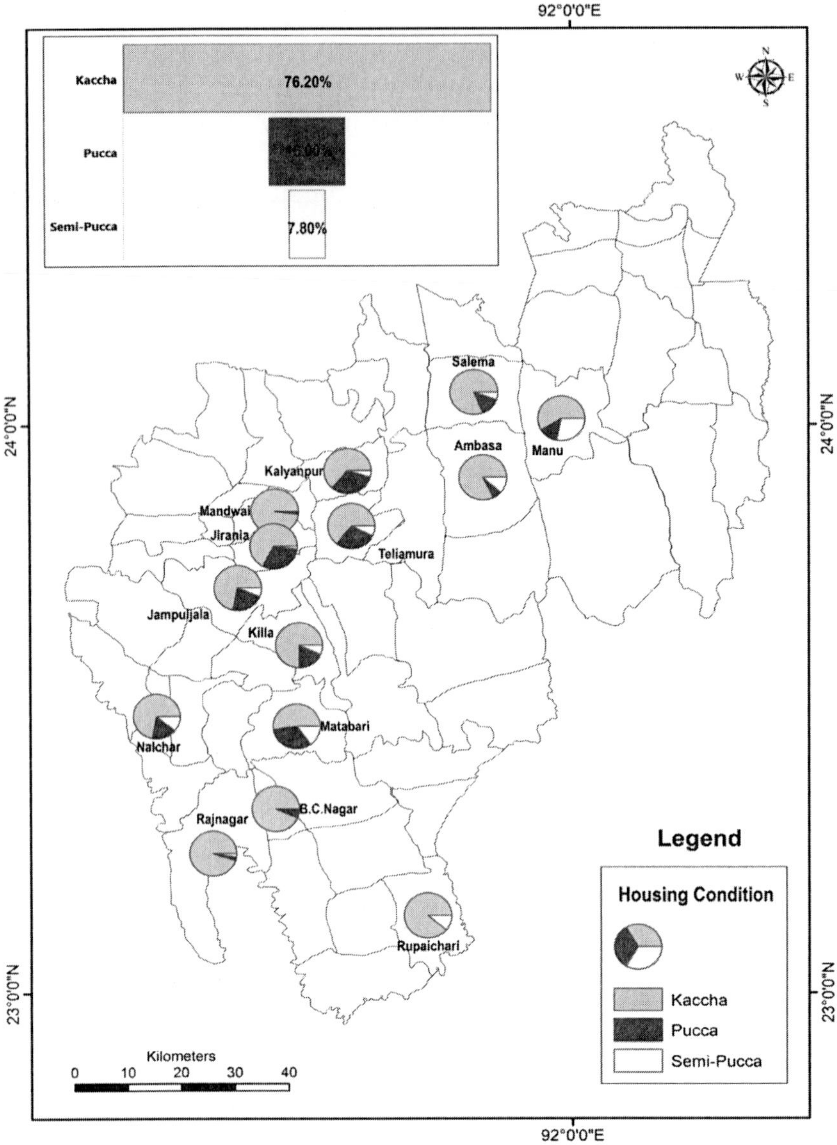

Figure 3.5: Mapping of Blocks Showing Housing Condition in the Study Area

Figure 3.6 and Figure 3.7 shows the sanitation condition and block-wise mapping of the sanitation condition of the sample beneficiary households in the study area.

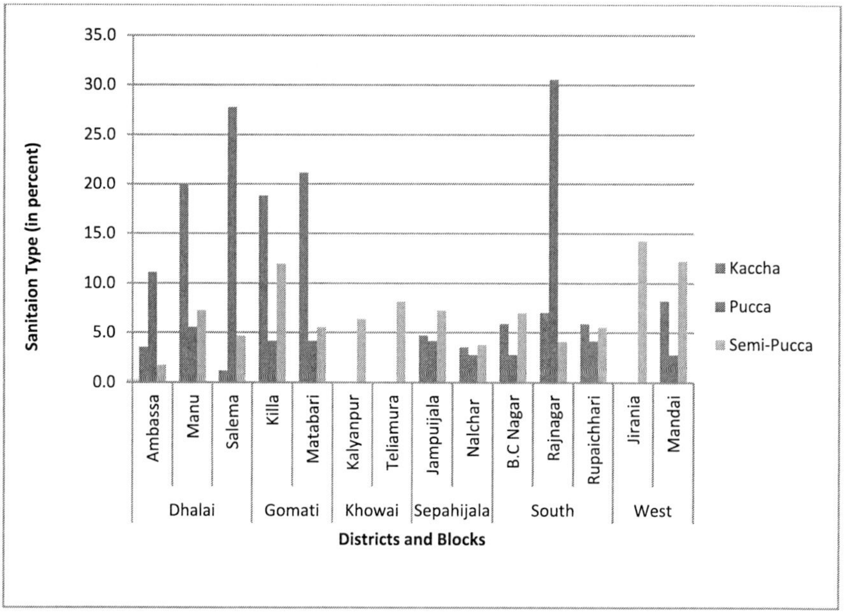

Figure 3.6: Sanitation Condition of the Beneficiary Households

Table 3.11 also reveals that the sanitary condition of the beneficiary households in the study area. It is found that out of the total 500 households, about 17 percent of the households do not have good sanitation and latrine facilities and they are still using kaccha latrine for their defecation purpose. Only around 14 percent of the households have pucca sanitation facility and the remaining 68.6 percent have semi-pucca sanitation and latrine facilities. Block wise data on the type of sanitation reveals that the use of kachha sanitation facilities is the found highest in Matabari block (45 percent) of the Gomati district which is followed by Manu block (37 percent) of Dhalai district which establishes the low awareness about health and hygienic living condition of the households. Highest percentage of pucca sanitation is available in Salema block (54.1 per cent) of Dhalai district which is followed by Rajnagar block (52.4 per cent) of South Tripura district, Ambasa block (47.1 per cent) under Dhalai district. Significantly, no kachha and pucca sanitation facilities are found Kalyanpur and Teliamura block of the Khowai district and in Jirania block of West Tripura district. In these blocks all household have semi-pucca sanitation facilities.

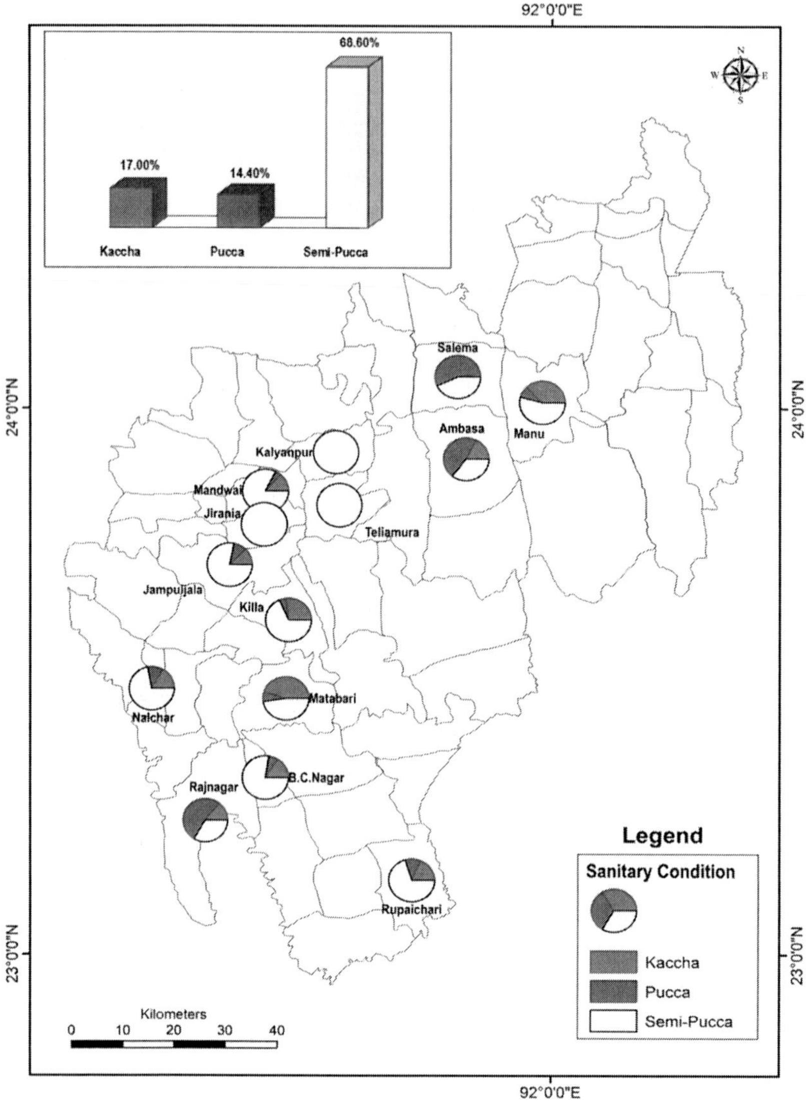

Figure 3.7: Mapping of Blocks Showing Sanitary Condition in the Study Area

Table 3.12 shows the block-wise number of rooms having in the houses of the sample tribal beneficiaries. The availability of housing space for the sample households, as reported in Table 3.12, reveals that majority of the households (65.2 per cent) possess two rooms each, followed by 22.2 percent have four rooms, 6.6 per cent have six rooms, 3.2 per cent have single room houses, 2.2 per cent have three rooms and only 0.6 per cent possess five rooms in their houses.

Table 3.12: Block-wise Number of Rooms having in the Houses of Sample Households (in percent)

District	*Block*	*No of Rooms*					
		1	*2*	*3*	*4*	*5*	*6*
Dhalai	Ambassa	0.0	70.6	11.8	5.9	5.9	5.9
	Manu	2.2	41.3	2.2	23.9	2.2	28.3
	Salema	0.0	56.8	10.8	27.0	0.0	5.4
Gomati	Killa	1.7	68.3	1.7	23.3	0.0	5.0
	Matabari	0.0	52.5	0.0	32.5	0.0	15.0
Khowai	Kalyanpur	0.0	63.6	0.0	31.8	0.0	4.5
	Teliamura	0.0	64.3	0.0	28.6	0.0	7.1
Sepahijala	Jampuijala	0.0	78.1	0.0	18.8	0.0	3.1
	Nalchar	0.0	94.4	0.0	5.6	0.0	0.0
South Tripura	B.C Nagar	0.0	67.7	0.0	29.0	0.0	3.2
	Rajnagar	7.1	83.3	2.4	7.1	0.0	0.0
	Rupaichhari	7.4	74.1	7.4	7.4	3.7	0.0
West Tripura	Jirania	2.0	61.2	0.0	32.7	0.0	4.1
	Mandai	15.7	62.7	0.0	19.6	0.0	2.0
Total		**3.2**	**65.2**	**2.2**	**22.2**	**0.6**	**6.6**

Source: Computed on the basis of Field Survey, December, 2021.

Block-wise comparison shows that 15.7 per cent of the households in Mandai block possess only one room in their houses, 94.4 per cent in Nalchar block have two rooms, 11.8 per cent households from Ambassa block possess three rooms, 32.7 per cent in Jirania block have four rooms, 5.9 per cent in Ambassa block have five rooms and 28.3 per cent in Manu possess six rooms in their houses.

Table 3.13 shows the housing area details of the sample beneficiary families. It is seen that out of the total sample households, 67 per cent possess a household area of 220–330 sq. ft each, followed by 23 per cent of the households having a housing area of 440–550 sq. ft. Only

Table 3.13: Block-wise Housing Area Details of the Beneficiary Households (in Sq. ft)

District	*Block*	*220–330 sq. ft*	*330–440 sq. ft*	*440–550 sq. ft*	*550–660 sq. ft*	*Above660 sq. ft*
Dhalai	Ambassa	70.6	11.8	5.9	5.9	5.9
	Manu	43.5	2.2	23.9	2.2	28.3
	Salema	56.8	8.1	27.0	0.0	8.1
Gomati	Killa	70.0	1.7	23.3	0.0	5.0
	Matabari	52.5	0.0	32.5	0.0	15.0
Khowai	Kalyanpur	63.6	0.0	31.8	0.0	4.5
	Teliamura	64.3	0.0	28.6	0.0	7.1
Sepahijala	Jampuijala	75.0	0.0	21.9	0.0	3.1
	Nalchar	94.4	0.0	5.6	0.0	0.0
South Tripura	B.C. Nagar	61.3	0.0	32.3	3.2	3.2
	Rajnagar	88.1	2.4	9.5	0.0	0.0
	Rupaichhari	70.4	11.1	11.1	3.7	3.7
West Tripura	Jirania	63.3	0.0	32.7	0.0	4.1
	Mandai	78.4	0.0	19.6	0.0	2.0
Total		**67.0**	**2.2**	**23.0**	**0.8**	**7.0**

Source: Computed on the basis of Field Survey, December, 2021.

2.2 per cent of the households have reported to possess a household area of 330–440 sq. ft and only 0.8 per cent possesses an area of 550–660 sq. ft. A household area of 660 sq. ft and above is possessed by only seven per cent of the total households. Block-wise comparison shows that about 94 per cent households in Nalchar block of Sepahijala district have reported to possess a household area of 220–330 sq. ft each, about 12 per cent households in Ambassa block having an area of 330–440 sq. ft and nearly 33 per cent households in Jirania block having an area of 440–550 sq. ft. Similarly, Manu block (28.30 per cent) of Dhalai district has the highest percentage of households having an area of household of 660 sq. ft and above. It is also observed that in Nalchar block of Sepahijala district and Rajnagar block area of South Tripura district, no household have a housing area of more than 550 sq. ft area.

Table 3.14 shows the distribution of total area of bastu among the sample households.

Table 3.14: Block-wise Average Area of Bastu of the Sample Households (in Kani)*

District	*Block*	*No. of Households*	*Average Area of Bastu*
Dhalai	Ambassa	17	0.9
	Manu	46	1.3
	Salema	37	1.1
Gomati	Killa	60	1.0
	Matabari	40	1.1
Khowai	Kalyanpur	22	1.0
	Teliamura	28	1.0
Sepahijala	Jampuijala	32	1.4
	Nalchar	18	0.8
South Tripura	B.C Nagar	31	1.5
	Rajnagar	42	0.9
	Rupaichhari	27	0.9
West Tripura	Jirania	49	1.4
	Mandai	51	1.1
Total		**500**	**1.1**

Source: Computed on the basis of Field Survey, December, 2021.
Note: *1 Kani = 1.322 Acres.

The mean area of bastu for the sample households is found to be 1.1 kani. Block-wise data shows that the average area of bastu is the highest (1.5 kani) for the sample households belong to B.C. Nagar block of South Tripura whereas it is the lowest (0.8 kani) for households belong to Nalchar block of the Sepahijala district.

Availability of Drinking Water Facilities of the Household Beneficiaries in the Study Area

Table 3.15 shows the sources of drinking water and the average distance of it from their home in the study area. It is evident that majority (79.2 per cent) of the sample households having the access to supply water for their drinking. However, 11.4 per cent of the

Table 3.15: Block-wise Sources of Drinking Water (in per cent) and Average Distance from Drinking Water Source (in meter)

District	*Block*	*Tube Wells*	*Supply Water*	*Bore Wells*	*Pond*	*Other*	*Average Distance (in meter)*
Dhalai	Ambassa	29.4	41.2	11.8	11.8	5.9	168.2
	Manu	4.3	91.3	0.0	4.3	0.0	108.5
	Salema	5.4	81.1	10.8	0.0	2.7	149.8
Gomati	Killa	23.3	56.7	5.0	11.7	3.3	112.7
	Matabari	7.5	55.0	0.0	37.5	0.0	599.8
Khowai	Kalyanpur	0.0	100.0	0.0	0.0	0.0	19.7
	Teliamura	0.0	100.0	0.0	0.0	0.0	20.5
Sepahijala	Jampuijala	9.4	90.6	0.0	0.0	0.0	16.4
	Nalchar	5.6	94.4	0.0	0.0	0.0	33.6
South Tripura	B.C Nagar	9.7	90.3	0.0	0.0	0.0	84.8
	Rajnagar	28.6	57.1	4.8	2.4	7.1	95.6
	Rupai-chhari	22.2	74.1	0.0	3.7	0.0	221.1
West Tripura	Jirania	0.0	100.0	0.0	0.0	0.0	100.4
	Mandai	11.8	86.3	0.0	0.0	2.0	90.5
Total		**11.4**	**79.2**	**2.2**	**5.6**	**1.6**	**136.87**

Source: Computed on the basis of Field Survey, December, 2021.

households collect their drinking water from tube wells. Only 2.2 per cent of the respondents have reported that they use bore wells for drinking water. It is worth mentioning that 5.6 per cent of the total sample households still depend on unsafe sources of drinking water such as pond. 1.6 per cent of the respondents have reported that they rely on other sources like hand pump, use of motor in house etc. for their drinking water.

Block-wise data on sources of drinking water show that supply water is the main source of drinking water for the people (Table 3.15). It is found that cent per cent household belongs to Kalyanpur, Teliamura of Khowai district and Jirania block of West Tripura district use supply water for their drinking which is followed Nalchar block (94.4 per cent) of Sepahijala district, Manu block (91.3 per cent) of Dhalai district and B.C. Nagar block (90.3 per cent) of South Tripura district. Whereas, highest percentage of households belong to Ambassablock (29.4 per cent) use drinking water sources from tube wells. Use of bore well as the main source of drinking water is also the highest in Ambassablock (11.8 percent) of Dhalai district while dependency on unsafe sources of drinking water like pond, river etc. is the highest in Matabariblock (37.5 percent) of the

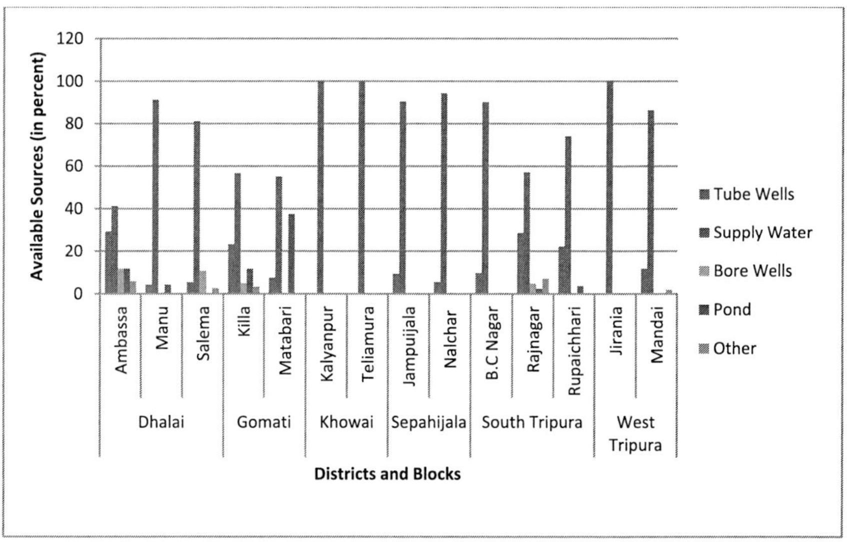

Figure 3.8: Available Sources of Drinking Water for the Beneficiary Households

Gomati district. The household belongs to Matabari block the walks the highest average distance (599.8 meter) to collect their drinking water, which is followed by Rupaichhari block (221.1 meter) of South Tripura district. The minimum distance is covered by the household of Jampuijala block (16.4 meter) of the Sepahijala district.

Figure 3.8 shows the available sources of drinking water for the beneficiary households.

Status of Electrification Gas Connection of the Household Beneficiaries in the Study Area

Proportion of households using electricity for domestic lighting instantaneously reflects the social status of the households as well as the success of welfare state. Table 3.16 shows the block-wise status of electrification and gas connection of the beneficiary households in the state.

Table 3.16: Block-wise Electricity and Gas Connection Details of the Households (in percent)

District	*Block*	*Electricity*	*Ujjala*	*Cylinder*	*No. Connection*
Dhalai	Ambassa	100.0	70.6	5.9	23.5
	Manu	100.0	65.2	6.5	28.3
	Salema	100.0	75.7	5.4	18.9
Gomati	Killa	100.0	93.3	5.0	1.7
	Matabari	100.0	90.0	0.0	10.0
Khowai	Kalyanpur	100.0	100.0	0.0	0.0
	Teliamura	100.0	100.0	0.0	0.0
Sepahijala	Jampuijala	100.0	90.6	9.4	0.0
	Nalchar	100.0	83.3	16.7	0.0
South Tripura	B.C Nagar	100.0	90.3	9.7	0.0
	Rajnagar	100.0	76.2	2.4	21.4
	Rupaichhari	100.0	66.7	14.8	18.5
West Tripura	Jirania	100.0	100.0	0.0	0.0
	Mandai	100.0	96.1	0.0	3.9
Total		**100.0**	**86.4**	**4.6**	**9.0**

Source: Computed on the basis of Field Survey, December, 2021.

Table 3.16 also reveals that all the sample households have electricity connection in their own houses for domestic lighting purpose. Table 3.16 also reflects that 86.4 percent have Ujjala gas connection and 4.6 percent the households avail cylinder gas connection. Nine percent of the sample households neither have Ujjala nor cylinder gas connection for cooking purpose. They mostly depend on conventional sources like kerosene, cow dung, wood etc. for cooking purpose. Block-wise data on gas connection reveals that cent per cent households from Kalyanpur block, Teliamura block and Jirania block avail Ujjala gas connection at their houses for cooking purpose. The availability of gas connection is found negligible in Manu and Ambassa block as 28.3 percent and 23.5 percent of the respondents have reported that they do not avail any kind of gas connection facility.

Status of Household Assets of the Beneficiaries in the Study Area

Table 3.17 reveals the use of consumer durable goods which indicates the social status of the sample beneficiary households in Tripura. It also provides the pattern of the possession of household assets by the sample households. It is observed that out of the total sample households, 75.2 per cent have reported to possess television, 97.6 per cent possess smart phone and 69.8 per cent of the households have reported to possess bicycle. Only three percent of the households are found possessing refrigerator and sound system. Similarly, a very few percentage of people is found possessing four wheelers (0.2 per cent) and three wheelers (1.2 per cent). It is also found that 18.4 percent of the sample households have reported to possess motor bike. Block-wise data shows that cent per cent sample households from B.C. Nagar block of South Tripura district have reported to possess television which is followed by Jirania block (95.9 per cent) of West Tripura district, Salema block (91.9 per cent) of Dhalai district. In case of smart phone, the trend is more or less similar in all the blocks and most of the households are found possessing smart phones. A minimum of 86.3 per cent people have smart phone belongs to Mandai block of West Tripura district. About 93 percent households in Teliamurab lock of Khowai district have reported to possess bicycle followed by Nalchar block (88.9 per cent) of Sepahijala district, Matabari block (83.8 per cent)

Table 3.17: Block-wise Details of Household Assets (Consumer Durable Goods) Possessed by the Households (in per cent)

District	*Block*	*TV*	*Refrigerator*	*Sound System*	*Smart Phone*	*Four Wheeler*	*Three Wheeler*	*Motor Bike*	*Bicycle*
Dhalai	Ambassa	82.4	0.0	5.9	94.1	0.0	0.0	5.9	52.9
	Manu	82.6	0.0	2.2	95.7	0.0	0.0	6.5	45.7
	Salema	91.9	0.0	0.0	100.0	0.0	0.0	13.5	83.8
Gomati	Killa	58.3	3.3	0.0	100.0	0.0	1.7	15.0	73.3
	Matabari	55.0	5.0	0.0	100.0	0.0	0.0	17.5	87.5
Khowai	Kalyanpur	63.6	0.0	0.0	100.0	0.0	0.0	27.3	81.8
	Teliamura	60.7	0.0	0.0	100.0	0.0	0.0	7.1	92.9
Sepahijala	Jampuijala	71.9	0.0	0.0	100.0	3.1	6.3	18.8	81.3
	Nalchar	83.3	0.0	0.0	100.0	0.0	0.0	22.2	88.9
South Tripura	B.C Nagar	100.0	0.0	0.0	100.0	0.0	0.0	25.8	83.9
	Rajnagar	61.9	2.4	0.0	100.0	0.0	0.0	11.9	61.9
	Rupaichhari	66.7	0.0	3.7	92.6	0.0	0.0	25.9	29.6
West Tripura	Jirania	95.9	0.0	6.1	100.0	0.0	0.0	36.7	59.2
	Mandai	82.4	0.0	7.8	86.3	0.0	5.9	21.6	66.7
Total		**75.2**	**1.0**	**2.0**	**97.6**	**0.2**	**1.2**	**18.4**	**69.8**

Source: Computed on the basis of Field Survey, December, 2021.

of Gomati district; whereas Jirania block (36.7 per cent) of West Tripura district has the highest percentage of households possessing motor bikes followed by Kalyanpur block (27.3 per cent) of Khowai district. The possession of two-wheeler or three-wheeler by the sample households is found very negligible in the studied blocks. Only 3.1 per cent people belongs to Jampuijala block of Sepahijala district have four wheelers; however only in three blocks people have three wheelers viz; Jampuijala block (6.3 per cent) of Sepahijala district, Mandai block (5.9 per cent) of West Tripura district and Killa block (1.7 per cent) of Gomati district.

3.2.2 *Economic Status of the Surveyed Household Beneficiaries in the Study Area*

The economic status of the surveyed household beneficiaries in the study area can be discussed in the following sub-heads.

Household Economic Category of the Beneficiaries in the Study Area

Table 3.18 reveals the block-wise economic category of the household. This category has been done by the state government on the basis of ration card details. It is observed that out of the 500 sample households, 29.2 per cent of the households are living under the above poverty line (APL) category, 35.2 per cent are living under the below poverty line (BPL) category and only 19 per cent are Ad-hoc families. The rest of the households belong to either Antyodaya (15.6 per cent) or Arnapurna (one per cent) category.

From the Table 3.18, it is also found that the highest percentage of the households belonging to the APL category is found in Jampuijala block (53.1 per cent) followed by Kalyanpur (50 per cent) of Khowai district, B.C. Nagar (45.2 per cent) of the South Tripura district; while Mandai has the lowest percentage (2 per cent). In terms of below poverty level, Mandai block of the West Tripura district has the highest percentage of the sample households being BPL (56.9 per cent) followed by Manu (45.7 per cent) of the Dhalai district, Rajnagar (40.5 per cent) of the South Tripura district. The percentage of household beneficiary under the Annapurna card is very few; only in three blocks this is found. Households belong to Ad-hoc category are the highest in Nalchar block (38.9 per cent) of

Table 3.18: Block-wise Economic Category as per Ration Card Profile of the Beneficiary Households in Tripura (in per cent)

District	*Block*	*Household*	*APL*	*BPL*	*Arnapurna*	*Ad-Hoc*	*Antyodaya*
Dhalai	Ambassa	17	35.3	17.6	5.9	29.4	11.8
	Manu	46	19.6	45.7	0.0	15.2	19.6
	Salema	37	24.3	27.0	2.7	29.7	16.2
Gomati	Killa	60	18.3	38.3	3.3	11.7	28.3
	Matabari	40	42.5	30.0	2.5	20.0	5.0
Khowai	Kalyanpur	22	50.0	18.2	0.0	9.1	22.7
	Teliamura	28	39.3	25.0	0.0	21.4	14.3
Sepahijala	Jampuijala	32	53.1	31.3	0.0	9.4	6.3
	Nalchar	18	22.2	33.3	0.0	38.9	5.6
South	B.C. Nagar	31	45.2	35.5	0.0	6.5	12.9
	Rajnagar	42	28.6	40.5	0.0	28.6	2.4
	Rupaichhari	27	25.9	37.0	0.0	25.9	11.1
West	Jirania	49	34.7	26.5	0.0	28.6	10.2
	Mandai	51	2.0	56.9	0.0	7.8	33.3
Total		**500**	**29.2**	**35.2**	**1.0**	**19.0**	**15.6**

Source: Computed on the basis of Field Survey, December, 2021.

Sepahijala district, which is followed by Ambassa block (29.4 per cent), Jirania block (28.6 per cent) under the West Tripura district. Antyodaya category is found highest percentage in Mandai block (33.3 per cent) of the West Tripura district, which is followed by Killa block (28.3 per cent) of the Gomati district, Kalyanpur block (22.7 per cent) under the Khowai district.

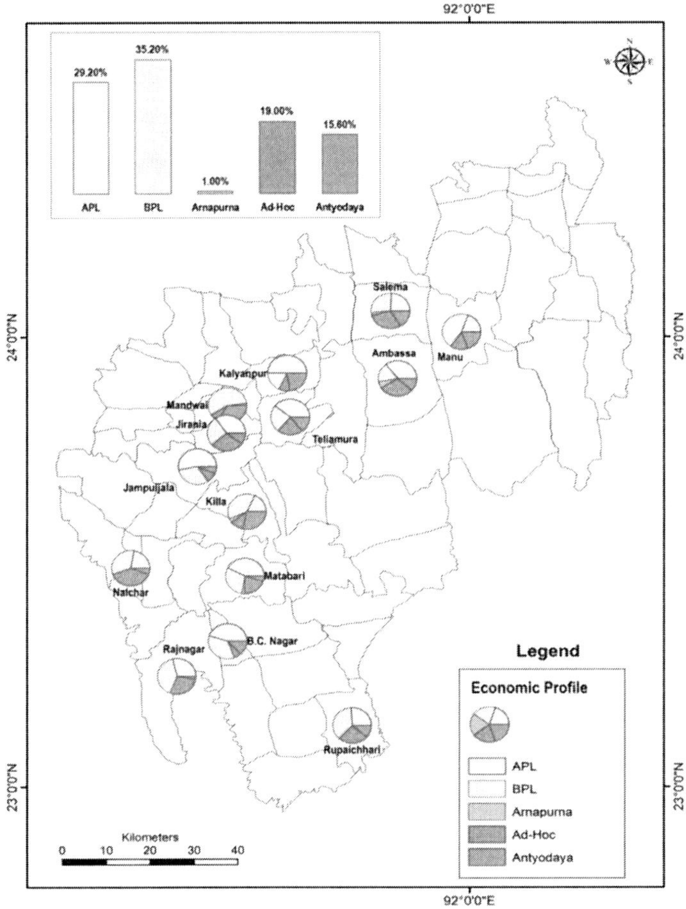

Figure 3.9: Mapping of Blocks with Diverse Economic Profile in the Study Area

Household Land Details of the Beneficiaries in the Study Area

Household landed property shows the economic status of the households. Table 3.19 shows the household land details of the tribal

Table 3.19: Block-wise Land Property Details of the Beneficiary Households in the State Tripura

District	*Blocks*	*Up to 1 Kani*	*1–2 Kani*	*2–3 Kani*	*3–4 Kani*	*4–5 Kani*	*Above 5 Kani*	*No Land but Lease in*	*Total*
Dhalai	Ambassa	6 (35.29)	2 (11.76)	5 (29.41)	1 (5.88)	2 (11.76)	0	1 (5.88)	17 (100.0)
	Manu	12 (26.09)	10 (21.74)	9 (19.57)	13 (28.26)	2 (4.35)	0	0	46 (100.0)
	Salema	12 (32.43)	9 (24.32)	9 (24.32)	3 (8.11)	2 (5.41)	0	1 (2.70)	37 (100.0)
Gomati	Killa	14 (23.33)	19 (31.67)	12 (20.0)	8 (13.33)	6 (10.0)	1 (1.67)	0	60 (100.0)
	Matabari	10 (25.0)	9 (22.50)	9 (22.50)	7 (17.50)	5 (12.50)	0	0	40 (100.0)
Khowai	Kalyanpur	4 (18.19)	6 (27.28)	6 (27.28)	3 (13.63)	3 (13.63)	0	0	22 (100.0)
	Teliamura	7 (25.00)	6 (21.43)	5 (17.86)	5 (17.86)	5 (17.86)	0	0	28 (100.0)
Sepahijala	Jampuijala	7 (21.88)	8 (25.00)	6 (18.75)	6 (18.75)	4 (12.5)	0	1 (3.13)	32 (100.0)
	Nalchar	7 (38.89)	6 (33.33)	2 (11.11)	0	1 (5.56)	0	2 (11.11)	18 (100.0)
South	B.C. Nagar	6 (19.35)	5 (16.13)	9 (29.03)	5 (16.13)	6 (19.35)	0	0	31 (100.0)

District	*Blocks*	*Up to 1 Kani*	*1–2 Kani*	*2–3 Kani*	*3–4 Kani*	*4–5 Kani*	*Above 5 Kani*	*No Land but Lease in*	*Total*
	Rajnagar	14 (33.33)	15 (35.71)	8 (19.05)	3 (7.14)	1 (2.38)	1 (2.38)	0	42 (100.0)
	Rupaichhari	10 (37.04)	5 (18.52)	3 (11.11)	2 (7.41)	1 (3.70)	1 (3.70)	5 (18.52)	27 (100.0)
West	Jirania	14 (28.57)	16 (32.65)	10 (20.41)	4 (8.16)	4 (8.16)	0	1 (2.04)	49 (100.0)
	Mandai	21 (41.18)	15 (29.41)	2 (3.92)	3 (5.88)	1 (1.96)	0	9 (17.64)	51 (100.0)
	Total	**145 (29.0)**	**131 (26.2)**	**95 (19.0)**	**63 (12.6)**	**43 (8.6)**	**3 (0.60)**	**21 (4.20)**	**500 (100.0)**

Source: Primary Survey, December, 2021.

Note: Percentages are given in the parentheses.

agricultural beneficiary of the state Tripura. In Tripura, land is measured in terms of local unit kani, so for this measuring unit of land kani is taken.[3]

From Table 3.19, it is observed that out of total respondent beneficiaries, most of the beneficiary farmers are marginal farmers (29 per cent) and they have only up to one kani of land which is followed by small farmers (26.2 per cent) those have only 1–2 kani of own land, 19 per cent respondents have 2–3 kani of own agricultural land, 12.6 per cent have 3–4 kani own agricultural land and very few (only 0.60 per cent) have own land of above five kani agricultural land. However, 4.20 per cent beneficiaries have no own land, though they are getting agricultural schemes as they are cultivating by taking lease in land. The table also reveals that most of the marginal farmers (up to 1 kani of own land) belong to Mandai block (41.18 per cent) of West Tripura district which is followed by Nalchar block (38.89 per cent) of Sepahijala district, Rupaichhari block (37.04 per cent) of South Tripura district. Most of the small farmers (those have only 1–2 kani of own land) belong to Rajnagar block (35.71 per cent) of South Tripura district which is followed by Nalchar block (33.33 per cent) of Sepahijala district, Jirania block (32.65 per cent) of West Tripura district. Most of the farmers who are land less but cultivated land by taking lease in belong to Rupaichhari block (18.52 per cent) of South Tripura district which is followed by Mandai block (17.64 per cent) of West Tripura district.

Occupational Pattern of the Household Beneficiaries in the Study Area

Occupational pattern is one of the most important aspects for showing economic status. Table 3.20 reveals the occupation-wise distribution of the working population of the sample households.The survey data indicates that out of the total (2206) population of the households under study, 67.14 percent (1481 numbers) belongs to the age group of 19–60 years, the effective working age group considered here. Male constitute 49.83 percent of this potential workforce while female potential workforce is constituted by the remaining 50.17 per cent. The section of sample population reported to have main occupation is, however, 60.7 per cent of the total

[3] 1 kani of land is equal to 1.322 acres.

Table 3.20: Occupational Distribution of Working Population of the Sample Households (in per cent)

District	*Block*	*Farmer*	*Daily Labour*	*Driver*	*Service*	*Business*	*Total*
Dhalai	Ambassa	32.69	17.31	1.92	1.92	1.92	55.77
	Manu	30.63	6.88	0.00	0.00	0.00	37.50
	Salema	35.58	20.19	0.00	0.00	0.00	55.77
Gomati	Killa	46.29	13.71	0.00	0.00	0.00	60.00
	Matabari	54.39	13.16	0.00	0.00	0.00	67.54
Khowai	Kalyanpur	31.88	17.39	1.45	0.00	0.00	50.72
	Teliamura	35.00	15.00	0.00	0.00	0.00	50.00
Sepahijala	Jampuijala	35.56	12.22	4.44	4.44	0.00	56.67
	Nalchar	33.33	31.48	0.00	0.00	0.00	64.81
South	B.C Nagar	77.01	4.60	2.30	0.00	0.00	83.91
	Rajnagar	81.58	7.02	0.00	0.00	0.00	88.60
	Rupaichhari	50.60	13.25	0.00	0.00	0.00	63.86
West	Jirania	32.67	25.33	0.00	0.67	0.67	59.33
	Mandai	34.23	26.85	0.67	0.67	0.00	62.42

Source: Calculated on the basis of Field survey, December, 2021.

population of the working age group. The work participation rate is, therefore, estimated at 60.7 per cent. Block-wise data shows that Rajnagar block has the highest work participation rate (88.60 per cent), followed by B.C. Nagar block (83.91 per cent) and Matabari (67.54 per cent), while Manu has the lowest (37.5 percent). Farming being the largest source of livelihood absorbs 43.75 percent of the total workforce. This is followed by 15.75 percent of the total workforce who are working as daily labour. The proportion of total working population engaged in different non-agricultural activities is found negligible; 0.67 percent is working as driver, 0.14 percent is found running their own business establishments and 0.47 percent is engaged in services of different kinds.

Block-level comparison reveals that Rajnagar block has the highest proportion of total workforce engaged in agricultural activities, followed by B.C. Nagar, whereas Nalchar block has the highest proportion of total workforce who are working as daily labour, followed by Mandai and Jirania block of West Tripura district. The proportion of total working age population employed in salaried jobs is found highest in Jampuijala block of Sepahijala district. Block-wise distribution of the total sample population engaged in different occupations is presented in Table 2. Out of the total (2206) sample population, 40.75 percent (899 numbers) are reported to have their main occupation and they are engaged in different agricultural and non-agricultural activities. Of the total sample population reported to have their occupation, almost three-fourth (72.08 per cent) are engaged in agriculture and allied activities and 25.92 per cent are working as daily labour. A very negligible percent of them is found to engage in different non-agricultural activities like driving, service and business.

Block-wise comparison of the occupational distribution reveals that Rajnagar block has the highest proportion of the engaged population working as farmers, followed by B.C. Nagar and Manu block, whereas Nalchar block has the lowest. The proportion of engaged population working as daily labour is found highest in Nalchar block, followed by Mandai and lowest in B.C. Nagar block of South Tripura district. Further, the proportion of engaged population having their occupation as services of different kinds and driving is found highest in Jampuijala block of Sepahijala district.

Only 2 out of 14 selected blocks, namely Ambassa and Jirania, respectively have 3.45 percent and 1.12 percent of the total engaged population who are running their own business establishments.

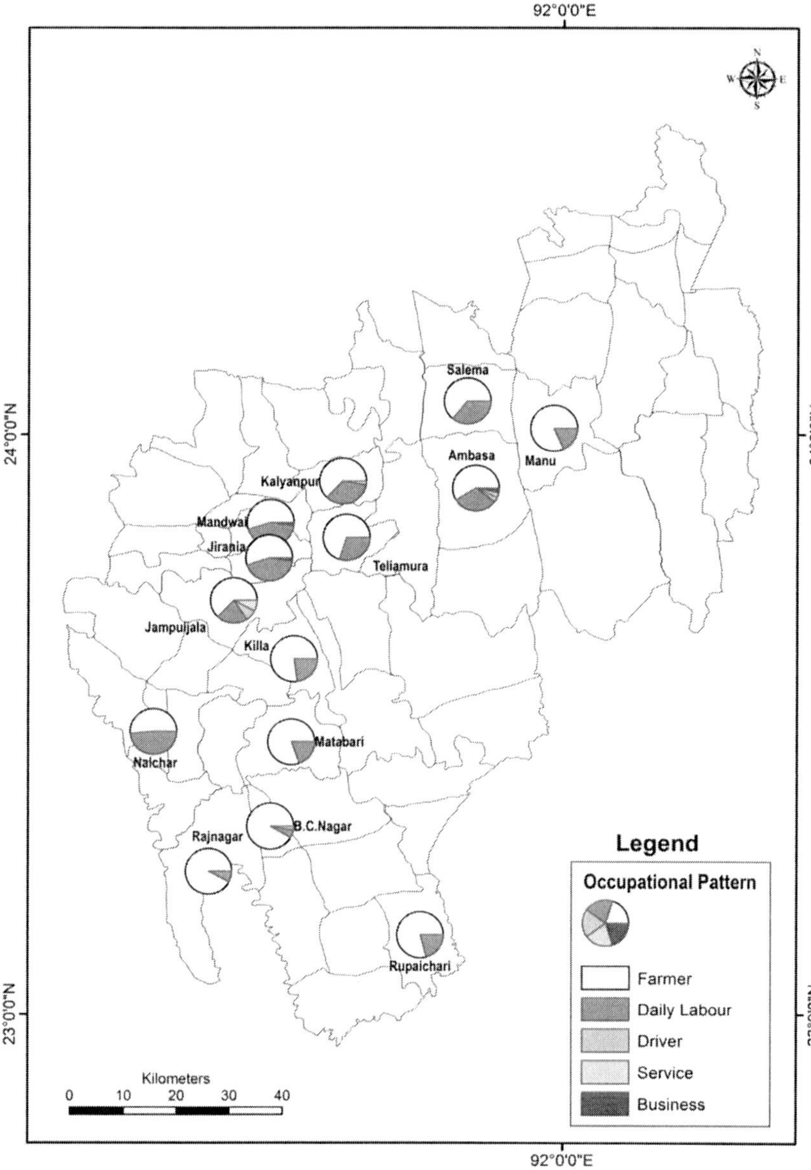

Figure 3.10: Mapping of Blocks showing Diverse Occupational Pattern in the Study Area

Table 3.21: Block-wise Occupational Distribution of the Engaged Population of the Sample Households

District	*Block*	*Farmer*	*Daily Labour*	*Driver*	*Service*	*Business*
Dhalai	Ambassa	58.62	31.03	3.45	3.45	3.45
	Manu	81.67	18.33	0.00	0.00	0.00
	Salema	63.79	36.21	0.00	0.00	0.00
Gomati	Killa	77.14	22.86	0.00	0.00	0.00
	Matabari	80.52	19.48	0.00	0.00	0.00
Khowai	Kalyanpur	62.86	34.29	2.86	0.00	0.00
	Teliamura	70.00	30.00	0.00	0.00	0.00
Sepahijala	Jampuijala	62.75	21.57	7.84	7.84	0.00
	Nalchar	51.43	48.57	0.00	0.00	0.00
South Tripura	B.C. Nagar	91.78	5.48	2.74	0.00	0.00
	Rajnagar	92.08	7.92	0.00	0.00	0.00
	Rupaichhari	79.25	20.75	0.00	0.00	0.00
West Tripura	Jirania	55.06	42.70	0.00	1.12	1.12
	Mandai	54.84	43.01	1.08	1.08	0.00
Total		**72.08**	**25.92**	**1.00**	**0.78**	**0.22**

Source: Calculated on the basis of Field survey, December, 2021.

Household Livestock's Details of the Beneficiaries in the Study Area

Income from livestock is a supportive income to the beneficiary households. Livestock is also used for both own consumption as well as additional supportive income for the family for their better livelihood. When the livestock rearing are done in small scale, then it is used only for their own consumption; however if it is in large scale, then it is used for both self-consumption as well as for market selling.

Table 3.22 shows the block-wise livelihood status in physical units of the beneficiary families in the study area. From the following Table, it is observed that poultry, piggery, cow, goat, duck and broiler are the common livestock almost in all blocks. Rearing of Buffalo and sheep are very rare in the study area; buffalo is found only in two beneficiary families belong to Salema block of Dhalai district; however, rearing of only three sheep is found only in two blocks viz; Jampuijala block and Jirania block (only in one family).

Table 3.23 shows the block-wise income details of the sample beneficiary households from the livestock.

Table 3.22: Block-wise Livestock Details of the Sample Beneficiary Household (in Physical units)

District	*Block*	*Broiler*	*Poultry*	*Duck*	*Piggery*	*Cow*	*Buffalo*	*Goat*	*Sheep*	*Others*
Dhalai	Ambassa	13	38	2	11	18	0	18	0	0
	Manu	52	57	19	83	37	0	93	0	0
	Salema	39	36	5	47	28	2	50	0	0
Gomati	Killa	0	127	41	50	62	0	46	0	0
	Matabari	0	123	42	10	59	0	20	0	0
Khowai	Kalyanpur	0	51	47	0	19	0	0	0	0
	Teliamura	4	64	55	0	24	0	2	0	0
Sepahijala	Jampuijala	1	69	65	9	31	0	1	3	14
	Nalchar	0	39	7	18	17	0	34	0	0
South	B.C Nagar	0	70	32	12	45	0	32	0	0
	Rajnagar	48	78	5	39	39	0	68	0	0
	Rupachari	22	52	2	20	37	0	29	0	0
West	Jirania	0	129	5	110	35	0	0	1	0
	Mandai	0	94	39	100	8	0	6	0	0
Total		**179**	**1027**	**366**	**509**	**459**	**2**	**399**	**4**	**14**

Source: Primary Survey, December, 2021.

Table 3.23: Block-wise Income Details Livestock of the Sample Beneficiary Household (in Rs.)

District	*Block*	*Broiler*	*Poultry*	*Duck*	*Piggery*	*Cow*	*Buffalo*	*Goat*	*Sheep*	*Others*
Dhalai	Ambassa	1400	13050	1000	120000	221000	0	68000	0	0
	Manu	17800	18800	7900	895000	476000	0	388000	0	0
	Salema	11800	13300	1700	448000	359000	28000	215000	0	0
Gomati	Killa	0	52500	19200	514500	902000	0	136000	0	0
	Matabari	0	86900	17000	88000	788000	0	85000	0	0
Khowai	Kalyanpur	0	18100	23400	0	284000	0	0	0	0
	Teliamura	1200	25200	26200	0	360000	0	10000	0	0
Sepahijala	Jampuijala	300	27000	30300	75000	475000	0	1003	15000	2400
	Nalchar	0	12100	1900	220000	272000	0	111500	0	0
South	B.C. Nagar	0	25400	21201	224200	673000	0	105500	0	0
	Rajnagar	14000	25400	2000	414000	560000	0	206200	0	0
	Rupachhari	5800	13800	800	142000	518000	0	63900	0	0
West	Jirania	0	38900	2500	1458000	565000	0	0	1000	0
	Mandai	0	25350	11500	1460000	200000	0	9000	0	0
Total		**52300**	**395800**	**166601**	**6058700**	**6653000**	**28000**	**1399103**	**16000**	**2400**

Source: Primary Survey, December, 2021.

Household Agricultural Cultivation and Production Details of the Beneficiaries in the Study Area

This section shows the cultivation and production details of the tribal beneficiaries of the state Tripura. Cultivated land of the farmers are of two types viz; cultivated on their own land, cultivated on the lease in land taken from the land owner for the production subject to some negotiation about the share of cropping between lease in farmer and land owner.

Table 3.24 shows the block-wise cultivated land details of the beneficiary farmers of the study area. It is observed that a total of 1212.25 kani of land is cultivated by the sample beneficiaries of the study area.It is observed that out of the total 1212.25 kani of cultivated land, only 37 kani of land is cultivated by the farmers taking lease in land from the land owner and rest of the land is cultivated by the farmers who have their own land. It is found that only total 20 kani of large size of own land holding (above 5 kani) is cultivated. Most of the land is cultivated under medium size of own land holding (2–3 kani and 3–4 kani of land) or under small size of own land holding (up to two kani of land) by the farmers. The Table also reveals that block-wise information of cultivation of land. It is observed that maximum 156.5 kani of land is cultivated under Killa block in the Gomati district which is followed by Manu block (119.5 kani) of Dhalai district, Jirania block (113 kani) of West Tripura district, Matabari block (108 kani) of Gomati district. The least amount of land is cultivated in Nalchar block (only 29 kani of land).It is found that large size of land (10 kani) is cultivated by taking lease in only in Rupaichhari block of the South Tripura district.

Table 3.25 shows block-wise the annual agricultural production (mainly production of rice) of the beneficiary households. The Table reveals that out of the total production of rice, the maximum 45 per cent rice is produced by the small farmers, which is under the production limit of 1000–2000 Kg. The next highest 31 per cent rice is produced by the marginal farmers which are under the lowest production limit of (up to 1000 Kg.) which is followed by the production limit of 2000–3000 Kg. (22 per cent) and only 1.80 per cent production belongs to the production group of above 3000 Kg.

Table 3.24: Block-wise Cultivated Land Details of the Beneficiary Households in the State Tripura (in Kani)

District	Block	Upto 1 Kani		1–2 Kani		2–3 Kani		3–4 Kani		4–5 Kani		Above 5 Kani		Total Cultivated Land
		Own	Lease in	Own	Lease in	Own	Lease in	Own	Lease in	Own	Lease in	Own	Lease in	
Dhalai	Ambassa	6	1	4		14.5		4		10		0	0	39.5
	Manu	12		20		25.5		52		10		0		119.5
	Salema	12	1	18	2	26.5		12		10		0		81.5
Gomati	Killa	13.5	1	37.5	0	35.5	0	32	0	30	0	7	0	156.5
	Matabari	10	0	18	0	27	0	28	0	25	0	0	0	108
Khowai	Kalyanpur	4		12		18		12		15		0		61
	Teliamura	7		12		15		20		25		0		79
Sepahijala	Jampuijala	6.5		16		18		24		20		0		84.5
	Nalchar	7	0.5	11.5		6		0		4		0		29
South	B.C. Nagar	6		10		26.5		20		30		0		92.5
	Rajnagar	13.75		27.5		23.5		11.5		5		6		87.25
	Rupaichhari	10		10	6	8.5		8	4	5		7	10	68.5
West	Jirania	14	1	32		30		16		20		0	0	113
	Mandai	20	3	29	9.5	6	8	12		5		0	0	92.5
Total		**141.75**	**7.5**	**257.5**	**17.5**	**280.5**	**8**	**251.5**	**4**	**214**	**0**	**20**	**10**	**1212.25**

Source: Primary Survey, December, 2021.

Note: Percentages are given in the parentheses.

Table 3.25: Block-wise Agricultural Annual Production of the Beneficiary Households in the Study Area (in per cent)

District	*Block*	*Up to 1000Kg*	*1000 Kg–2000 Kg*	*2000 Kg–3000 Kg.*	*Above 3000 Kg.*	*Total*
Dhalai	Ambassa	47.06	35.29	17.65	0.00	100.00
	Manu	26.09	36.96	34.78	2.17	100.00
	Salema	37.84	48.65	13.51	0.00	100.00
Gomati	Killa	23.33	43.33	26.67	6.67	100.00
	Matabari	22.50	45.00	30.00	2.50	100.00
Khowai	Kalyanpur	18.18	54.55	27.27	0.00	100.00
	Teliamura	25.00	39.29	35.71	0.00	100.00
Sepahijala	Jampuijala	21.88	46.88	31.25	0.00	100.00
	Nalchar	55.56	38.89	5.56	0.00	100.00
South Tripura	B.C Nagar	19.35	48.39	32.26	0.00	100.00
	Rajnagar	42.86	47.62	7.14	0.00	100.00
	Rupaichhari	40.74	37.04	11.11	11.11	100.00
West Tripura	Jirania	28.57	53.06	18.37	0.00	100.00
	Mandai	41.18	47.06	11.76	0.00	100.00
Total		**31.00**	**45.00**	**22.00**	**1.80**	**100.00**

Source: Calculated from the Field Survey, December, 2021.

Table 3.26: Block-wise Agricultural Annual Consumption of the Beneficiary Households in the Study Area (in per cent)

District	*Block*	*Up to 1000 Kg*	*1000Kg–2000 Kg*	*2000 Kg–3000 Kg.*	*Above 3000 Kg.*	*Total*
Dhalai	Ambassa	52.94	41.18	5.88	0.00	100.00
	Manu	54.35	39.13	0.00	0.00	100.00
	Salema	37.84	62.16	0.00	0.00	100.00
Gomati	Killa	55.00	45.00	0.00	0.00	100.00
	Matabari	42.50	57.50	0.00	0.00	100.00
Khowai	Kalyanpur	22.73	77.27	0.00	0.00	100.00
	Teliamura	32.14	67.86	0.00	0.00	100.00
Sepahijala	Jampuijala	40.63	59.38	0.00	0.00	100.00
	Nalchar	66.67	16.67	5.56	0.00	100.00
South	B.C Nagar	16.13	80.65	0.00	0.00	100.00
	Rajnagar	45.24	54.76	0.00	0.00	100.00
	Rupaichhari	40.74	33.33	7.41	3.70	100.00
West	Jirania	30.61	67.35	2.04	0.00	100.00
	Mandai	41.18	58.82	0.00	0.00	100.00
Total		**41.60**	**55.20**	**1.00**	**0.20**	**100.00**

Source: Calculated from the Field Survey, December, 2021.

Table 3.26 shows the block-wise agricultural consumption of the beneficiary households. It is observed that most of the households' especially marginal farmers have used their production for their own consumption. 55.2 per cent households have used for own consumption within 1000 kg–2000 kg and 41.6 per cent household consume within 1000 kg. Block-wise it is found that most of marginal farmers belong to Nalchar block of Sepahijala district consume within 1000 kg which is followed by farmers of Killa block (55 per cent) of the Gomati district. However, within the 1000–2000 kg group of self-consumption, the highest percentage of farmers belong to B.C. Nagar block (80.65 per cent) of South Tripura district which is followed by Teliamura block (67.86 per cent) of Khowai district, Salema block (62.16 per cent) of the Dhalai district.

Household Horticultural Cultivation and Production Details of the Beneficiaries in the Study Area

Table 3.27 shows the block-wise horticultural practices by the beneficiary farmers of the selected study area. From the Table 3.27, it is found that out of the total sample beneficiaries only small percentage beneficiaries are doing horticultural practices and mainly they are doing rubber plantation, banana and betel nut. It is observed that out of the total 500 sample beneficiaries, only 14.40 per cent households have rubber plantation, 1.80 per cent households have betel nut and only 0.40 per cent households are doing banana. Block-wise analysis reveals that no horticultural practices are found in both Teliamura and Kalyanpur block of Khowai district and Jirania block of West Tripura district.

Table 3.27 also reveals that maximum rubber plantation is found in Jampuijala block (40.63 per cent) of Sepahijala district, which is followed by B.C. Nagar block (38.71 per cent) of South Tripura district and Nalchar block (27.78 per cent) of Sepahijala district. However, maximum betel nut beneficiary is found in Ambassa block (17.65 per cent) of Dhalai district which is followed by Rajnagar block (4.76 per cent) of South Tripura district.

Table 3.28 reveals the block-wise annual production and income details of the sample beneficiaries. From the Table it is observed that a sizable amount of production and income is found from the rubber

Table 3.27: Block-wise Horticultural Beneficiary Farmers in the Study Area

District	*Block*	*Rubber*	*Banana*	*Betel Nut*
Dhalai	Ambassa	4 (23.53)	1 (5.88)	3 (17.65)
	Manu	4 (8.70)	0 (0.00)	1 (2.17)
	Salema	7 (18.92)	0 (0.00)	3 (8.11)
Gomati	Killa	9 (15.00)	0 (0.00)	0 (0.00)
	Matabari	9 (22.50)	0 (0.00)	0 (0.00)
Khowai	Kalyanpur	0 (0.00)	0 (0.00)	0 (0.00)
	Teliamura	0 (0.00)	0 (0.00)	0 (0.00)
Sepahijala	Jampuijala	13 (40.63)	0 (0.00)	0 (0.00)
	Nalchar	5 (27.78)	0 (0.00)	0 (0.00)
South Tripura	B.C Nagar	12 (38.71)	0 (0.00)	0 (0.00)
	Rajnagar	7 (16.67)	0 (0.00)	2 (4.76)
	Rupachhari	1 (3.70)	0 (0.00)	0 (0.00)
West Tripura	Jirania	0 (0.00)	0 (0.00)	0 (0.00)
	Mandai	1 (1.96)	1 (1.96)	0 (0.00)
Total		**72 (14.40)**	**2 (0.40)**	**9 (1.80)**

Source: Calculated from the Field Survey, December, 2021.

Note: Percentages are given in the parentheses.

plantation. A total of 47,159 kg of rubber production (rubber sheet) comes out annually from 72 beneficiaries and they earned total revenue Rs. 59,62,050.00 per annum. A total of 168 kg betel nut is produced annually by nine sample beneficiaries and they have earned revenue of Rs. 56,400.00 per annum.

Block-wise comparison shows that annual rubber production is highest in Matabari block (8050 kg.) which is followed by Killa block (7350 kg.) of Gomati district, Jampuijala block (5775 kg.) of Sepahijala district. Though in B.C. Nagar highest percentage of farmers are doing rubber plantation, but they are producing only 4354 kg of rubber sheet as they have done their plantation in small are of land.The income earned from the rubber plant is highest in Matabari block (Rs. 10,46,500.00), which is followed by Killa block (Rs. 9,55,500.00), Jampuijala block (Rs. 7,52,500.00), etc. The least income earned from rubber plant is in the Mandai block (Rs. 7250.00) of West Tripura district.

Table 3.28: Block-wise Annual Production and Income of the Sample Beneficiaries from Major Horticultural Production in the Study Area

District	*Block*	*Rubber*		*Banana*		*Betel Nut*	
		Production (Kg.)	*Income (Rs.)*	*Production (Quantity)*	*Income (Rs.)*	*Production (Kg.)*	*Income (Rs.)*
Dhalai	Ambassa	2475	329250	4	1000	48	11200
	Manu	3850	500500	0	0	10	4000
	Salema	4025	523250	0	0	30	9200
Gomati	Killa	7350	955500	0	0	0	0
	Matabari	8050	1046500	0	0	0	0
Khowai	Kalyanpur	0	0	0	0	0	0
	Teliamura	0	0	0	0	0	0
Sepahijala	Jampuijala	5775	752500	0	0	0	0
	Nalchar	5500	715000	0	0	0	0
South	B.C Nagar	4354	585500	0	0	0	0
	Rajnagar	4130	516500	0	0	80	32000
	Rupaichhar i	1600	30300	0	0	0	0
West	Jirania	0	0	0	0	0	0
	Mandai	50	7250	1	350	0	0
Total		**47159**	**5962050**	**5**	**1350**	**168**	**56400**

Source: Calculated from the Field Survey, December, 2021.

Income Distribution and its Sources of the Household Beneficiaries in the Study Area

Table 3.29 reveals percentage frequency distribution of block-wise agricultural income of the sample beneficiaries. It is found that most of the beneficiary farmers earn up to Rs. 10000 income and between Rs. 10000–20000 income group from their agriculture. 29.4 per cent sample beneficiary farmers earn up to Rs. 10000 income by selling their agricultural product and 29.6 per cent sample beneficiary farmers earn Rs. 10000–20000 income by selling their agricultural products. 17.6 per cent farmers earn Rs. 20000–30000 income and 13.4 per cent farmers earn Rs. 30000–40000 income and 8.6 per cent farmers earn Rs. 40000–50000 income by selling their agricultural products. Only very negligible percentage of sample beneficiary farmers earn more than Rs. 50000 income by selling their agricultural products which implies that there are very few large land holding farmers in the study area. Block-wise analysis reveals that highest percentage of beneficiary farmers belong to Nalchar block (61.11 per cent) of Sepahijala district earn only up to Rs. 10000 income by selling their agricultural products which is followed by the farmers of Rupaichhari block (48.15 per cent) of South Tripura district, Ambassa block (41.18 per cent) of Dhalai district. In case of earning income group of Rs. 10000–20000 from agricultural products, the highest percentage of farmers belong to Mandai block (45.10 per cent) of West Tripura district which is followed by Rajnagar block (40.48 per cent) of South Tripura district. A maximum of 27.27 per cent farmers belong to Kalyanpur block of Khowai district earn Rs. 20000–30000 income by selling their agricultural products. However, a maximum of 30.43 per cent farmers belong to Manu block of Dhalai district earn Rs. 30000–40000 income by selling their agricultural products which is followed by Matabari block (20 per cent) of Gomati district. A maximum of 19.35 per cent farmers belong to B.C. Nagar block of South Tripura district earn Rs. 40000–50000 income by selling their agricultural product which is followed by Teliamura block (17.86 per cent) of Khowai district. Only few farmers of two blocks Rupaichhari (7.41 per cent) and Rajnagar block (2.38 per cent) of South Tripura district earn Rs. 50000–60000 income be selling their agricultural products. However, only few farmers of two blocks Matabari (5 per cent) and Killa block (2.5 per cent) of Gomati district earn more than Rs. 60000 income be selling their agricultural products.

Table 3.29: Block-wise Agricultural Income of the Sample Beneficiary Households in the Study Area (in per cent)

District	*Block*	*Up to Rs. 10000*	*Rs. 10000– Rs. 20000*	*Rs. 20000– Rs. 30000*	*Rs. 30000– Rs. 40000*	*Rs. 40000– Rs. 50000*	*Rs. 50000– Rs. 60000*	*Above Rs. 60000*	*Total*
Dhalai	Ambassa	41.18	17.65	23.53	5.88	11.76	0.00	0	100.0
	Manu	23.91	28.26	13.04	30.43	4.35	0.00	0	100.0
	Salema	35.14	32.43	18.92	8.11	5.41	0.00	0	100.0
Gomati	Killa	23.33	28.33	20.00	15.00	8.33	0.00	5	100.0
	Matabari	22.50	22.50	20.00	20.00	12.50	0.00	2.5	100.0
Khowai	Kalyanpur	18.18	27.27	27.27	13.64	13.64	0.00	0	100.0
	Teliamura	25.00	21.43	17.86	17.86	17.86	0.00	0	100.0
Sepahijala	Jampuijala	25.00	25.00	18.75	18.75	12.50	0.00	0	100.0
	Nalchar	61.11	22.22	11.11	5.56	0.00	0.00	0	100.0
South Tripura	B.C Nagar	19.35	19.35	25.81	16.13	19.35	0.00	0	100.0
	Rajnagar	23.81	40.48	23.81	7.14	2.38	2.38	0	100.0
	Rupaichhari	48.15	25.93	11.11	7.41	0.00	7.41	0	100.0
West Tripura	Jirania	28.57	34.69	18.37	8.16	10.20	0.00	0	100.0
	Mandai	39.22	45.10	3.92	5.88	5.88	0.00	0	100.0
Total		**29.4**	**29.6**	**17.6**	**13.4**	**8.6**	**0.6**	**0.8**	**100.0**

Source: Calculated from the Field Survey, December, 2021.

Consumption Pattern of the Household Beneficiaries in the Study Area

Household consumption pattern is important aspect of economic status of the households. Table 3.30 shows the block-wise monthly average household expenditure of the beneficiary farmers in the study area. Table 3.30 reveals that beneficiary farmers spend their major monthly expenditures on food, education, gas, electricity, mobile, DTH cable etc. It is found that monthly average household expenditure on foodis Rs. 3186.55, which is followed by average expenditure on gas (Rs. 784.25), average educational expenditure (Rs. 568.60), average mobile expenditure (Rs. 391.35), average electricity expenditure (Rs. 245.24)etc. Block-wise analysis reveals that highest monthly average household food expenditure is found in Manu (Rs. 4192.44) which is followed by Ambassa block (Rs. 4000.88) of Dhalai district, Rajnagar block (Rs. 3588.12) of South Tripura district, Nalchar block (Rs. 3297.83) of Sepahijala district etc. However, farmers belong to Rupaichhari district of South Tripura district spend highest monthly average education expenditure (Rs. 1081.48) for their children's education which is followed by Killa block (Rs. 955.00) of Gomati district and Rajnagar block (Rs. 911.90) etc. In case of monthly average household expenditure on gas is highest in Ambassa block (Rs. 1005.88) of Dhalai district which is followed by Jampuijala block (Rs. 876.56) of Sepahijala district, Matabari block (Rs. 871.25) of Gomati block etc. Monthly average mobile expenditure on household's smart phone is highest in Matabari block (Rs. 593.75) of Gomati district which is followed by Teliamura block (Rs. 535.71) and Kalyanpur block (Rs. 500.00) of Khowai district. Monthly average electricity expenditure is highest in Kalyanpur block (Rs. 390.91) of Khowai district which is followed by B.C. Nagar block (Rs. 293.29) of South Tripura district. Estimation of monthly average health expenditure is very difficult, because household spend monthly health expenditure if they fall in ill health in that particular month.

Table 3.31 reveals the block-wise monthly average expenditure of the household on different addiction. Table 3.31 shows that monthly average expenditure on alcohol addiction is highest (Rs. 137.97) compare to other habit. Apart from alcohol addiction they are habituated to take pan, the monthly average expenditure on pan is Rs. 127.30 which is followed by monthly average expenditure on bidi (Rs. 63.31). Block-wise analysis reveals that monthly average

Table 3.30: Block-wise Monthly Average Household Expenditure of the Beneficiary Households in Tripura (in Rs.)

District	*Block*	*Food*	*Education*	*Health*	*Electricity*	*Gas*	*Kerosene*	*Fuel*	*Cosmetics*	*Mobile*	*DTH Cable*
Dhalai	Ambassa	4000.88	741.18	88.24	191.18	1005.88	91.76	34.12	150.00	402.94	194.12
	Manu	4192.44	502.17	65.22	206.52	461.74	157.61	37.83	140.22	339.13	208.70
	Salema	2937.16	486.49	27.03	231.89	674.32	99.46	52.43	151.35	404.05	214.86
Gomati	Killa	3048.50	955.00	38.33	247.00	859.67	64.57	129.00	103.65	463.83	161.68
	Matabari	2831.00	550.00	0.00	272.50	871.25	57.50	76.75	57.50	593.75	188.75
Khowai	Kalyanpur	2540.91	340.91	0.00	390.91	850.00	52.27	166.36	0.00	500.00	190.91
	Teliamura	2544.64	339.29	0.00	271.43	850.00	51.79	41.79	0.00	535.71	192.86
Sepahijala	Jampuijala	2746.69	281.25	37.50	259.38	876.56	51.88	64.69	25.00	468.72	220.31
	Nalchar	3297.83	494.44	272.22	200.00	808.33	84.44	130.56	66.67	222.22	238.89
South Tripura	B.C Nagar	3035.48	758.06	41.94	293.29	851.61	74.19	109.03	232.26	393.48	325.81
	Rajnagar	3588.12	911.90	92.86	195.24	726.33	111.43	154.76	217.86	327.69	155.95
	Rupachhari	3177.48	1081.48	103.70	238.15	727.78	146.11	185.19	337.04	262.48	104.81
West Tripura	Jirania	3247.39	263.27	0.00	265.31	850.00	67.35	169.18	240.82	378.57	244.90
	Mandai	3205.20	245.10	192.16	210.78	766.67	94.12	161.96	45.10	198.04	193.14
Average Household Exp.		3186.55	568.60	63.40	245.24	784.25	86.94	111.50	129.34	391.35	200.76

Source: Primary Survey, December, 2021.

Table 3.31: Block-wise Monthly Average Household Expenditure on Different Addiction of the Beneficiary Households in Tripura (in Rs.)

District	*Block*	*Alcohol*	*Tobacco*	*Pan*	*Bidi*	*Gutkha*	*Khaini*
Dhalai	Ambassa	258.82	0.00	111.76	68.24	0.00	5.88
	Manu	143.48	11.96	164.57	83.70	0.00	4.35
	Salema	58.11	0.00	124.32	66.22	0.00	10.81
Gomati	Killa	153.33	1.67	80.50	78.75	0.00	6.67
	Matabari	222.50	10.00	105.00	80.00	0.00	10.00
Khowai	Kalyanpur	104.55	0.00	109.09	68.18	0.00	0.00
	Teliamura	117.86	0.00	110.71	66.07	0.00	0.00
Sepahijala	Jampuijala	137.50	3.13	103.13	46.88	0.00	0.00
	Nalchar	200.00	38.89	100.00	26.11	0.00	5.56
South Tripura	B.C Nagar	120.97	8.06	175.81	82.26	3.23	11.29
	Rajnagar	154.86	2.38	134.52	72.62	0.00	4.76
	Rupachhari	134.44	8.89	216.67	98.15	0.00	32.59
West Tripura	Jirania	34.69	0.00	179.59	24.49	8.16	0.00
	Mandai	167.65	15.69	82.35	29.41	3.92	0.00
Average Household Exp.		**137.97**	**6.48**	**127.30**	**63.31**	**1.40**	**6.06**

Source: Primary Survey, December, 2021.

expenditure of alcohol addicted people is highest in Ambassa block (Rs. 258.82), Matabari (Rs. 222.50) and Nalchar block (Rs. 200.00).

Table 3.31 also reveals that the minimum monthly average expenditure on alcohol is in Jirania block (Rs. 34.69). The monthly average expenditure on pan is in Rupaichhari block (Rs. 216.67) which is followed by Jirania block (Rs. 179.59) of West Tripura district, B.C. Nagar block (Rs. 175.81) of South Tripura district. The monthly average expenditure on bidi is highest in Rupaichhari block (Rs. 98.15), which is followed by B.C. Nagar block (Rs. 82.26), Matabari block (Rs. 80.00) of Gomati district.

A composite Socio-economic Index (SEI) is calculated be taking a weighted average of two dimensions viz; social dimension and economic dimension. The social dimension consists with eight indicators viz; level of education, housing type, sanitation type, gas connection, area of bastu, housing space, water source and distance of water source from their house. The formula for Social Index (SI) is given in the following equation.

$$SI = \frac{\sum_{i=1}^{8} X_i}{8}$$

where, X's are index value of different social indicators.

The economic dimension consists with eight indicators viz; annual average income, economic profile, work participation rate, availability of consumer durable goods, average expenditure, cultivated land, horticultural income and agricultural income. The formula for Economic Index is given in the following equation.

$$EI = \frac{\sum_{i=1}^{8} Y_i}{8}$$

where, Y's are index value of different economic indicators.

From these two equations a composite Socio-economic Index (SEI) can be constructed in the following.

$$SEI_i = \frac{SI_i + EI_i}{2}$$

Table 3.32 shows the beneficiary households' social index in the selected blocks of Tripura. It is observed that composite social index (SI) ishighest in Jirania block (0.708), which is followed by Teliamura block (0.544), B.C. Nagar block (0.521), Jampuijala block

(0.518), Matabari block (0.513), Kalyanpur block (0.509), Salema block (0.488), whereas the value of social index is minimum in Rupaichari block (0.270) which implies that the social status of the beneficiary households belong to Rupaichari block is poor and that is due to poor level of education, housing type, poor availability of gas connection and lesser area of bastu. The social index for Rajnagar (0.289), Ambassa (0.316), Nalchar (0.326) and Killa (0.334) are also not impressive. The level of education is worst in Nalchar block among 14 selected sample blocks in Tripura. The housing type in Mandai block is worst among all 14 selected blocks. The social index of Jirania block is very high due to better level of education, gas connection, easy water sources and area of bastu compare to other blocks; only the sources of drinking water is far away from their residence. Housing condition is best in Matabari block whereas sanitation condition is best in Salema block of Dhalai district.

Table 3.33 reveals the Households' economic index of the selected sample blocks. It is found that highest value of composite households' economic index is in B.C Nagar block (0.807) which is followed by Matabari block (0.713), Rajnagar block (0.642), Killa block (0.625), Jampuijala block (0.595), Nalchar block (0.528) whereas the minimum value is found in Mandai block (0.177) of South Tripura district which implies that economic status of the beneficiary households in Mandai block is very poor compare to beneficiary households of other selected blocks. The economic status of Teliamura block (0.328), Salema block (0.366), Ambassa block (0.369), Manu block (0.374), Jirania block (0.391), Kalyanpur block (0.392) are not impressive. The economic index of B.C. Nagar block is highest due to high agricultural income, work participation, annual income of the beneficiaries, average expenditure, having more consumer durable goods and high economic profile. It is also observed that work participation rate is highest in Rajnagar block; however it is lowest in Manu block. The annual income of the Jampuijala block is highest compare to other selected blocks. The horticultural income status is highest in Matabari block among these selected blocks.

Table 3.32: Beneficiary Households' Social Index of the Selected Blocks in Tripura

District	*Blocks*	*Education Level*	*House Type*	*Sanitation*	*Gas Connect*	*Water Source*	*Distance of Water Source*	*Housing Space*	*Area of Bastu*	*Composite Index (SI)*
Dhalai	Ambassa	0.662	0.258	0.753	0.160	0.069	0.260	0.338	0.030	0.316
	Manu	0.105	0.663	0.104	0.000	0.855	0.158	1.000	0.633	0.440
	Salema	0.342	0.375	1.000	0.314	0.685	0.229	0.527	0.430	0.488
Gomati	Killa	0.087	0.518	0.178	0.868	0.319	0.165	0.361	0.176	0.334
	Matabari	0.329	1.000	0.000	0.683	0.000	1.000	0.719	0.372	0.513
Khowai	Kalyanpur	0.126	0.845	0.422	1.000	1.000	0.006	0.446	0.225	0.509
	Teliamura	0.433	0.793	0.422	1.000	1.000	0.007	0.471	0.225	0.544
Sepahijala	Jampuijala	0.336	0.606	0.387	0.851	0.922	0.000	0.285	0.754	0.518
	Nalchar	0.000	0.533	0.360	0.736	0.954	0.029	0.000	0.000	0.326
South Tripura	B.C Nagar	0.374	0.118	0.313	0.847	0.919	0.117	0.480	1.000	0.521
	Rajnagar	0.421	0.042	0.851	0.282	0.385	0.136	0.065	0.134	0.289
	Rupaichhari	0.058	0.095	0.339	0.178	0.722	0.351	0.304	0.115	0.270
West Tripura	Jirania	1.000	0.780	0.422	1.000	1.000	0.144	0.445	0.869	0.708
	Mandai	0.499	0.000	0.312	0.876	0.837	0.127	0.227	0.382	0.407

Source: Calculated from Primary Survey, December, 2021.

Table 3.33: Beneficiary Households' Economic Index in the Selected Blocks

District	*Block*	*AAI*	*EPI*	*WPRI*	*CDI*	*AEI*	*CLI*	*HII*	*AII*	*Composite EI*
Dhalai	Ambassa	0.484	0.379	0.358	0.387	0.833	0.082	0.326	0.104	0.369
	Manu	0.829	0.341	0.000	0.393	0.015	0.710	0.482	0.222	0.374
	Salema	0.396	0.211	0.358	0.731	0.242	0.412	0.509	0.073	0.366
Gomati	Killa	0.677	0.158	0.440	0.515	0.840	1.000	0.913	0.453	0.625
	Matabari	1.000	0.763	0.588	0.573	0.513	0.620	1.000	0.651	0.713
Khowai	Kalyanpur	0.713	0.598	0.259	0.678	0.352	0.251	0.000	0.284	0.392
	Teliamura	0.449	0.520	0.245	0.542	0.161	0.392	0.000	0.311	0.328
Sepahijala	Jampuijala	0.415	1.000	0.375	0.652	0.167	0.435	0.719	1.000	0.595
	Nalchar	0.623	0.321	0.535	0.774	0.399	0.000	0.683	0.889	0.528
South Tripura	B.C Nagar	0.978	0.829	0.908	0.876	0.890	0.498	0.559	0.913	0.807
	Rajnagar	0.917	0.603	1.000	0.465	0.720	0.457	0.524	0.450	0.642
	Rupaichhari	0.677	0.421	0.516	0.342	1.000	0.310	0.029	0.280	0.447
West Tripura	Jirania	0.221	0.469	0.427	0.844	0.341	0.659	0.000	0.164	0.391
	Mandai	0.000	0.000	0.488	0.426	0.000	0.498	0.007	0.000	0.177

Source: Calculated from Primary Survey, December, 2021.

Note: AAI = Annual Agricultural Income Index, EPI = Economic Profile Index, WPRI = Work Participation Rate Index, CDI = Consumer Durable goods Index, AEI = Average Expenditure, CLI = Cultivated Land Index, HII = Horticultural Income Index, AII = Annual Income Index.

Table 3.34 reveals the Households' socio-economic index (SEI). It is found that highest value of composite households' socio-economic index is in B.C. Nagar block (0.6638) of South Tripura district and this block is ranked 1 as per the socio-economic index value because social status is best compare to other blocks due to high value of economic index. This implies that the socio-economic status is best in B.C. Nagar block compare to other selected blocks in the study area. The second best socio-economic index value is found in Matabari block (0.6132) which is followed by Jampuijala block (0.5565), Jirania block (0.5491), Killa block (0.4793), Rajnagar (0.4658), Kalyanpur block (0.4502) etc. However, the worst socio-economic condition is found in Mandai block (0.2924) of West Tripura district. The socio-economic condition is also poor in Ambassa block (0.3427) which is ranked 13th Rupaichhari block (0.3585) which is ranked 12th, and Manu block (0.4069) is ranked 11th.

Table 3.34: Beneficiary Households' Socio-economic Index in the Selected Blocks

District	*Block*	*Social Index*	*Economic Index*	*Socio-economic Index (SEI)*	*Rank*
Dhalai	Ambassa	0.316	0.369	0.3427	13
	Manu	0.440	0.374	0.4069	11
	Salema	0.488	0.366	0.4270	10
Gomati	Killa	0.334	0.625	0.4793	5
	Matabari	0.513	0.713	0.6132	2
Khowai	Kalyanpur	0.509	0.392	0.4502	7
	Teliamura	0.544	0.328	0.4357	8
Sepahijala	Jampuijala	0.518	0.595	0.5565	3
	Nalchar	0.326	0.528	0.4272	9
South Tripura	B.C Nagar	0.521	0.807	0.6638	1
	Rajnagar	0.289	0.642	0.4658	6
	Rupaichhari	0.270	0.447	0.3585	12
West Tripura	Jirania	0.708	0.391	0.5491	4
	Mandai	0.407	0.177	0.2924	14

Source: Calculated from Primary Survey, December, 2021.

Figure 3.11 shows the block-wise comparison of socio-economic index value in the study area which shows the comparative status of socio-economic condition.

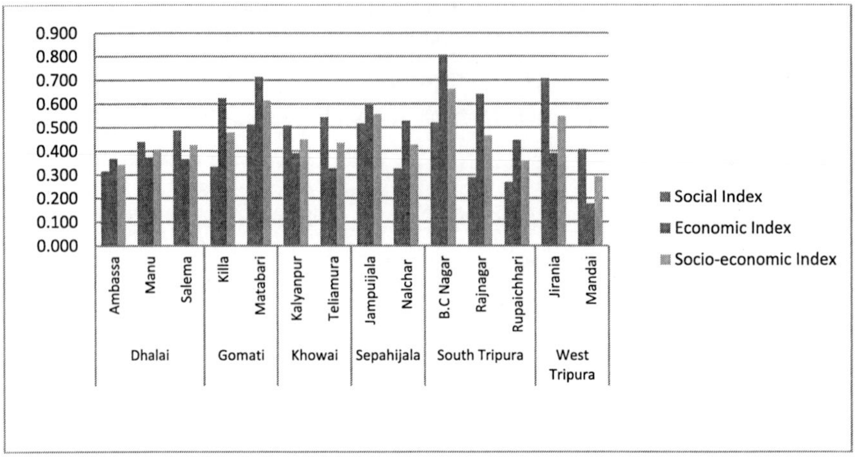

Figure 3.11: Beneficiary Households' Socio-economic Index in the Selected Blocks
Source: Calculated from Primary Survey, December, 2021.

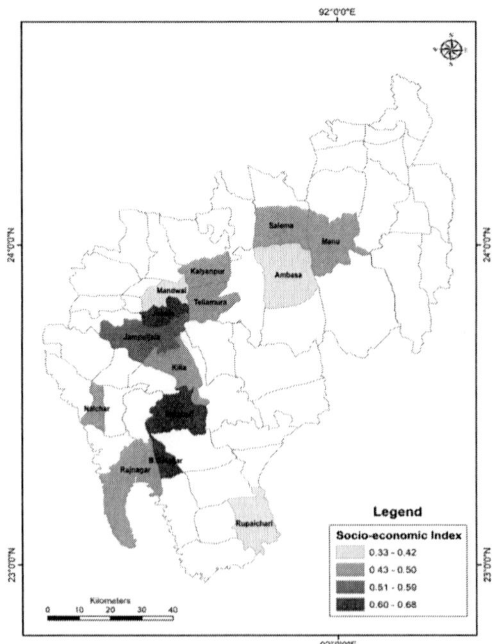

Figure 3.11: Mapping of Blocks showing Socio-economic Index in the Study Area

3.3 Conclusion

Based on the secondary as well as primary findings the following conclusions can be mentioned briefly.

The health infrastructure in the TTAADC areais very poor as there are only two hospital and one health sub-centre which is not sufficient for the area of 7132.56 square km. However, the educational infrastructure is relatively better than health infrastructure.

From the primary survey, it is found that male percentage of population is much higher than the female percentage of population. The sex ratio among these selected 14 blocks of Tripura is found very poor in B.C. Nagar block and Rajnagar block of South Tripura district. It is observed that 64.20 percentages of the sample households are Hindu, followed by 20.60 Christian households and remaining 15.20 percentage households are the believers of Buddhist religion. Buddhist believers are mainly found in Manu and Rupaichhari block.

From the primary survey, it is found that respondents' level of education is very poor. 37.80 per cent of them are illiterate, 28.60 per cent have only primary level of education. After secondary education, the enrolment rate in higher classes is found to be very poor. As the survey data indicates, 4.40 per cent of the respondents have completed higher secondary level of education and a mere 0.40 per cent is found to have studied up to graduate level.

It is found that housing condition of the beneficiary farmers is very poor. More than 76 per cent households are living in kaccha houses and only 16 per cent live in pucca houses and rest are in semi-pucca houses. Most of the houses have only two rooms and they are living in very small area of house and their average area of bastu is in only around one kani of land. Though most of them are living in kaccha house, but their sanitation condition is improved. It is found that 68.6 per cent households are using semi-pucca sanitation facilities and only 17 per cent households have kaccha sanitation facilities. Majority (79.2 per cent) of the sample households having the access to supply water for their drinking and only 11.4 per cent of the households collect their drinking water from tube wells. It is worth mentioning that 5.6 per cent of the total sample households still depend on unsafe sources of drinking water such as pond. 1.6 per cent of the respondents have reported that they rely on other sources like hand pump, use of motor in house etc. for their drinking water.

Most of the beneficiary farmers are marginal farmers (29 per cent) and they have only up to one kani of land. Most of the farmers have livestock for their both own consumption as well as additional supportive income for the family. It is observed that poultry, piggery, cow, goat, duck and broiler are the common livestock almost in all blocks. It is found that out of the total production of rice, the maximum 45 per cent rice is produced by the small farmers, which is under the production limit of 1000–2000 Kg. It is found that out of the total sample beneficiaries only small percentage beneficiaries are doing horticultural practices and mainly they are doing rubber plantation, banana and betel nut.

CHAPTER 4

Development of Agricultural and Horticultural Production in Tripura

The economy of Tripura is mainly dependent on agricultural production and horticultural production. Around 60 percent of the household belongs to the rural area and they totally depend on agricultural economy for their livelihoods. Agricultural and horticultural development may be deemed as the critical aspect of inclusive growth and proves to be a smooth path for achieving social and economic inclusion. This chapter is divided into three sections viz; Agricultural Development in Tripura (Section 4.1), Horticultural Development in Tripura (Section 4.2) and the Importance of Agriculture and Horticulture in developing the Tribal economy of Tripura (Section 4.3). These sections are discussed in the following.

4.1 Agricultural Development in Tripura

Agriculture is the primary sector contributing to about 64 percent of the total employment in the state and 48 percent of the State Domestic Product. The agricultural production and productivity depends largely on the quality of land and sustainable practices. A balance between efficient and productive agricultural enterprise and environmental protection and sustainability is important to make agriculture sector an economically viable venture. In recent years, the achievement of self-sufficiency in food production in various states has been accorded high priority in the food policies of the country. Tripura, one among the north eastern states, is also successful in achieving self-sufficiency in various sectors by increasing its food production in manifolds.

Table 4.1 shows the land use pattern of Tripura has undergone quite interesting changes during the last few years. The state has a total geographical area of 10,49,169 hectares (Table 4.1). Out of the total geographical area of the state, 59.99 percent (6,29,437 hectares) land is

Table 4.1: Land Use Classification in Tripura, 2014–15 to 2019–20 (Area in Hectares)

Land Use Classification (Yearly)	*2014–15*	*2015–16*	*2016–17*	*2017–18*	*2018–19*	*2019–20*
Geographical Area	1049169	1049169	1049169	1049169	1049169	1049169
Forest Area	629426	629426	629426	629426	629426	629426
Land not Available for Agricultural Use	146155	146920	147413	147979	148304	148691
Land under Misc. Tree Crops, Groves not including in Net Area Sown	11213	10687	10525	10423	10125	10037
Permanent Pasture & other Grazing	1130	1070	944	944	944	925
Cultivable Waste land	3020	2878	2878	2878	2578	2578
Current Fallow	1150	1096	898	890	1055	955
Fallow Land Other than Current fallow	1715	1635	1595	1534	1189	1189
Net Cropped Area	255360	255450	255490	255095	255548	255368
Gross Cropped Area	483488	485677	490540	486770	488500	487000
Area Sown More Than Once	228128	230227	235050	231675	232952	231632
Cropping Intensity (%)	189	190	192	191	191	191
Cultivable Land	273588	272823	272330	271764	271439	271052

Source: Directorate of Agriculture, Govt. of Tripura.

under the forest covering, which remains same throughout the period 2014–15 to 2019–20. The area of land not available for agricultural use was 1,46,155 hectares in 2014–15 which has increased to 1,48,691 hectares in 2019–20, thereby adding a total area of 2,536 hectares during a period of last six years. The area under permanent pastures and other grazing lands has greatly reduced over the years. The area of land under this use was 1,130 hectares in 2014–15, which fell down to 925 hectares in 2019–20, thereby registering a decline of 205 hectares during the last six years. Similarly, there has been a substantial decline of 1,176 hectares in the land under miscellaneous tree crops and groves not included under net sown agricultural area over the period 2014–15 to 2019–20. The area under cultivable waste land has also reduced over the years.

The area cultivable waste land use has declined from 3,020 hectares in 2014–15 to 2,578 hectares in 2019–20, there by registering a decline of 442 hectares during the last six years. The total current fallow land in Tripura is found to decline from 1,150 hectares to 955 hectares during 2014–15 to 2019–20, there by registering a decline of 195 hectares. Similarly, the area under fallow land other than current fallow has declined from 1,715 hectares in 2014–15 to 1189 in 2019–20, there by displaying a decline of 526 hectares over a period of six years. The net cropped area and the area sown more than once have increased by eight hectares and 3,504 hectares, respectively, during the last six years resulting into an increase of 3508 hectares in the gross cropped area. The increase in area sown more than once has also improved the intensity of cropping in the state from 189 per cent in 2014–15 to 191 per cent in 2019–20. The total area under cultivable land in Tripura is found to decline constantly from 2,73,588 hectares in 2014–15 to 2,71,052 hectares in 2019–20, there by registering a decline of 2,536 hectares over a period of six years.

Table 4.2 shows the size of operational holding and land used in Tripura for cultivation. As per agriculture census, the operational holdings are categorized into five size classes, viz. marginal, small, semi–medium, medium and large. The total number of operational holdings in Tripura is estimated at 5,73,194 holding (Table 4.2). The total area of operational holdings is 2,81,785.165 hectares which accounts for 26.86 percent of the total geographical area of the state. Average size of operational holdings in the state is 0.49 hectare and it is the lowest among the eight north eastern states as well as that of the national average of 1.08 hectare. It is observed from Table 4.2 that the size of operational holdings in Tripura is dominated by marginal and small categories of farmers, and as a consequence, most of the agricultural activities in the state are confined to subsistence farming. Out of the total operational holdings, 87.95 percent (5,04,105 holding) belong to 'marginal' farmers, holding less than one hectare of land, and they operate 52.80 percent of the total operated area. About 8.37 percent (47,987 holding) of operational holdings belong to 'small' farmers (holding between 1–2 hectares of land) and they operate 24.88 percent of the operated area. Further, there are 18,538 holding (3.23 percent) 'semi-medium' and 2,491 holding (0.43 percent) 'medium' farmers in Tripura, owning between 4–10 hectares of land and operating 17.46 percent and 4.48 percent of the total operated area, respectively. Only 0.01 percent (73 holding) of the total operational holdings belongs to 'large farmers'. They are in the size class of 10 hectares and above with only 0.38 percent of operated area. The distribution of land according to different sizes of operational holdings is also shortlisted in Table 4.2. It is observed that out of the total net cultivated area of the state, 52.90 percent (1,35,745.35 hectares) is operated by marginal farmers, 24.24 percent by small farmers, 18.16 percent by semi-medium farmers, 4.38 percent by medium farmers and only 0.32 percent of the net cultivated area is operated by large farmers. Similarly, the highest proportion i.e. 51.79 percent of the total area under uncultivated land excluding fallow land belongs to marginal holdings, followed by small holdings (31.34 percent), semi-medium holdings (10.31 percent), medium holdings (5.51 percent) and large holdings (1.05 percent).

In India, the climatic conditions like temperature, humidity and rainfall varies across region as a result of there is crop diversification. Hence a diversity of crop production is also found in Tripura which includes different type of crops like rice, maize, wheat, gram, pulses, oil seeds etc. Table 4.3 reveals the total area and total annual production of some important crops grown in Tripura during the period 2005–06 to 2019–20. Rice is the principal staple food in Tripura and is cultivated in 54.54 percent of the total cropped area. It is grown in both hilly and valley regions of the state. Jhum or

Table 4.2: Operational Holdings by Size Class and Land Use in Tripura (Agriculture Census, 2005–06)

Sl.	*Size Class (in Ha.)*	*Total Holding*		*Net Area Sown*	*Area under Current Fallows*	*Net Area Cultivated*	*Un-cultivated Land Excluding Fallow*
		No.	*Area*				
1.	Below 0.5	416092	91568.12	85662.17	167.30	85829.47	5738.65
2.	(0.5–1.0)	88013	57209.40	49681.21	234.67	49915.88	7293.52
	Marginal	504105	148777.52	135343.38	401.97	135745.35	13032.17
3.	(1.0–2.0)	47987	70095.55	62005.71	203.50	62209.21	7886.35
	Small	47987	70095.55	62005.71	203.50	62209.21	7886.35
4.	(2.0–3.0)	14662	35865.79	33934.52	91.27	34025.79	1840.00
5.	(3.0–4.0)	3876	13330.49	12441.07	134.84	12575.91	754.58
	Semi-Medium	18538	49196.28	46375.59	226.11	46601.70	2594.59
6.	(4.0–5.0)	1595	7028.86	6008.43	46.83	6055.26	973.60
7.	(5.0–7.5)	746	4287.17	3936.63	0.00	3936.63	350.54
8.	(7.5–10.0)	150	1317.72	1256.42	0.00	1256.42	61.30
	Medium	2491	12633.75	11201.48	46.83	11248.31	1385.44
9.	(10.0–20.0)	62	786.18	742.15	0.00	742.15	44.04
10.	20 & Above	11	295.88	64.71	11.14	75.85	220.00
	Large	73	1082.06	806.85	11.14	817.99	264.04
11.	All Classes	573194	281785.17	255733.01	889.55	256622.56	25162.58

Source: Directorate of Land Records, Govt. of Tripura.

shifting cultivation is practiced in the hill region and settled farming in the plains. Rice is grown in three seasons, viz. Aus (pre-Kharif), Aman (Kharif) and Boro (Summer). The total area under rice cultivation has increased marginally from 2,56,078 hectares in 2005–06 to 2019–20 with at 0.67 growth rate. The total annual production of rice is found to increase significantly from 6,07,780 MT in 2005–06 to 8,10,244 MT in 2019–20. The CAGR has recorded at 2.34 percent during the reference period. Maize is the second most important food grain grown in Tripura. It is mostly grown under rainfed hilly upland conditions and jhum fields and is used both for direct consumption and as well as feed ingredient for pig and poultry farming of the state. The area under maize production has increased from 2150 hectares in 2005–06 to 14635 hectares in 2019–20 with a growth rate of 18.68 percent. Similarly, there has been an increase of about 20861 MT of maize production during the last 15 years, registering a growth of 22.83 percent. Wheat is another important cereal crop being cultivated in Tripura. The total production of wheat in Tripura is found to show a declining trend along with decline in area. The total area under wheat production has declined from 2610 hectares in 2005–06 to only 148 hectares in 2019–20 with a decrease in growth rate of 17.21 per cent. Similarly, the total annual production is found to decline from 5259 MT in 2005–06 to only about 330 MT in 2019–20, registering a negative growth rate of 16.04 per cent during the last 15 years. Gram (also known as chickpea) is another major pulse crop being cultivated in Tripura.

From Table 4.3, it is also found that the total area under gram cultivation in Tripura has declined considerably from 939 hectares in 2005–06 to 291 hectares in 2019–20. Similarly, there has been a decline of about 436 MT of gram during the last 15 years. Pulses are consumed as dal, which is the cheapest source of protein, and therefore occupy an important position in balancing human dietary needs. The trend of production of pulses in Tripura is found to increase along with increase in area. The total area under pulses has increased from 8544 hectares in 2005–06 to 24570 hectares in 2019–20 and the total annual production has increased from 5608 MT to about 18661 MT during the same period.

Table 4.3: Area and Production of Some Important Crops in Tripura, 2005–06 to 2019–20
(Area in Ha & Production in MT)

Year	Rice		Maize		Wheat		Gram		Total Pulses	
	Area	*Production*	*Area*	*Production*	*Area*	*Production*	*Area*	*Production*	*Area*	*Production*
2005–06	256078	607780	2150	2113	2610	5259	939	616	8544	5608
2006–07	250980	620500	2450	2420	984	1827	–	–	8081	5290
2007–08	252897	640422	2123	2125	1023	1889	–	–	5361	3496
2008–09	242966	627174	2093	2046	635	1195	91	88	5796	4181
2009–10	244853	640948	1918	1909	701	1328	121	87	6170	4126
2010–11	262320	701562	3100	4101	800	1600	–	–	7500	5085
2011–12	265999	718304	3743	5058	274	536	–	–	8582	6005
2012–13	254743	713222	3948	5176	334	827	164	127	8439	5958
2013–14	254254	711831	4589	5863	150	300	125	95	12150	8696
2014–15	257273	746954	4519	5963	135	304	250	131	11664	8426
2015–16	269793	794848	8646	12095	182	407	250	195	22327	15463
2016–17	277106	814644	14696	20495	200	460	250	195	24327	16717
2017–18	274290	812092	15736	22473	171	376	235	186	27234	19358
2018–19	269364	793200	15982	22696	157	332	257	171	25854	18918
2019–20	267335	810244	14635	22974.48	148	330.45	291	180.4	24570	18660.83

Source: Directorate of Agriculture, Govt. of Tripura.

The growth rate over time has recorded at 12.64 per cent and 13.52 per cent in case of area and production, respectively, during the last 15 years. The phenomenal increase in the production of pulses has been due to adoption of high yielding varieties and modern agricultural inputs which significantly improved productivity.

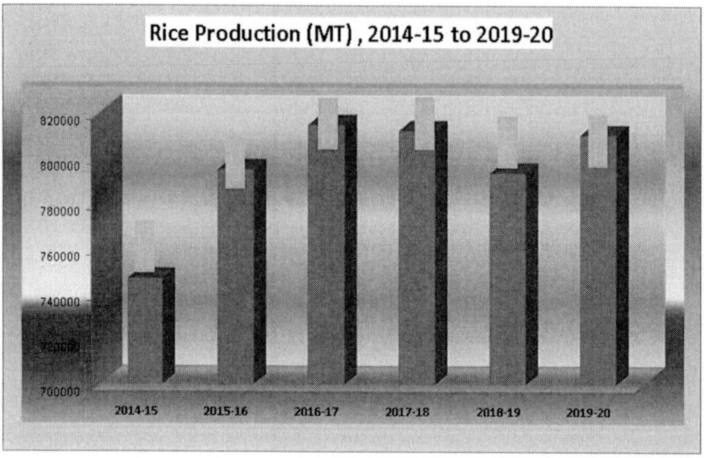

Figure 4.1: Rice Production from 2014–15 to 2019–20

Table 4.4 depicts the trends in area and production of some important oilseed crops in Tripura during 2005–06 to 2019–20. The total production of oilseeds in Tripura is found to increase significantly along with increase in area. The total area under oilseed crops has increased from 3384 hectares to 17180 hectares during 2005–06 to 2019–20, resulting in an increase of 13796 hectares of total area over a period of 15 years. Similarly, there is an increase in the production of oilseeds from 1990 MT in 2005–06 to about 14478 MT in 2019–20, thereby registering an increase of about 12488 MT of oilseed production in the state over the years. The level of productivity has risen from 0.59 MT/Ha in 2005–06 to 0.84 MT/Ha in 2019–20. The highest oilseed production has been recorded in 2019–20. Groundnut, sesamum and rape/mustard are the major important oilseed crops grown in Tripura. The area under groundnut cultivation is found to increase from 379 hectares in 2005–06 to 2367 hectares in 2019–20, thereby adding a total area of 1988 hectares during a period of 15 years. Similarly, there has been an increase of about 2961 MT of

Table 4.4: Area and Production of Some Important Oilseed Crops & Potato in Tripura, 2005–06 to 2019–20 (Area in Ha& Production in MT)

Year	*Groundnut*		*Sesamum*		*Rape/Mustard*		*Total Oil Seed*		*Potato*	
	Area	*Production*	*Area*	*Production*	*Area*	*Production*	*Area*	*Production*	*Area*	*Production*
2005–06	379	400	1526	700	1479	890	3384	1990	5425	66741
2006–07	590	610	2077	1048	1744	1360	4411	3018	5380	80858
2007–08	679	687	1776	896	1451	1062	3906	2645	5800	84563
2008–09	486	539	1392	780	1588	1191	3466	2510	5336	93030
2009–10	423	483	1532	801	1467	1078	3422	2363	5653	88645
2011–12	369	480	1942	1095	2131	1683	2500	2163	6500	104000
2012–13	597	731	2085	1188	2132	1701	4814	3620	8312	149046
2013–14	613	725	2824	1706	2617	2159	6054	4590	3366	62843
2014–15	735	801	2468	1543	5934	4925	9137	7269	9040	159466
2015–16	1375	1587	3898	2261	6418	5166	12044	9303	7684	138512
2016–17	1833	2675	5590	3276	7500	6188	15373	12508	7948	143577
2017–18	2239	3207	7035	4151	7893	6630	17546	14279	7985	144534
2018–19	2251	3098	6967	4332	7729	6425	17101	13973	8005	144935
2019–20	2367	3361.39	6611	4208.82	7895	6669.73	17180	14478.19	8050	145866

Source: Directorate of Agriculture, Govt. of Tripura.

groundnut production in the state during the last 15 years. The production of sesamum has also shown an increasing trend along with increase in area. The area under this crop has increased from 1526 hectares in 2005–06 to 6611 hectares in 2019–20, thereby registering an increase of 5085 hectares during 2005–06 to 2019–20.

The total annual production of sesamum is found to increase from 700 MT in 2005–06 to about 4209 MT in 2019–20 with marked year to year fluctuations. The highest area under sesamum is found in 2017–18, while the highest production is found in 2018–19. Another oilseed crop in which significant increase in area and production has taken place is rapeseed/mustard. The total area under this crop has increased from 1479 hectares in 2005–06 to 7895 hectares in 2019–20, thereby adding a total area of 6146 hectares over a period of 15 years. Similarly, the total production has increased substantially from 890 MT to about 6670 MT during 2005–06 to 2019–20. Potato is another important cash crop being cultivated in Tripura. The state has achieved remarkable progress in the production of potato which has increased spectacularly from 66741 MT in 2005–06 to 145866 MT in 2019–20. The phenomenal increase in production has been partly due to increase in the area under cultivation, which has increased from 5425 hectares to 8050 hectares during 2005–06 to 2019–20 and partly due to increase in productivity, which has increased from 12.30 MT/Ha to 18.12 MT/Ha during the same period.

The suitable agro climatic conditions of Tripura also favour the cultivation of different types of non-foodgrain crops like jute, mesta, cotton and sugarcane in the state. The trends in area and production of these crops during the period 2005–06 to 2019–20 are presented in Table 4.5. Jute and mesta crop together known as raw jute as their uses are almost same and they are important natural fibre crops being cultivated in Tripura. Raw jute being a natural annual renewal source of raw material, bio-degradable, non-toxic and environment friendly, offer excellent fibre as raw material for different textiles and other utility products, apart from as raw material in the packaging industry.

From the Table 4.5, it is observed that there is a gradual decline in the area coverage of jute while production is showing an increasing trend. From a level of 685 hectares in 2005–06, the area under jute

Table 4.5: Area and Production of Some Important Non-food Grain Crops in Tripura, 2005–06 to 2019–20 (Area in Ha)

Year	*Jute*		*Mesta*		*Cotton*		*Sugar cane*	
	Area	*Production (180 kg of Bale)*	*Area*	*Production (180 kg of Bale)*	*Area*	*Production (170 kg of Bale)*	*Area*	*Production (MT)*
2005–06	685	5410	1170	8522	1143	1610	874	43334
2006–07	466	3966	1064	7798	1148	1598	869	42373
2007–08	458	3734	949	6810	1110	1504	959	46678
2008–09	450	3678	638	4814	997	1355	991	48423
2009–10	466	3550	728	5453	965	1341	859	41892
2010–11	479	4139	776	6255	1063	1488	900	44955
2011–12	639	5483	628	5212	949	1348	921	45002
2012–13	640	5261	641	5077	922	1341	899	45436
2013–14	643	5369	854	7003	949	1395	964	49598
2014–15	650	5564	627	5079	904	1347	793	41510
2015–16	650	5701	627	5530	904	1365	793	40492
2016–17	590	5369	583	4961	870	1358	822	44100
2017–18	551	4695	541	4804	805	1160	875	46862
2018–19	656	5838	493	4117	812	1215	662	35914
2019–20	623	5731	430	3838	760	1138.51	687	36372.09

Source: Directorate of Agriculture, Govt. of Tripura.

has decreased to 623 hectares in 2019–20, thereby registering a decline of 62 hectares over a period of 15 years. The production of jute from a level of 5410 bales in 2005–06 has increased to 5731 bales in 2019–20, registering thereby growth rate of 2.67 per cent during the reference period. However, there have been some fluctuations year to year in both area and production under the crop. The decrease in area under jute coverage seems due to diversion of area to other competitive and remunerative short duration crops including horticultural crops. The total area under mesta has declined significantly from 1170 hectares in 2005–06 to 430 hectares in 2019–20 with a negative growth of 5.34 per cent. Similarly, there has been a significant decline in the production of mesta from 8522 bales in 2005–06 to 3838 bales in 2019–20, thereby registering a negative growth of 3.89 per cent during the period of 15 years. Cotton is another important fibre crop being cultivated in Tripura. From the table it is found that there has been a continuous decline in both area and production of this crop.

From a level of 1143 hectares in 2005–06, the area under cotton has come down to 760 hectares during 2019–20. Similarly, the production is found to decline from 1610 bales in 2005–06 to about 1139 bales in 2019–20. The growth rate of area and production is recorded at –2.68 per cent and –1.93 per cent respectively. The decline in area under cotton cultivation seems due to switching over to other remunerative short duration crops like maize, sesamumetc. Sugarcane is another important agricultural crop grown in Tripura. The trends in area and production of sugarcane in Tripura, as reported in Table 4.5, reveal that over the years its production has declined along with decline in area. From a level of 874 hectares in 2005–06, the area under sugarcane cultivation has declined to 687 hectares in 2019–20, while production has declined from 43334 MT to about 36372 MT during the same period. However, there have been some fluctuations year to year in both area and production under this crop. The growth rate of area and production over the period of 15 years is recorded at –1.76 per cent and –0.97 per cent respectively. The significant decline in both production and area under this crop in recent years appears to be due to low level of profitability and instability in sugarcane yield, which has resulted in switching to other commercial crop such as rubber.

4.2 Development of Horticulture in Tripura

The good agro climatic conditions, deep fertile soils, subtropical humid climate with abundance of rainfall offer tremendous scope for the development of horticulture in Tripura. At present, the total area under horticulture in the state is 1,21,160 hectares with a production of 14,58,245 MT. Among the important horticultural crops, pineapple grown in Tripura is widely acclaimed as the best in the country. There is huge potential of growing fruits and plantation crops like litchi, mango, pineapple, orange, guava, jackfruit, banana, lemon, cashew nut, coconut and areca nut commercially, which may cater to the needs of other North Eastern States and neighboring country like Bangladesh as well. Recent development in Indo-Bangla relationship has also opened up new avenues for export possibilities.

The area and production of major fruits and plantation crops in Tripura during the period from 2005–06 to 2019–20 are reported in Table 4.6. The area coverage of litchi is found to decline from 2346 hectares in 2005–06 to 933 hectares in 2019–20 with a negative growth rate of 4.57 per cent during the study period. The production of litchi is also found to decline from 14255 MT in 2005–06 to 3219 MT in 2019–2020 with a negative growth of 8.65 per cent during the reference period. The trend of production of mango is found to increase along with increase in area. The area under mango production has increased from 3868 hectares in 2005–06 to 10272 hectares in 2019–20 and the corresponding production is found to increase from 12340 MT to 52284 MT during the same period. It is estimated that the growth of area and production of mango over time is recorded at 9.89 per cent and 15.61 per cent respectively. Among the different tropical and sub-tropical fruits, pineapple grown in Tripura is widely known for its excellent quality. Since 2018 pineapple is being exported to many other countries. The area and production of pineapple, as reported in Table 4.6, show an increasing trend during the studied period. The area under pineapple cultivation is found to increase from 5180 hectares in 2005–06 to 9785 hectares in 2019–20 with a growth of 4.85 per cent over time. The production of pineapple has increased from 106406 MT in 2005–06 to the peak of 181208 MT in 2015–16 and then to 142665 MT in 2019–20. The growth of pineapple production is estimated to be 2.24 percent during the reference period. Orange is another important fruit which is significant in terms of increase in area and production. The area coverage of orange has increased from 2811 hectares in 2005–06 to 4763 hectares in 2019–20 and the production is found to increase from 18150 MT to 21319 MT during the same period. The estimated growth of area and production is recorded at 6.15 percent and 2.58 percent over time respectively. Comparatively lesser increase in production than that in area seems to be due to larger areas under new plantations which are yet to come to full bearing stage. Another important horticultural crop in Tripura is Guava. The trend of production of guava is found to increase along with increase in area. The area under guava production has increased from 356 hectares in 2005–06 to 665 hectares in 2019–20 with a growth of 8.35 percent. Similarly, the production of guava has increased from 1560 MT in 2005–06 to a peak of 6300 MT in 2014–15 and then to 3119 MT in 2019–20 with a growth of 8.97 percent during the reference period. Jackfruit is another important fruit grown in Tripura. The agro-climatic conditions, fertile and acidic soil with abundant rainfall favour the cultivation of jackfruits in Tripura. Diverse forms of jackfruits have been cultivated in hilly slopes and plains and exported to neighbouring countries like Bangladesh and neighbouring states like Assam. It is one of the major commercial fruit crops in Tripura and has high local demand. The farming community of the state earns a lot of money from it, as its cultivation is easy, hardy in nature, producing fruits even under adverse soil and climatic conditions. However, the area under jackfruit cultivation is found to decline from 8645 hectares in 2005–06 to 5487 hectares in 2019–20 with a negative growth of 2.11 percent. Similarly, there has been a decline in the production of jackfruit from 2,56,280 MT in 2005–06 to 1,33,154 MT in 2019–20 with a negative growth of 4.40 percent during the reference period.

Banana is another important horticultural crop grown in Tripura. Its year round availability, affordability, varietal range, taste and nutritive value makes it the favourite fruit among all classes of people. It is consumed in fresh or cooked form both as ripe and raw fruit. Chini Champa (Ney Poovan), Champa (Poovan), Jahaji (Dwarf Cavendish) and Morthomon (Sabri) are some of the important cultivars grown in Tripura. There has been an increasing trend in both area and production of banana over the years. The total area

Table 4.6: Area and Production of Fruits and Plantation Crops in Tripura, 2005–06 to 2019–20 (Area in Ha & Production in MT)

(a)

Year	*Litchi*		*Mango*		*Pineapple*		*Orange*		*Guava*		*Jackfruit*	
	Area	*Production*	*Area*	*Production*	*Area*	*Production*	*Area*	*Production*	*Area*	*Production*	*Area*	*Production*
2005–06	2346	14255	3868	12340	5180	106406	2811	18150	356	1560	8645	256280
2006–07	2475	14400	3700	11358	6184	115829	2882	19445	333	1496	7430	249265
2007–08	2722	16032	3981	11925	6247	108009	2972	20383	336	1510	7666	252384
2008–09	2762	16165	4190	12706	6336	110487	3098	20926	348	1636	7627	250619
2009–10	2762	16972	4254	13170	6476	117531	3162	22230	350	1727	7636	251569
2010–11	2935	16566	5408	23861	6789	153310	3845	23592	384	2008	7796	279033
2011–12	3200	16566	7400	23861	11600	153709	4650	23592	352	2008	9000	245773
2012–13	3464	17980	8382	28849	11842	165010	5284	28414	525	2740	9021	269404
2013–14	3888	20179	10559	56279	11590	162260	6302	33905	997	5204	10120	302183
2014–15	3921	20578	11180	62559	11948	170890	6704	36521	1220	6300	10410	300000
2015–16	3991	20945	12224	68409	12669	181208	7301	39790	1013	5367	10079	302600
2016–17	2372	8710	10640	57035	8848	128971	6342	29352	881	4557	6096	150117
2017–18	1811	6278	10325	54929	8728	126994	5620	25328	700	3397	5560	135493
2018–19	931	3206	10231	52042	9628	140184	4780	21403	665	3117	5482	133033
2019–20(P)	933	3219	10272	52284	9785	142665	4763	21319	665	3119	5487	133154

(b)

Year	Banana		Lemon		Cashew nut		Coconut		Areca nut		Other Fruits	
	Area	*Production*	*Area*	*Production*	*Area*	*Production*	*Area*	*Production*	*Area*	*Production*	*Area*	*Production*
2005–06	5717	79250	2025	11070	3814	1855	5201	2997	4465	9580	1120	14245
2006–07	6219	80160	2034	11115	3814	1726	5382	3167	4349	9564	2366	18828
2007–08	7323	95259	2071	11380	4078	2084	5567	7882	4434	8361	–	–
2008–09	7416	96787	2106	11712	4087	2122	5746	8216	4443	8354	2290	19216
2009–10	7486	105615	2106	11716	4387	2345	5746	11384	4443	8600	2290	27694
2010–11	7754	124968	2234	15461	4746	3061	5902	18605	4699	16137	2751	38409
2011–12	12900	124968	3250	15461	5185	3132	6216	18068	5600	17726	3948	38409
2012–13	13587	133699	3857	18424	5301	3237	6467	18892	6008	19050	4183	3361
2013–14	13644	134257	4836	23116	5368	4047	6912	19483	6443	20095	6442	48964
2014–15	13990	141313	5544	27805	5376	4032	6932	19548	6635	20701	1672	1254
2015–16	15060	152117	5959	29888	5401	4051	7202	20310	7056	22015	1877	14275
2016–17	10804	115274	5041	25805	2211	1519	4610	13163	5943	20934	1659	15098
2017–18	10289	109398	4772	24208	848	327	4568	12538	5986	20409	1297	11586
2018–19	10590	109521	4972	23970	656	79	4607	12669	6731	23020	2188	19036
2019–20(P)	10658	110204	4972	23965	691	269	4610	12678	7167	24511	2188	19036

Source: Directorate of Horticulture, Govt. of Tripura.

under banana cultivation is found to increase from 5717 hectares in 2005–06 to 10658 hectares in 2019–20. Similarly, the production has increased from 79250 MT in 2005–06 to the peak of 152117 MT in 2015–16 and then to 110204 MT in 2019–20. The estimated growth of area and productivity of banana is recorded at 5.16 per cent and 2.53 per cent. Comparatively less increase in the production of banana is possibly due to large areas yet to come to bearing. Another horticultural crop in which significant increase in area and production has been taken place is lemon. The total area under lemon cultivation is found to increase from 2025 hectares in 2005–06 to 4972 hectares in 2019–20 while the production is found to increase from 11070 MT to 23965 MT during the same period. The estimated of area and production lemon is recorded at 9.20 per cent and 7.92 per cent respectively.

Cashew nut is a commercially important plantation crop being cultivated in Tripura, which offers considerable scope for enhancing the state economy by generating more income and employment potential. The state has nearly 5,000 registered cashew nut growers, out of which 3,000 are from Rajnagar alone. They usually sell raw cashew to wholesale dealers, who privately process it. BLA-39-4, Priyanka (H-1591), Vengurla-4, Ullal-1, Ullal-3, Dhana (H-1608), NRCC Selection-2, BPP-8, Jhargram-1, V.R.I-3 and Bhashkara are some of the important cultivars grown in Tripura. The area under cashew cultivation in Tripura was 3814 hectares in 2005–06 with an annual production of 1855 MT. However, in recent years, there has been a decline in both area and production. The total area under cashew cultivation is estimated at 691 hectares in 2019–20 with an annual production of only 269 MT. The estimated growth of area and production is recorded at –10.77 percent and –13.37 percent respectively during the reference period. Due to dwindling prices and heavy investment in cashew farming, a substantial number of cashew growers have migrated to rubber in recent years, resulting in a considerable decline in both area and production. Coconut is another important plantation crop in Tripura. The total cultivated area of coconut is found to decline from 5201 hectares in 2005–06 to 4610 hectares in 2019–20.However, there has been a significant increase in its production from 2997 MT in 2005–06 to 12678 MT in 2019–20 with a growth of 9.16 percent during the same period. The suitable climatic conditions of Tripura also favour the cultivation of areca nut across the state. The process of areca nut development in terms of area and production, as reported in Table 4.6 shows that the area under areca nut cultivation has been increasing more or less consistently over the years. However, the production is found to be fluctuating more often than the area. The area under areca nut cultivation is found to increase from 4465 hectares in 2005–06 to 7167 hectares in 2005–06 with a growth of 3.94 percent. Similarly, there has been a substantial increase in the production from 9580 MT in 2005–06 to 24511 MT in 2019–20 with a growth of 8.73 percent. The phenomenal increase in production has been due to adoption of high yielding varieties and modern agricultural inputs which significantly improved productivity. There are a large number of indigenous fruits such as mosambi, berry, palm, jamun, bael etc. being cultivated in Tripura. These fruits have diverse uses, besides being hardy and well adapted to different agro-climatic conditions and stress situations. The total cultivated area under these fruits in Tripura is found to increase from 1120 hectares in 2005–06 to 2188 hectares in 2019–20 while the total annual production is found to increase from 14,245 MT in 2005–06 to an all time high record of 48,964 MT in 2013–14 and then reach to 19,036 MT in 2019–20.

Development of Rubber in Tripura

Tripura occupies a pivotal position in India's rubber map in terms of relative shares in area, production as well as potential area identified for natural rubber cultivation. Tripura is also credited with higher utilization of potential area identified for rubber cultivation among the non-traditional rubber-growing regions in the country. Natural rubber (Heave brasiliensis) cultivation was initially introduced in Tripura as a soil conservation project by the Tripura Forest Department in 1963 and in course of time, it has been developed as the most commercially viable crop of thestate. Tripura has now become the second largest producer of natural rubber in the country, after Kerala, accounting for about 9 percent of the total rubber production of the country. The state also has the second largest rubber growing area in the country, after Kerala. The trends in area and production of natural rubber in Tripura during the period 2005–06 to 2019–20 are given in the following Table 4.7.

Table 4.7: Area, Production and Value of Rubber in Tripura, 2005–06 to 2019–20

Year	*Area (ha)*	*Production (MT)*	*Value (Rs. in Crore)*
2005–06	16937	17122	102.73
2006–07	19859	19650	157.20
2007–08	21760	23088	196.25
2008–09	23313	25588	255.88
2009–10	25313	27276	354.59
2011–12	57620	32332	600
2012–13	61231	37277	600
2013–14	34628	42489	634
2014–15	36855	46806	578
2015–16	41616	52020	571
2016–17	46986	56380	552
2017–18	54441	65330	640
2018–19	85100	74139	890
2019–20	85454	83701	1004

Source: Rubber Board, Agartala, Tripura.

From Table 4.7, it is observed that there has been gradual increase in the production of natural rubber along with increase in area. From a level of 16,937 hectares in 2005–06, the area under rubber plantation has increased to 85,454 hectares in 2019–20. Therefore, the area under rubber plantation increases from 16,917 ha in 2005–06 to 85454 in 2019–20. Similarly, the total annual production of rubber is found to increase from 17122 MT in 2005–06 to 83,701 MT during 2019–20, registering thereby an increase of 66,579 MT of rubber production in the state over the years. Though, there is some fluctuations in area under rubber cultivation, but the production is found to show a gradual increasing trend throughout the years. The phenomenal increase in production and area under rubber cultivation in Tripura can largely be attributed to factors such as good agro-climatic conditions suitable for rubber plantation, shifting of farmers from other crops to natural rubber, high market prices of rubber and most importantly the policy interventions by the state administration.

4.3 Importance of Agriculture and Horticulture for the Development of Tribal Economy

Agriculture is backbone of the economy especially for the tribal people. A large section of tribal people depend on agriculture for their livelihood. Whatever they produce from their cultivated land, mostly it is used for their own livelihoods which are already given in Table 3.26 and discussed in Chapter 3. However, the production of horticulture is mostly they sell it to the market and earned a sizable amount of revenue from it which is also given in Table 3.28 and discussed in the earlier chapter (Chapter-3). From the primary survey, it is observed that beneficiary households produce agricultural product especially paddy in their cultivated land. In the chapter 3, already it is found that block-wise cultivated land and agricultural production. Some beneficiary households are also concentrated on horticultural production especially rubber production in the study area.

Table 4.8 reveals the block-wise annual agricultural and horti-cultural production of the beneficiary households in the study area.

It is found that total agricultural production (paddy) is highest in Killa block (99650 kg) which is followed by Manu block (71400 kg), Jirania (69600 kg), Matabari (65000 kg) etc. and accordingly rank of the blocks in terms of value of production is also found. The least amount production of paddy is found in Nalchar block. However, in case of horticulture, the value of horticultural production (mainly rubber) is highest in Matabari block (Rs. 1046500.00) which is followed by Killa block (Rs. 955500.00), Jampuijala block (Rs. 752500.00), Nalchar block (Rs. 715000.00), Salema block (Rs. 523250.00) etc. No horticultural production is found among the sample beneficiaries belong to Jirania, Teliamura and Kalyanpur block.

Table 4.9 shows the block-wise average value of production and average cost of agricultural production in the study area.

It is found that the average value of production per kani of land is highest in Mandai block (Rs. 9500.54) of West Tripura district which is followed by Manu block (Rs. 9414.23), Rajnagar block (Rs. 9130.66) etc. The least average value of production is found in Rupaichhari block (Rs. 7644.25) of South Tripura district. It is found that average cost of irrigation for cultivation of per kani land is found very high in B.C. Nagar block (Rs. 344.32) which is followed

Table 4.8: Block-wise Annual Production of Agricultural and Horticultural of the Beneficiary Households in the Study Area at Present (in per cent)

District	*Block*	*Agricultural Production (in Kg)*	*Agricultural Production (in Value)*	*Horticultural Production (in Kg)*	*Horticultural Production (in Value)*
Dhalai	Ambassa	22920	324780	2475	329250
	Manu	71400	1125000	3850	500500
	Salema	47700	697800	4025	523250
Gomati	Killa	99650	1426850	7350	955500
	Matabari	65000	981000	8050	1046500
Khowai	Kalyanpur	36600	549000	0	0
	Teliamura	47400	711000	0	0
Sepahijala	Jampuijala	53100	769500	5775	752500
	Nalchar	17400	246500	5500	715000
South	B.C Nagar	53400	794000	4354	585500
	Rajnagar	51480	796650	4130	516500
	Rupaichhari	44470	523631	1600	30300
West	Jirania	69600	1028300	0	0
	Mandai	57850	878800	50	7250
Total		**737970**	**10852811**	**47159**	**5962050**

Source: Calculated from the Field Survey, December, 2021.

Table 4.9: Block-wise Average Value of Production and Average Cost of Agricultural Production of the Beneficiary Households in Tripura (in Rs.)

District	*Block*	*Production*	*Machinery*	*Self-Labour*	*Hired Labour*	*Seed*	*Fertilizer*	*Pesticides*	*Irrigation*
Dhalai	Ambasa	8222.28	481.01	603.80	603.80	20.81	767.09	134.18	0.00
	Manu	9414.23	495.40	640.17	640.17	29.67	961.51	160.92	0.00
	Salema	8561.96	461.35	552.15	552.15	23.28	748.47	133.13	0.00
Gomati	Killa	9117.25	519.49	427.48	427.48	23.90	781.79	141.85	77.02
	Matabari	9083.33	442.59	274.07	274.07	24.22	733.33	149.91	118.06
Khowai	Kalyanpur	9000.00	462.30	240.98	240.98	24.00	1293.44	216.39	0.00
	Teliamura	9000.00	463.29	269.62	269.62	23.70	1241.77	150.00	0.00
Sepahijala	Jampuijala	9106.51	495.86	262.72	262.72	24.57	776.33	160.65	0.00
	Nalchar	8500.00	582.76	737.93	737.93	23.03	789.66	127.76	0.00
South Tripura	B.C Nagar	8583.78	396.76	284.32	284.32	22.83	1151.89	138.05	344.32
	Rajnagar	9130.66	551.29	801.15	801.15	43.07	838.97	149.11	290.54
	Rupachhari	7644.25	767.88	590.67	590.67	23.91	1070.38	206.57	119.71
West Tripura	Jirania	9100.00	384.07	378.76	378.76	24.35	1292.92	145.13	0.00
	Mandai	9500.54	691.89	732.43	732.43	23.72	935.46	135.78	0.00

Source: Calculated from the Field Survey, December, 2021.

by Rajnager block (Rs. 290.54), Rupaichhari block (Rs. 119.71) of South Tripura district which implies that there is a lack of irrigation facilities in these blocks. Average cost of fertilizer in is highest in Kalyanpur block (Rs. 1293.44) compare to other block which is followed by Jirania block (Rs. 1292.92), Teliamura block (Rs. 1241.77), B.C. Nagar block (Rs. 1151.89), Rupaichhari block (Rs. 1070.38) etc. However least average cost of fertilizer is found in Matabari block (Rs. 733.33) of Gomati district. The farmers belong too Rupaichhari block, Jirania block, B.C. Nagar, Matabari, Jampuijala, Teliamura, Killa and Kalyanpur block use more higher labour than self-labor. The cost of hired labour for the production is highest in Rupaichhari block which is followed by Jirania block and B.C. Nagar block.

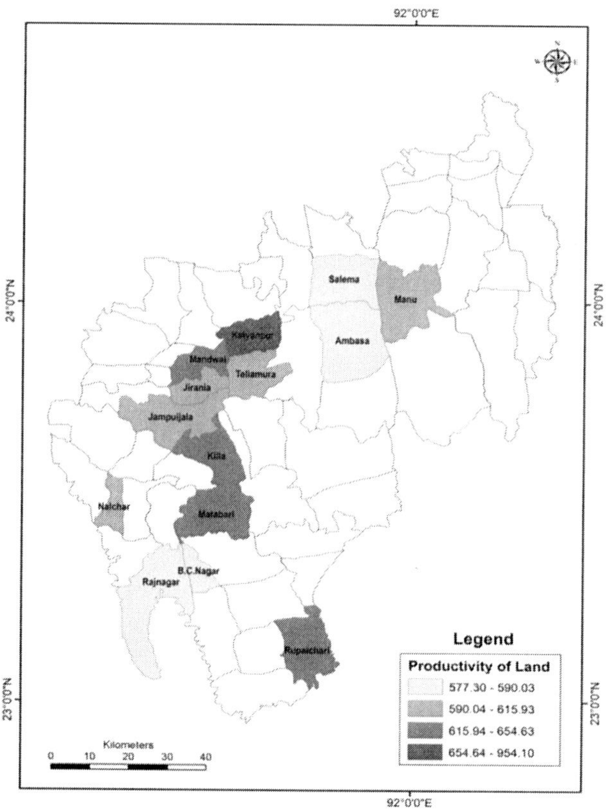

Figure 4.2: Mapping of Blocks showing Productivity of Land in the Study Area

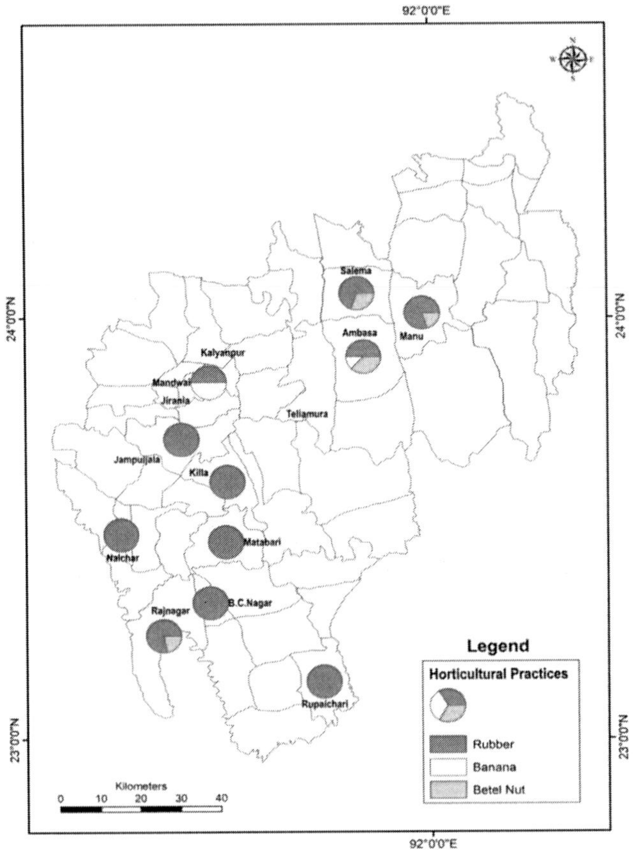

Figure 4.3: Mapping of Blocks Showing Horticultural Practices in the Study Area

4.4 Conclusion

This chapter focuses on the development of agriculture and horticulture in Tripura which is discussed on the basis of relevant secondary informations mainly. From the above discussion, it is concluded that out of the total operational holdings in Tripura, 87.95 per cent holding belong to 'marginal' farmers, holding less than one hectare of land, and they operate 52.80 per cent of the total operated area. Rice is the principal staple food in Tripura and is cultivated in 54.54 per cent of the total cropped area. It is grown in both hilly and valley regions of the state. Jhum or shifting cultivation is practiced in the hill region and settled farming in the plains.

Maize is the second most important food grain grown in Tripura. It is used both for direct consumption and as well as feed ingredient for pig and poultry farming of the state. The area under maize production has increased from 2150 hectares in 2005–06 to 14635 hectares in 2019–20 with a growth rate of 18.68 per cent.

The total production of oilseeds in Tripura is found to increase significantly along with increase in area. Groundnut, sesamum and rape/mustard are the major important oilseed crops grown in Tripura. The area under groundnut cultivation is found to increase from 379 hectares in 2005–06 to 2367 hectares in 2019–20. The highest oilseed production has been recorded in 2019–20.

The suitable agro climatic conditions of Tripura also favour the cultivation of different types of non-foodgrain crops like jute, mesta, cotton and sugarcane in the state. It is observed that there is a gradual decline in the area coverage of jute while production is showing an increasing trend.

Cotton is another important fibre crop being cultivated in Tripura. It is found that there is a continuous decline in both area and production of this crop. The decline in area under cotton cultivation seems due to switching over to other remunerative short duration crops like maize, sesamum etc. Sugarcane is another important agricultural crop grown in Tripura but over the years its production has declined along with decline in area.

The good agro climatic conditions, deep fertile soils, subtropical humid climate with abundance of rainfall offer tremendous scope for the development of horticulture in Tripura. Among the important horticultural crops, pineapple grown in Tripura is widely acclaimed as the best in the country.

There is huge potential of growing fruits and plantation crops like litchi, mango, pineapple, orange, guava, jackfruit, banana, lemon, cashew nut, coconut and areca nut commercially, which may cater to the needs of other North Eastern States and neighbouring country like Bangladesh as well. Recent development in Indo-Bangla relationship has also opened up new avenues for export possibilities.

The trend of production of mango is found to increase along with increase in area. Among the different tropical and sub-tropical fruits, pineapple grown in Tripura is widely known for its excellent quality. Since 2018 pineapple is being exported to many other countries.

Orange is another important fruit which is significant in terms of increase in area and production. Jackfruit is another important fruit grown in Tripura. The agro-climatic conditions, fertile and acidic soil with abundant rainfall favour the cultivation of jackfruits in Tripura. It is one of the major commercial fruit crops in Tripura and has high local demand. However, the area under jackfruit cultivation is found to decline from 8645 hectares in 2005–06 to 5487 hectares in 2019–20 with a negative growth of 2.11 per cent. Cashew nut is a commercially important plantation crop being cultivated in Tripura, which offers considerable scope for enhancing the state economy by generating more income and employment potential. The state has nearly 5,000 registered cashew nut growers, out of which 3,000 are from Rajnagar alone. There are a large number of indigenous fruits such as mosambi, berry, palm, jamun, bael etc. being cultivated in Tripura. Tripura occupies a pivotal position in India's rubber map in terms of relative shares in area, production as well as potential area identified for natural rubber cultivation.

CHAPTER 5

Impact of Agricultural & Horticultural Schemes on the Tribal Livelihoods

In order to achieve the sustainable development goals, the Govt. of India has launched several schemes throughout the country. These schemes are also implemented in the state of Tripura, a one of the smallest state in the North-eastern region of the country. This chapter discusses about the several agricultural and horticultural schemes implemented in Tripura which is discussed in Section 5.1 and their impact on the livelihood of the tribal farmers belongs to Tripura which is discussed in Section 5.2.

5.1 Agricultural and Horticulture Schemes Implemented in Tripura

Though the Govt. of India has launched the several agricultural and horticultural schemes throughout the nation, but only few of these schemes are successfully implemented especially in Tripura. On the basis of field survey some of these schemes are mentioned in detail in the following.

Pradhan Mantri Kisan Samman Nidhi (PM-KISAN)

In order to provide income support to all land holding farmers and their families, Govt. of India has taken a scheme named 'PM-KISHAN' through which Govt. provides Rs. 6000.00 per annum to the land holding agricultural farmers. This Rs. 6000.00 is divided in three installments and given to the farmers through Direct Beneficiary Transfer (DBT). PM-KISAN scheme also aims to supplement the financial needs of the farmers in procuring various inputs to ensure proper crop health and appropriate yields, commensurate with the anticipated farm income. It is fully funded by the central government; only the list of the land holding beneficiaries of this scheme is provided by the state government. Total payment for the state of Tripura for the financial year 2021 is Rs. 31271.00.

Table 5.1: Financial Year-wise Status of Implementation of PM-KISHAN in Tripura

Financial Year	*No. of Beneficiaries*	*Payment given to (No.)*	*Payment given to (in percent)*
2018–19	244792	151862	62.00
2019–20	244792	185470	76.00
2020–21	244792	222357	91.00
2021–22	244792	231177	94.00

Source: www.pmkisan.gov.in

Table 5.1 reveals the year-wise status of implementation since its inception. It is observed that in the year 2018–19, the benefit of this scheme is given only to 62 per cent family, in the next financial year 76 per cent families have got the benefit of this scheme. In the financial year 2020–21 91 per cent families have got the benefit of this scheme, however in 2021–22, the percentage is more and it is 94 per cent.

Pradhan Mantri Fasal Bima Yojana (PMFBY)

PMFBY will provide a comprehensive insurance cover against failure of the crop and thus help in stabilizing the income of the farmers and encourage them for adoption of innovative practices. This scheme also ensures the flow of credit to the agricultural sector. This scheme covers all food and oil seed crops and also horticultural crops. This is compulsory for loanee farmer obtaining Crop Loan/KCC account for notified crops. The losses due to localized perils such as hailstorm, landslide and inundation and also post-harvest losses due to specified perils, like cyclone, unseasonal rains) shall be assessed at the affected insured field of the individual insured farmer.The existing State Level Co-ordination Committee on Crop Insurance (SLCCCI), Sub-Committee to SLCCCI, District Level Monitoring Committee (DLMC) is responsible for proper management of the scheme.It is a Central Assistance Sponsored Programme with 90:10 sharing with state.

Table 5.2: Financial Year-wise Status of Implementation of PMFBY Scheme in Tripura

Financial Year	*Farmers Application Insured (Lakh*	*Area Insured (Lakh ha)*	*Sum Insured(Rs. Crore)*	*Farmers Share in Premium (Rs. Crore)*	*Gross Premium (Rs. Crore)*	*Reported Claims (Rs. Crore)*	*Paid Claims (Rs. Crore)*	*Farmer Application Benefitted (Lakh)*
2016–17	0.118	0.028	17.64	0.292	0.39	0.71	0.71	0.037
2017–18	0.117	0.030	21.14	0.593	0.74	1.00	1.00	0.027
2018–19	0.021	0.003	2.06	0.048	0.09	0.02	0.02	0.002
2019–20	0.364	0.061	37.17	0.756	1.07	0.81	0.80	0.077

Source: www.pmfby.gov.in

Table 5.2 shows the year-wise status of implementation of PMFBY in Tripura. It is observed that in the financial year 2019–20, 36400 farmers have applied for getting insurance and out of that only 7700 farmers have benefitted in the same financial year. It is also found that only 6100 hector area is insured in 2019–20 financial year under this PMFBY scheme. The efficacy is comparatively better in 2019–20 compare to earlier periods. A total of 2,06,092 farmers for 31,235 ha. paddy area insured under the scheme during Kharif, 2020.[1]

Pradhan Mantri Krishi Sinchayee Yojana (PMKSY)

Pradhan Mantri Krishi Sinchayee Yojana (PMKSY) is launched to enhance the physical access of water on the farm and expand cultivable area under assured irrigation (har khet ko pani), to enhance recharge of aquifers and introduce sustainable water conservation practices and to promote extension activities relating to water harvesting, water management and crop alignment for farmers and grass root level field functionaries. It ensures the integrated development of rainfed areas using the watershed approach towards soil and water conservation,

[1]*Source:* https://agri.tripura.gov.in/achievements_treda

regeneration of ground water, arresting runoff, providing livelihood options and other NRM activities. It improves water use efficiency of the farm and through reducing wastage of water. It also explores the feasibility of reusing treated municipal waste water for peri-urban agriculture, and open up greater private investments in irrigation. It encourages community irrigation through registered user groups/ farmer producers' organizations/NGOs. It is a Central Assistance Sponsored Programme with 90:10 sharing with state. Table 5.3 reveals the achievements under PMKSY in Tripura during 2020–21.

Table 5.3: Achievement under PMKSY in Tripura during 2020–21

New rain water harvesting structure	472 Nos.
Renovation/re-excavation of old WHS/Water bodies etc.	255 Nos.
Additional are abrougth under irrigation	288.23 Ha
Creation of irrigation channel	6738 mtr.
Soil & Moisture Conservation works	2016 Ha

Source: Economic Survey, 2020–21.

From the Table 5.3, it is observed that 472 rain water harvesting structure has been newly constructed during 2020–21. It is also found that additional 288.23 hector area is irrigated and soil and moisture conservation works is done in Tripura during 2020–21 under this scheme. In addition to that 6738 meter irrigation channel has been constructed under this scheme.

Rashtriya Krishi Vikas Yojana (RKVY)

Rashtriya Krishi Vikas Yojana (RKVY) scheme was initiated in 2007 as an umbrella scheme for ensuring holistic development of agriculture and allied sectors. The scheme has come a long way since its inception and has been implemented across 11th and 12th plan periods. The basic objective of this scheme is to strengthen the farmers' efforts through creation of required pre and post-harvest agro-infrastructure that increases access to quality inputs, storage, market facilities etc. and enables farmers to make informed choices and to promote value chain addition linked production models that will help farmers increase their income as well as encourage production/productivity. The objective of this scheme also to mitigate risk of farmers with focus on additional income generation activities – like integrated farming, mushroom cultivation, bee keeping, aromatic plant cultivation, floriculture etc. It provides the autonomy and flexibility to the state to execute the scheme as per the local needs. It is a Central Assistance Sponsored Programme with 90:10 sharing with state. The estimated financial allocation under RKVY scheme for the Tripura for five year plan (2015–2020) is Rs. 953.4764 crore for different sectors.

Table 5.4 reveals the year-wise allocation and release of fund under RKVY scheme in Tripura. From the Table 5.4, it is significantly observed that release of fund out of total fund allocated is near about 50 per cent. It would have better for more development of the agro-infrastructure if more fund releases in this scheme.

Table 5.4: Year-wise Allocation and Release of Fund under RKVY Scheme in Tripura

Year	*Allocation of Fund (Crore)*	*Release of Fund (Crore)*	*Release Date*	*Release (in per cent)*
2014	80.27	40.13	Dec. 14	49.99
2015	27.1	13.55	Aug. 15	50.00
2016	34.41	17.2	Dec. 16	49.99
2017	39.55	19.77	Aug. 17	49.99
2018	55.45	25.91	Jul. 18	46.73
2019	56.61	27.35	Jun. 19	48.31
2020	NA	11.05	Dec. 20	–
2021	NA	26.14	Nov. 21	–

Source: www.rkvy.gov.in

It is also found that highest amount of fund of Rs. 40.13 crore has been released during the 2014–15 financial year whereas it is surprising that the least amount of fund of Rs. 11.05 crore has been released during the pandemic period i.e., 2020–21 financial year. In order to develop better agro infrastructure in the state, the concerned department of the government should look after the issue, so that favourable infrastructure such as storage, warehouses, mandi etc. can be developed.

ATMA (Agricultural Technology Management Agency)

Agricultural Technology Management Agency (ATMA) scheme is benefitting the majority of farmers in overwhelming the technological gaps in the industry. The scheme has been launched during 2005–06. The basic objectives of these scheme is to provide an effective mechanism for co-ordination and management of activities of different agencies involved in technology adaption/validation and dissemination at the district level and below, to increase the quality and type of technologies being disseminated and to develop new partnerships with the private institutions including NGOs. Under this scheme, Farmer's Advisory Committee has been set up to improve the technology of the farmers. The scheme is a central government scheme though 90 per cent is funded by central government and 10 per cent is funded by state government. During 2021, training has been given to 2300 farmers, 275 farm schools has been constructed under this scheme.[2]

Kisan Credit Card (Crop Production Loan)

Kishan Credit Card (KCC) is a scheme to provide timely and adequate credit to farmers to meet their production credit needs and expenses related to ancillary activities through simplified procedure facilitating the borrowers for availing loans as and when it is needed. It offers credit to the farmers up to three lakhs with a very low interest rate at three per cent per annum. This credit is of two types viz; cash credit and term credit. Cash credit is given for a short period (crop period) or marketing period whereas the term credit is given for allied activities

Table 5.5: Year-wise KCC Sanctioned Credit and Amount Disbursed (in Lakh)

Components	*2017–18**	*2018–19**	*2019–20**	*2020–21**
Kisan Credit Cards sanctioned for credit	50333	56040	56651	88512
Amount disbursed (Rs. in Lakhs)	23644.08	36321.91	25700.75	32552.86

Source: Economic Review of Tripura, 2020–21.

[2] *Source:* https://www.pib.gov.in/PressReleasePage.aspx?PRID=1778910 site visited on 24.06.22.

such as pump sets, land development, plantation, drip irrigation etc. The credit is given to both agricultural as well as horticultural farmers.

National Food Security Mission (NFSM)

National Food Security Mission has been launched during 2007–08 to increase the production of rice by ten million tonnes, wheat by eight million tonnes and pulses by two million tonnes, respectively by the end of 11th Plan through area expansion and productivity enhancement; restoring soil fertility and productivity; creating employment opportunities; and enhancing farm level economy. Coarse cereals (Maize and Barley) and Commercial crops viz., Cotton, Jute and Sugarcane have been included under NFSM scheme. NFSM-coarse cereal is also being implemented in the state of Tripura.

Scheme Available for the Sample Beneficiary Households in Tripura

During survey it is observed all beneficiary households in the selected blocks of the study area have received Rs. 6000.00 annually from the PM Kishan scheme. Apart from that the beneficiary farmers have received assistance from Rashtriya Krishi Vikas Yojana (RKVY) scheme and benefit from National Food Security Mission (NFSM) scheme. Following Table 5.6 reveals the block-wise getting benefit from this scheme and average amount of assistance amount for their agricultural as well horticultural farming. From Table 5.6, it is observed that maximum average benefit of the RKVY scheme is received by the beneficiary households from Matabari block (Rs. 449.00), followed by Killa block (Rs. 398.00), B.C. Nagar block (Rs. 390.45), Taliamura (Rs. 383.71), Kalyanpur (Rs. 377.09) etc. whereas the minimum average amount of money is received by the beneficiary households from the Nalchar block (Rs. 220.89). In case of NFSM scheme, the beneficiaries from Kalyanpur block of Khowai district have received the highest amount of benefit of Rs. 1793.18 which is followed by Teliamura block (Rs. 1773.21), Rupaichhari block (Rs. 1593.19), B.C. Nagar block (Rs. 1487.10), Jirania block (Rs. 1471.43) etc. whereas the beneficiary farmers of Nalchar block of Sepahijala district have received the minimum amount of Rs. 677.78 from NFSM scheme.

Table 5.6: Block-wise Availability of RKVY and NFSM Assistance for the Beneficiary Households in Study Area

District	*Block*	*Amount from PMKISAN*	*Amount from RKVY*	*Amount from NFSM*
Dhalai	Ambassa	6000.00	280.00	773.53
	Manu	6000.00	350.54	1231.63
	Salema	6000.00	262.16	755.41
Gomati	Killa	6000.00	398.00	1093.5
	Matabari	6000.00	449.00	1040.00
Khowai	Kalyanpur	6000.00	377.09	1793.18
	Teliamura	6000.00	383.71	1773.21
Sepahijala	Jampuijala	6000.00	367.63	1025.00
	Nalchar	6000.00	220.89	677.78
South Tripura	B.C Nagar	6000.00	390.45	1487.10
	Rajnagar	6000.00	287.38	778.57
	Rupaichhari	6000.00	319.85	1593.19
West Tripura	Jirania	6000.00	319.80	1471.43
	Mandai	6000.00	237.10	894.12

Source: Calculated from the Field Survey, December, 2021.

Figure 5.1 shows the block-wise average benefit from RKVY and NFSM scheme in the study area.

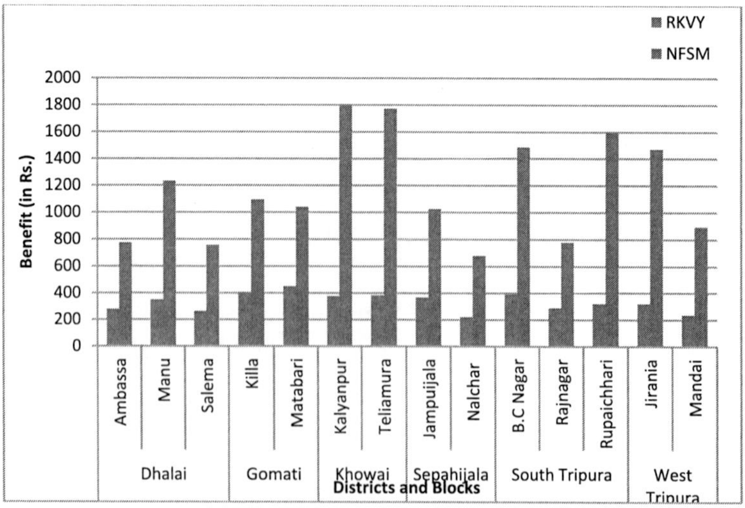

Figure 5.1: Average Benefit from RKVY and NFSM Scheme

5.2 Impact of Agricultural and Horticulture Schemes in Tripura

There are many agricultural and horticultural schemes mentioned above have been implemented in Tripura. Tribal are also the beneficiaries of these schemes. This section shows the impact of these schemes on changing their livelihoods. Already, from the secondary information it is observed that there is an improvement in the production of cereal production, cash crop production and horticultural production. From the field survey, it is mostly observed that tribal beneficiaries mainly concentrate on the production of paddy and their earning depended mostly on this principal crop production.

Table 5.7 reveals the agricultural productivity of land and labour in the selected study area of Triura. It is found that average productivity of land and labour is 612.43 kg./kani and 191.00 kg perlabour. Block-wise comparison reveals that productivity of land is highest in Killa block (654.63 kg/kani) which is followed by Rupaichhari block (548.47 kg/kani), Matabati block (638.89 kg/kani), Mandai block (626.49 kg/kani), Jirania block (615.93 kg/kani) etc. whereas the minimum productivity of land is in B.C. Nagar block (577.30 kg/kani). However, labur productivity is highest in Kalyanpur block (326.79 kg) which is followed by Matabari block (283.95 kg), Jampuijala block (277.05 kg), Teliamura block (270.86 kg), B.C. Nagar block (231.60 kg) etc. The least labour productivity is found in Nalchar block (117.57 kg) in Sepahijala district.

The beneficiary households produce agricultural output for both their self-consumption and earning income by selling of it. The rest amount of output after their self-consumption, they sell it to the market.

Table 5.8 reveals the block-wise agricultural sales of the beneficiary households in the study area of Tripura. It is observed 57.40 per cent beneficiary households do not sale their agricultural products rather they are used for their self-consumption. Only 42.60 per cent beneficiary households are selling their agricultural product into the market. Out of that 20.20 per cent sell yearly up to 1000kg, however 20.60 per cent beneficiary households sell within 1000–2000 kg. Very few percentage of beneficiary households sell their product above 2000 kg as it is already found that most of the beneficiaries are

Table 5.7: Block-wise Agricultural Productivity of Land and Labour in the Selected Study Area

District	*Block*	*Total Production*	*Land (Kani)*	*Total Labour*	*Productivity of Land (Kg./kani)*	*Productivity of Labour*
Dhalai	Ambassa	22920	39.5	157	580.25	145.99
	Manu	71400	119.5	487	597.49	146.61
	Salema	47700	81.5	287	585.28	166.20
Gomati	Killa	102450	156.5	501	654.63	204.49
	Matabari	69000	108	243	638.89	283.95
Khowai	Kalyanpur	58200	61	112	600.00	326.79
	Teliamura	47400	79	175	600.00	270.86
Sepahijala	Jampuijala	50700	84.5	183	600.00	277.05
	Nalchar	17400	29	148	600.00	117.57
South	B.C Nagar	53400	92.5	250	577.30	213.60
	Rajnagar	51480	87.25	400	590.03	128.70
	Rupaichhari	44420	68.5	348	648.47	127.64
West	Jirania	69600	113	363	615.93	191.74
	Mandai	57950	92.5	390	626.49	148.59
	Total	**742420**	**1212.25**	**3887**	**612.43**	**191.00**

Source: Calculated from the Field Survey, December, 2021.

Table 5.8: Block-wise Agricultural Annual Sales of the Beneficiary Households in the Study Area (in per cent)

District	*Block*	*No Sales*	*Up to 1000 Kg*	*1 k–2 k*	*2 k–3 k*	*Above 3 k*	*Total*
Dhalai	Ambassa	23.53	64.71	11.76	0.00	0.00	100.00
	Manu	47.83	13.04	36.96	0.00	2.17	100.00
	Salema	54.05	32.43	13.51	0.00	0.00	100.00
Gomati	Killa	41.67	25.00	26.67	3.33	3.33	100.00
	Matabari	42.50	27.50	27.50	0.00	2.50	100.00
Khowai	Kalyanpur	45.45	27.27	27.27	0.00	0.00	100.00
	Teliamura	46.43	17.86	35.71	0.00	0.00	100.00
Sepahijala	Jampuijala	43.75	25.00	31.25	0.00	0.00	100.00
	Nalchar	77.78	16.67	5.56	0.00	0.00	100.00
South	B.C Nagar	41.94	29.03	29.03	0.00	0.00	100.00
	Rajnagar	83.33	7.14	7.14	2.38	0.00	100.00
	Rupaichhari	70.37	11.11	11.11	3.70	3.70	100.00
West	Jirania	73.47	10.20	16.33	0.00	0.00	100.00
	Mandai	88.24	7.84	3.92	0.00	0.00	100.00
	Total	57.40	20.20	20.60	0.80	1.00	100.00

Source: Calculated from the Field Survey, December, 2021.

marginal, small and medium farmers. Block-wise analysis reveals that beneficiaries belong to Mandai block (88.24 per cent) of West Tripura district and Rajnagar block (83.33 per cent) of South Tripura district are used their agricultural product only for their own consumption. Whereas only 23.53 per cent beneficiary households belong to Ambassa block of Dhalai district is used their agricultural product for their own consumption and 64.71 per cent households of the same block are selling their agricultural product up to1000 kg. 36.96 per cent beneficiary households of Manu block sell their product within 1000–2000 kg which is followed by Teliamura block (35.71 per cent), of Khowai district, Jampuijala (31.25 per cent) of Sepahijala district etc. Only the highest 3.70 per cent beneficiary households of Rupaichhari block of South Tripura district sell more than 3000kg output followed by Killa block (3.33 per cent), Matabari block (2.50 per cent) of Gomati district and Manu block (2.17 per cent) of Dhalai district.

In order to examine the change in impact of agricultural scheme paired t-test has been used. The impact of agricultural schemes may have two types of impact viz; impact on change in agricultural income and impact on total household income.

Impact of Agricultural Schemes on Change in Agricultural Income

Before using paired t-test, descriptive statistics has been used. Table 5.10 reveals the block-wise descriptive statistics of beneficiaries' income before getting the agricultural schemes of the beneficiary households in the study area.

From the Table 5.10, it is observed that average income from agriculture before getting benefit from agricultural scheme is highest in Jampuijala block (Rs. 41990.63)of Sepahijala district which is followed by Nalchar (Rs. 41211.11), B.C. Nagar (Rs. 38700.00) of South Tripura district, Matabari block (Rs. 31443.75) of Gomati district etc. Table 5.8 also reveals that there is least standard deviation in Salema block in(Rs. 8436.98) though the average income before getting benefit from agricultural scheme is only Rs. 15470.27 which implies that there is lesser inequality among the beneficiary households belong to Salema block of Dhalai district. It is found that the skewness of agricultural income is positive for all blocks and high in all blocks

Table 5.9: Block-wise Descriptive Statistics of Beneficiary's Agricultural Income before Getting the Benefit

District	*Block*	*Mean*	*Median*	*Mode*	*Std. Deviation*	*Kurtosis*	*Skewness*	*Range*	*Minimum*	*Maximum*
Dhalai	Ambassa	16178.82	14400	7200	10540.57	–0.60	0.69	33600	2400	36000
	Manu	18626.09	14400	28800	9245.93	–1.36	0.21	28800	7200	36000
	Salema	15470.27	14400	7200	8436.98	0.11	0.91	28800	7200	36000
Gomati	Killa	25363.33	21600	14400	26757.29	16.68	3.62	173650	0	173650
	Matabari	31443.75	21600	7200	41471.53	5.92	2.64	159250	7200	166450
Khowai	Kalyanpur	19963.64	21600	21600	9409.142	–0.82	0.32	28800	7200	36000
	Teliamura	20314.29	21600	7200	10562.47	–1.35	0.18	28800	7200	36000
Sepahijala	Jampuijala	41990.63	28800	21600	39720.6	1.93	1.63	146150	3600	149750
	Nalchar	41211.11	14400	7200	61460.58	2.04	1.82	185600	3600	189200
South	B.C. Nagar	38700.00	21600	7200	34290.98	1.85	1.46	135350	7200	142550
	Rajnagar	27006.19	14400	7200	35224.6	8.17	2.85	157680	5400	163080
	Rupaichhari	19764.44	15360	15360	17604.51	4.08	2.01	73200	4800	78000
West	Jirania	17044.9	14400	14400	9142.143	–0.30	0.79	28800	7200	36000
	Mandai	13611.76	14400	7200	8244.699	1.58	1.34	34200	1800	36000

Source: Calculated from the Field Survey, December, 2021.

Table 5.10: Block-wise Descriptive Statistics of Beneficiary's Agricultural Income after Getting the Benefit

District	Block	Mean	Median	Mode	Std. Deviation	Kurtosis	Skewness	Range	Minimum	Maximum
Dhalai	Ambassa	27277.06	25072	15536	13952.04	–0.62	0.68	44680	9000	53680
	Manu	30864.78	25710	15636	12394.63	–1.40	0.21	38194	15486	53680
	Salema	26355.41	25072	34608	11161.94	0.07	0.89	38430	15000	53430
Gomati	Killa	37837.33	33515	25072	28452.98	11.87	2.92	177812	6510	184322
	Matabari	43807.75	34458	15486	43240.47	5.27	2.48	164958	15486	180444
Khowai	Kalyanpur	32718.27	35208	35208	12426.25	–0.60	0.40	38794	15886	54680
	Teliamura	33549.79	35208	15886	14209.88	–1.34	0.18	38794	15886	54680
Sepahijala	Jampuijala	54361.38	44044	44144	41152.41	2.09	1.61	156662	10768	167430
	Nalchar	51009.78	25072	15536	61786.96	1.92	1.78	186772	10764	197536
South	B.C. Nagar	51745.29	35608	15836	36155.52	1.41	1.31	142408	15486	157894
	Rajnagar	37749.29	24838	28808	36779.33	7.99	2.78	170230	13186	183416
	Rupaichhari	32618.59	26172	16136	23230.91	3.88	1.98	95724	13136	108860
West	Jirania	29097.35	25472	25472	12442.34	–0.29	0.80	39946	15434	55380
	Mandai	24145.92	24734	15886	10974.7	1.58	1.35	46296	8384	54680

Source: Calculated from the Field Survey, December, 2021.

except four blocks (all three in Dhalai district and other is Jirania block) which implies the agricultural income is evenly distributed. However, the value kurtosis is also high except these above mentioned four blocks. The data set with high kurtosis tend to have heavy tails or outliers. High kurtosis also implies that agricultural income distribution of these blocks is very high than the usual distribution. It is also found that there is small gap between mean agricultural income and its median in most of the blocks except Nalchar, Jampuijala of Sepahijala district, B.C. Nagar and Rajnagar blocks of South Tripura district. Large gap between mean and median (mean value is greater than median value) implies there are some farmers whose agricultural income is very high which is also supported by the high value of standard deviation.

Table 5.11 reveals the average income from agriculture after getting the benefit from agricultural schemes. It is also observed that the average income from agriculture after getting the benefit is comparatively higher than before getting the benefit. The standard deviation is also very high in Nalchar, Jampuijala, B.C. Nagar and Rajnagar blocks which implies that there is high dispersion in agricultural income among these blocks. It is also found that the skewness of agricultural income is positive for all blocks and high in all blocks except four blocks (all three in Dhalai district and other is Jirania block) which implies the agricultural income is evenly distributed. It is also found that the median value of agricultural income increases by more than Rs. 10000.00 on an average.

Table 5.11 reveals the descriptive statistics of growth of change in agricultural income. It is observed that average growth of change in agricultural income is highest in Mandai block (97.24 per cent) which is followed by Ambassa block (92.51 per cent), Nalchar block (89.15 per cent), Rupaichhari block (86.79 per cent), Salema block (82.29 per cent), Jirania block (82.22 per cent) etc. The median value of growth of change in household's agricultural income is highest in Mandai block (77.82 per cent) which is followed by Jirania block (76.89 per cent), Nalchar (74.81 per cent). The median growth percentage value is same (74.11) for Ambassa and Salema block of Dhalai district, Rajnagar and Rupaichhari block of South Tripura district. The least median growth percentage value (53.28) is for Jampuijala block of Sepahijala district. The highest measure of

Table 5.11: Block-wise Descriptive Statistics of Growth of Income Change of the Agricultural Beneficiary in the Study Area

District	*Block*	*Mean*	*Median*	*Mode*	*Std. Deviation*	*Kurtosis*	*Skewness*	*Range*	*Minimum*	*Maximum*
Dhalai	Ambassa	92.51	74.11	115.78	54.25	8.18	2.55	227.28	47.72	275.00
	Manu	76.63	70.39	117.17	24.77	–0.93	0.79	72.22	48.42	120.64
	Salema	82.29	74.11	60.22	24.96	–1.51	0.33	68.89	48.28	117.17
Gomati	Killa	73.98	60.22	74.11	47.16	24.92	4.15	358.85	6.15	365.00
	Matabari	70.98	60.22	115.08	32.89	–0.20	0.18	137.08	5.01	142.08
Khowai	Kalyanpur	73.96	64.04	63.00	25.77	0.21	0.73	95.64	25.00	120.64
	Teliamura	77.46	63.00	120.64	26.99	–0.95	0.84	68.75	51.89	120.64
Sepahijala	Jampuijala	55.27	53.28	53.28	40.06	4.20	1.60	188.06	11.05	199.11
	Nalchar	89.15	74.81	115.78	64.16	–0.54	0.45	194.71	4.41	199.11
South	B.C. Nagar	59.40	60.22	119.94	36.64	–1.00	0.47	109.18	10.76	119.94
	Rajnagar	73.75	74.11	66.71	35.86	–0.62	–0.13	137.68	6.50	144.19
	Rupaichhari	86.79	74.11	124.11	33.95	–0.10	0.64	134.10	39.56	173.67
West	Jirania	82.22	76.89	76.89	25.02	–1.19	0.63	69.44	51.89	121.33
	Mandai	97.24	77.82	120.64	50.67	15.54	3.34	318.81	46.97	365.78

Source: Calculated from the Field Survey, December, 2021.

dispersion is shown in Nalchar block (standard deviation 64.16) which indicates there is high inequality in terms of growth change in household's agricultural income. This is followed by Mandai block (50.67), Killa block (47.16) whereas the least inequality is shown in Salema block as the value of standard deviation is minimum 24.77. The minimum growth of change in household's agricultural income in Nalchar block (4.41 per cent) whereas the highest growth change in household's income 365.78 per cent is found in Mandai block of West Tripura district.

Table 5.12 reveals the block-wise impact of agricultural scheme on changing agricultural income. In order to check the impact of agricultural schemes for improving agricultural income, paired t-test is used. For this test the hypotheses are constructed in the following:

- ***Null Hypothesis:*** H_0: $\mu_1 - \mu_2 = 0$ (i.e., there is no difference in their average agricultural income parameters before and after getting the benefit of agricultural scheme.)
- ***Alternative Hypothesis:*** H_1: $\mu_1 - \mu_2 \neq 0$ (i.e., there is a difference in their average agricultural income parameters before and after getting the benefit of agricultural scheme.)

Where, μ_1 and μ_2 are the average agricultural income before and after getting benefits from different agricultural schemes. The test statistic is written in the following:

$$t = \frac{(\overline{X_1} - \overline{X_2}) - (\mu_1 - \mu_2)}{\sqrt{\frac{s_1^2}{n} + \frac{s_2^2}{n}}} \sim t_{(n-1)+(n-1)}$$

Where; $\overline{X_1}$ and $\overline{X_2}$ are the average sample parameter of agricultural incomeof the beneficiaries before getting and after getting benefits from different agricultural schemes in the concerned block; n is the number of beneficiaries in the village and s_1^2 and s_2^2 are the sample variance of agricultural income before and after getting benefits from different agricultural schemes.

$$s_j^2 = \frac{\sum_{i=1}^{n}(X_i - \bar{X}_j)^2}{(n-1)}$$

for all j = 1 and 2 (for two sample) and for all i = 1, 2, 3,..., n.

If the observed value of paired t-test exceeds the table value of t-distribution with (2n-2) degrees of freedom, then null hypothesis is rejected i.e., test is significant which means there is a difference in average income before and after getting benefits from different agricultural schemes. If the observed value is less than table value of t-distribution with (2n-2) degrees of freedom, then null hypothesis is accepted and test is insignificant.

Table 5.12: Block-wise Impact of Agricultural Schemes on Change in Agricultural Income of the Beneficiary Households

District	*Block*	*Mean Income Before*	*Mean Income After*	*t-test*	*Prob.*
Dhalai	Ambassa	16178.82	27277.06	13.38	0.00
	Manu	18626.09	30864.78	26.21	0.00
	Salema	15470.27	26355.41	24.18	0.00
Gomati	Killa	25363.33	37837.33	24.59	0.00
	Matabari	31443.75	43807.75	21.33	0.00
Khowai	Kalyanpur	31745.45	47852.09	5.09	0.00
	Teliamura	20314.29	33549.79	19.20	0.00
Sepahijala	Jampuijala	41990.63	54361.38	22.10	0.00
	Nalchar	41211.11	51009.78	18.19	0.00
South	B.C Nagar	38700.00	51745.29	23.31	0.00
	Rajnagar	27006.19	37749.29	25.29	0.00
	Rupaichhari	19764.44	32618.59	11.71	0.00
West	Jirania	17044.90	29097.35	25.50	0.00
	Mandai	13611.76	24145.92	27.36	0.00

Source: Calculated from the Field Survey, December, 2021.

From Table 5.12, it is observed that paired t-test is positive and highly significant in all blocks of the study area. This implies that agricultural schemes have positive impact on change in agricultural income of the beneficiary households in the study area.

Table 5.13 and Table 5.14 reveal the descriptive statistics of different agricultural schemes on the households' income of the beneficiaries. From Table 5.13, it is observed that mean value of

Table 5.13: Block-wise Descriptive Statistics of Household's Annual Income before Getting the Benefit

District	*Block*	*Mean*	*Median*	*Mode*	*Std. Deviation*	*Kurtosis*	*Skewness*	*Range*	*Minimum*	*Maximum*
Dhalai	Ambassa	165664.1	164240	#N/A	45682.43		–0.03	165100	89900	255000
	Manu	203137	177300	113400	73890.76	0.71	0.94	318500	104400	422900
	Salema	156140.5	137600	#N/A	64975.66	0.15	0.90	258000	56000	314000
Gomati	Killa	186048.3	157300	154800	81111.19	0.37	1.02	340800	64400	405200
	Matabari	221771.3	198900	128200	122648.7	–0.61	0.61	458600	41800	500400
Khowai	Kalyanpur	187018.2	144600	122400	90574.08	7.05	2.28	406800	103200	510000
	Teliamura	160814.3	138500	103200	54764.03	–0.61	0.89	159600	103200	262800
Sepahijala	Jampuijala	157087.5	150750	239800	65078.85	–0.42	0.14	261050	28200	289250
	Nalchar	182216.7	175850	#N/A	91498.62	0.75	0.60	374800	21600	396400
South	B.C. Nagar	219032.3	203400	#N/A	124057.2	8.51	2.49	640000	83900	723900
	Rajnagar	213806.2	208015	#N/A	70398.9	1.45	1.04	340340	100700	441040
	Rupaichhari	186071.9	141600	#N/A	108943.9	0.98	1.18	432000	67200	499200
West	Jirania	136461.2	131150	110400	43992.1	–0.60	0.05	190000	43200	233200
	Mandai	112942.2	107200	111000	50015.58	–0.13	0.77	185800	40800	226600

Source: Calculated from the Field Survey, December, 2021.

Table 5.14: Block-wise Descriptive Statistics of Household's Annual Income after Getting the Benefit

District	*Block*	*Mean*	*Median*	*Mode*	*Std. Deviation*	*Kurtosis*	*Skewness*	*Range*	*Minimum*	*Maximum*
Dhalai	Ambassa	169708.8	167000	#N/A	46009.8	–0.55	–0.06	166300	91700	258000
	Manu	207793.5	183900	132000	74810.79	0.60	0.91	318500	108000	426500
	Salema	160008.1	143000	#N/A	65222.76	0.27	0.95	259800	63200	323000
Gomati	Killa	191030.8	162000	162000	82111.55	0.39	1.01	347000	68000	415000
	Matabari	226646.3	202500	130000	123088.4	–0.65	0.59	460400	43600	504000
Khowai	Kalyanpur	194954.5	150000	126000	103005.1	9.35	2.68	477000	105000	582000
	Teliamura	165892.9	144500	105000	56305.61	–0.61	0.86	165000	105000	270000
Sepahijala	Jampuijala	162065.6	159550	245200	66293.42	–0.37	0.13	269150	29100	298250
	Nalchar	185116.7	178550	#N/A	92205.19	0.66	0.56	375700	22500	398200
South	B.C. Nagar	224200	207000	#N/A	124237.9	8.32	2.46	641800	85700	727500
	Rajnagar	217483.3	212175	#N/A	70978.12	1.45	1.04	344300	102500	446800
	Rupaichhari	191013	147200	#N/A	109573.4	0.77	1.11	432000	69000	501000
West	Jirania	140722.4	134750	123000	44611.75	–0.52	0.07	197200	45000	242200
	Mandai	116345.1	110000	75500	51081.07	–0.14	0.77	190750	41250	232000

Source: Calculated from the Field Survey, December, 2021.

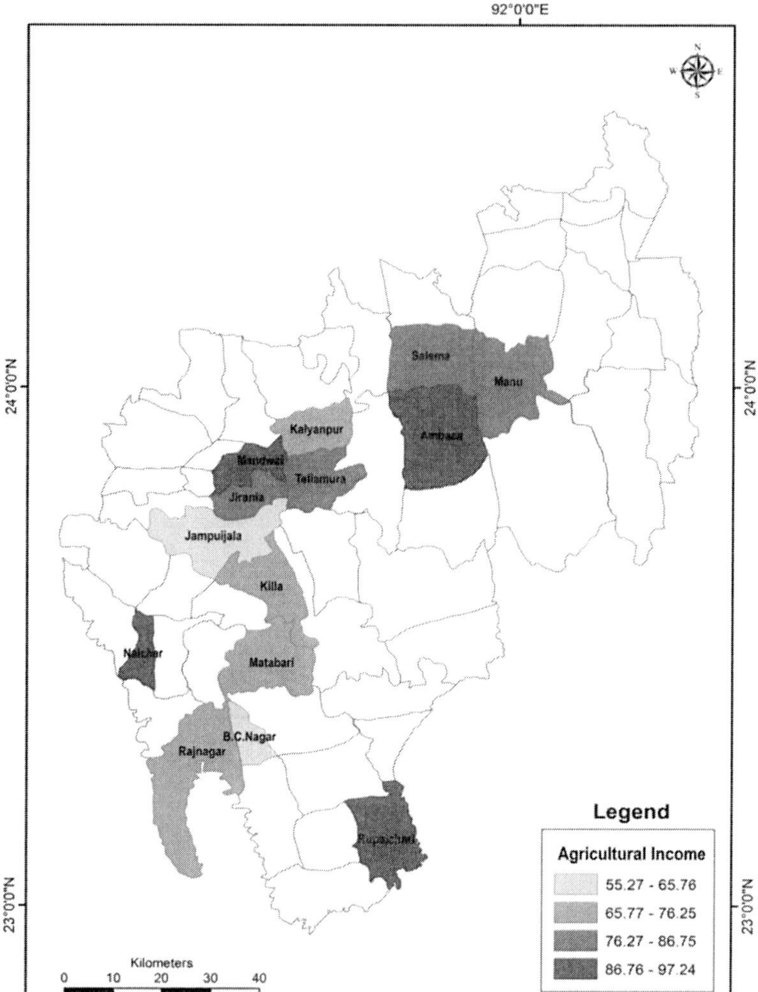

Figure 5.2: Mapping of Blocks Showing Impact of Growth on Agricultural Income

households' annual income is highest in the Matabari block (Rs. 221771.30) which is followed by B.C. Nagar block (Rs. 219032.30), Rajnagar block (Rs. 213806.20), Manu block (Rs. 203137.00), Kalyanpur block (Rs. 187018.20) etc. whereas the minimum value of average annual income is Mandai block (Rs. 112942.20) of West Tripura district. The value of standard deviation is very high in all blocks in the study area which implies that there is high dispersion among the beneficiary households. The value of absolute dispersion i.e., range is also very high. The highest annual income is found in one beneficiary household belongs to B.C. Nagar block (Rs. 723900.00) of South Tripura district whereas the minimum annual income is found in one beneficiary household belongs to Nalchar block (Rs. 21600.00) of Sepahijala district.

From Table 5.14, it is observed that, mean value of households' annual income is highest in the Matabari block (Rs. 226646.30) which is followed by B.C. Nagar block (Rs. 224200.00), Rajnagar block (Rs. 217430.30), Manu block (Rs. 207793.50), Kalyanpur block (Rs. 184954.50) etc. whereas the minimum value of average annual income is Mandai block (Rs. 116345.10) of West Tripura district. The value of standard deviation is very high in all blocks in the study area which implies that there is high dispersion among the beneficiary households. The value of absolute dispersion i.e., range is also very high. The highest annual income is found in one beneficiary household belongs to B.C. Nagar block (Rs. 727500.00) of South Tripura district whereas the minimum annual income is found in one beneficiary household belongs to Nalchar block (Rs. 22500.00) of Sepahijala district.

In order to check the impact of agricultural schemes for improving their average annual income, paired t-test is used. For this test the hypotheses are constructed in the following;

- ***Null Hypothesis:*** H_0: $\mu_1 - \mu_2 = 0$ (i.e., there is no difference in their average annual household's income parameters before and after getting the benefit of agricultural scheme.)
- ***Alternative Hypothesis:*** H_1: $\mu_1 - \mu_2 \neq 0$ (i.e., there is a difference in their average annual household's income parameters before and after getting the benefit of agricultural scheme.)

Where; μ_1 and μ_2 are the average annual household's income before and after getting benefits from different agricultural schemes. The test statistic is written in the following:

$$t = \frac{(\overline{X_1} - \overline{X_2}) - (\mu_1 - \mu_2)}{\sqrt{\frac{s_1^2}{n} + \frac{s_2^2}{n}}} \sim t_{(n-1)+(n-1)}$$

Where; $\overline{X_1}$ and $\overline{X_2}$ are the average sample parameter of average annual household's income of the beneficiaries before getting and after getting benefits from different agricultural schemes in the concerned block; n is the number of beneficiaries in the village and s_1^2 and s_2^2 are the sample variance of average annual household's income before and after getting benefits from different agricultural schemes.

$$s_j^2 = \frac{\sum_{i=1}^{n}\left(X_i - \bar{X}_j\right)^2}{(n-1)}$$

for all j = 1 and 2 (for two sample) and for all i = 1, 2, 3,..., n.

If the observed value of paired t-test exceeds the table value of t-distribution with (2n-2) degrees of freedom, then null hypothesis is rejected i.e., test is significant which means there is a difference in average annual household's income before and after getting benefits from different agricultural schemes. If the observed value is less than table value of t-distribution with (2n-2) degrees of freedom, then null hypothesis is accepted and test is insignificant.

Table 5.15: Block-wise Impact of Agricultural Schemes on Change in Household's Income

District	*Block*	*Mean Income Before*	*Mean Income After*	*t-test*	*Prob.*
Dhalai	Ambassa	165664.12	169708.82	6.329	0.000
	Manu	203136.96	207793.48	13.663	0.000
	Salema	156140.54	160008.11	11.154	0.000
Gomati	Killa	186048.33	191030.83	12.782	0.000
	Matabari	221771.25	226646.25	10.915	0.000
Khowai	Kalyanpur	187018.18	194954.55	2.569	0.018
	Teliamura	160814.29	165892.86	10.177	0.000
Sepahijala	Jampuijala	157087.50	162065.63	11.488	0.000
	Nalchar	182216.67	185116.67	6.985	0.000
South Tripura	B.C Nagar	219032.26	224200.00	11.754	0.000
	Rajnagar	213806.19	217483.33	11.225	0.000
	Rupaichhari	186071.85	191012.96	5.834	0.000
West Tripura	Jirania	136461.22	140722.45	13.051	0.000
	Mandai	112942.16	116345.10	11.790	0.000

Source: Calculated from the Field Survey, December, 2021.

Table 5.15 reveals that the paired t-test is positive and highly significant for all selected blocks in the study area. This implies that the different agricultural schemes have positive impact on change in households' annual income.

Figure 5.3 shows that block-wise impact of agricultural scheme on the beneficiary households' income in the study area.

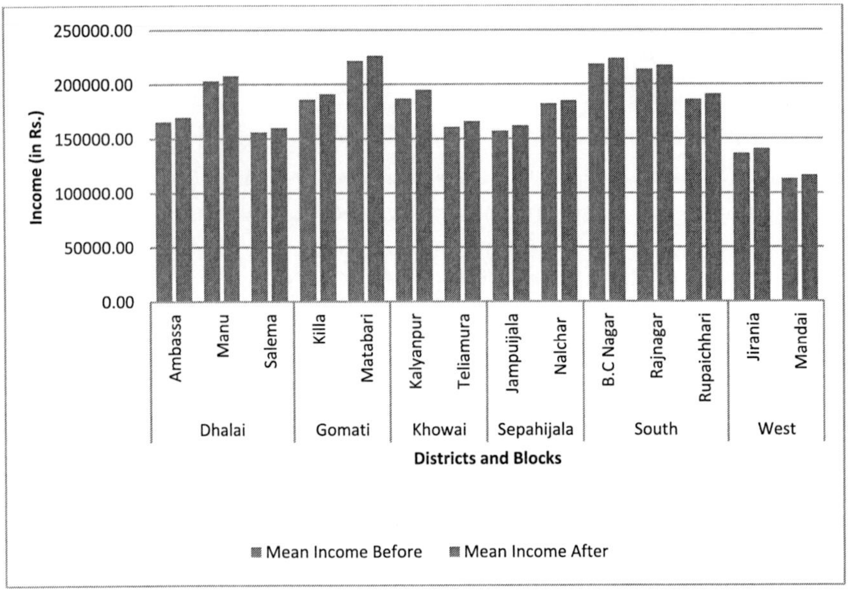

Figure 5.3: Impact of Agricultural Scheme on the Beneficiary Households' Income

Problems Faced the Beneficiaries in the Study Area

During field survey, the beneficiaries were asked about the problems facing related to their farming activites and others. The respondents are faced different type of problems related to their farming activities. Table 5.16 reveals the opinion given by the beneficiary farmers. From Table 5.16, it is observed that all beneficiaries are facing the problem inadequate availability and also low quality of seed/planting materials. All of them are also facing the problem of inadequate farm power and poor quality of machinery. Only 44 per cent are facing the problem of shortage of labour. Due to MGNREGA activities sometimes labour are not available for the farming activities. 62.40 per cent respondents are facing the problem of inadequate infrastructure during post-harvesting period. The beneficiary farmers are responded that there is non-existence of cold chain system, storage facility and unavialabilty of agro-processing industries. All of them are responded that packaging cost is very high due to shortage of packing materials.

Table 5.16: Opinion about the Problems Faced the Beneficiaries in the Study Area (in per cent)

1.	*Seeds/Planting Materials*	*in %*	7.	*Market*	*in %*
	Inadequate availability of seed/planting materials	100.00		Inadequate market information	100.00
	Low quality of seed/planting material	100.00		Limited market Information	100.00
2.	Farm Power	100.00		Higher commission charges	100.00
	Inadequate availability of farm power	100.00		Middlemen (brokers/village merchants) Problem	100.00
	Poor quality of implements/machinery available in the market	100.00		Higher marketing costs	100.00
	Shortage of labour for farming operations	44.00		Delay in Payment after selling	17.20
3.	Post-Harvest Infrastructure			Quote lower price than actual price	100.00
	Inadequate post-harvest facilities	62.40		Lack of MSP	100.00
	Cold chain system is virtually non-existent	100.00		Lack of competitive price	100.00
	Absence of agro-processing industry	100.00		Lack of transparency in transactions	100.00
	Shortage of packing Material	100.00		Lack of storage facility	100.00
	High prices of packing Material	100.00		Lack of online trading facility	100.00
	Inadequate modern packing material	100.00		Lack of grading and quality testing facility	100.00

	Inadequate storage facility	100.00	8.	Govt. Schemes	
	Lack of pre-cooling facility	100.00		Information about programme details are not easily available	100.00
4.	Climatic Constraints		9.	Capacity Building	
	Waterlogging	14.00		Capacity building/technical advice was not provided	100.00
	High Rainfall	11.00	10.	Subsidy	
	Persistent Drought	100.00		Eligibility or criteria for availing the subsidy not known	100.00
	Inadequate water for area expansion	100.00		Procedure for the subsidy very tedious	100.00
5.	Transport	100.00		Number of documents required for availing subsidy are too many	100.00
	Poor rural road connectivity	100.00		Subsidy paid after making entire cost of the benefit/component (for agro-credit)	100.00
	Lack of transport vehicles	100.00		Considerable time lag between the purchase and receiving the subsidy	100.00
	High transport charges	100.00		Difficulty faced while availing subsidy	100.00
	Lack of refrigerated vans	100.00	11.	Any other specify	100.00
6.	Banks/Credit linkage			Irrigation and others integrated inputs	100.00
	Relatively high interest rate for loans	100.00			
	Inadequate financial facility	100.00			
	Lack of commodity pledge loan facility	100.00			

Source: Primary Survey December, 2021.

Table 5.16 also reveals that climate change is another major problem and it beyond their control. Only 14 per cent and 11 per cent farmers are responded that about the problem of water logging and high rainfall. All beneficiaries are responded that inadequate water is a major problem to the tribal beneficiaries as mostly they belong to tilla and hilly land. All beneficiary farmers are responded that transportation such as poor road connectivity, lack of vehecles and due to the high transport charges are major problems in tribal area.

Agricultural credit is another serious problem. All beneficiaries are responded that they are not getting adequate financial facilities. Sometimes it is available at very higher rate of interest. There is also lack of commodity pledge loan facilities.

Marketing is another major problem to the beneficiary farmers in the study area. All farmers are facing the problem of inadequate market information even if it is very limited information. They are facing the middleman and also higher commission. They donot know how to test the quality of their product and give to proper grading against their product. They are also admitted that there is also lack of grading and quality testing facilities in their area. There is a problem of minimum support price as well as lack of competitive price. Due to digital illiteracy they are unable to access online trading facilities. Though young family member can operate smart phone but, they don't have an idea about online trading of the product. Poor network is also another issue.

Cent per cent respondents are admitted that they don't know about all govt. schemes. They are not aware how to get the benefit through these schemes. They are responded that no capacity building programme has been done in their area. Cent per cent respondents are admitted that they don't know about eligibility criteria of getting subsidy. In case of agricultural credit, they are facing the problem of getting the subsidy payment after making entire cost components. Irrigation is another serious problem faced by the tribal beneficiaries. All beneficiaries are facing this problem as they belong to the tilla or hilly area.

A Successful Case Study of the Beneficiary Farmer

A farmer 43 years old Apan Kumar Jamatiya has been doing agricultural activities from long days back as his family was associate with peasant related activities for living their life in Khupilong area under Killa Agricultural Sector of Matabari Agricultural Subdivision in Gomati District of Tripura. He has a total of five Kani agricultural land which is used for paddy cultivation. The other family members are also associated agricultural activities. A total of approximately 3000 kg paddy is produced every year and out of that they are using 1400 kg for their self consumption and remaining 1600 kg are sold it to the local middleman at the rate Rs. 15 or Rs. 18 per kg. As per the report given by Agricultural Sub-Division Office, he has received at amount of Rs. 1 lakh under PMKSY to purchase Tractor for doing agricultural activities. This support makes him to produce paddy with lesser cost of production. Though still he is suffering irrigation problem to produce paddy. However, Mr. Jamatia is hopeful that an appropriate intervention of the local administration or concerned office of Agricultural Sub-Division can solve the problem in future.

5.3 Conclusion

The Govt. of India has launched the several agricultural and horticultural schemes throughout the nation to improve the agricultural scenario of the nation as well as to improve the economic condition. But only few of these schemes are successfully implemented especially in Tripura. PM Kishan is most important scheme in Tripura and which is successfully implemented in the state. Pradhan Mantri Krishi Sinchayee Yojana (PMKSY) is another successful scheme implemented in Tripura and through this scheme irrigation has been developed in the state. Rashtriya Krishi Vikas Yojana (RKVY) scheme is also another important scheme through which the agro-infrastructure has been developed in the state. The farmers are benefited from this scheme; however there is a huge gap between allocation of fund and release of fund. There a high potential to develop the agro-infrastructure if the overtime gap between allocation of fund and release of fund reduces. The more release of fund under this scheme would develop the storage facilities and market facilities such as more mandi can be constructed and as a result farmers can be benefited. National Food Security Mission is also another important scheme implemented in Tripura.

From the field survey, it is found that the farmers are received the benefit mainly from three schemes viz; PM Kishan, RKVY and NFSM. It is observed that maximum average benefit of the RKVY scheme is received by the beneficiary households from Matabari block, followed by Killa block, B.C. Nagar block, Taliamura, Kalyanpur etc. whereas the minimum average amount of money is received by the beneficiary households from the Nalchar block. In case of NFSM scheme, the beneficiaries from Kalyanpur block of Khowai district have received the highest amount of benefit which is followed by Teliamura block, Rupaichhari block, B.C. Nagar block, Jirania block etc.

Finally, it is also concluded that agricultural schemes have positive impact on change in agricultural income of the beneficiary households in the study area. The impact is also positive and significant on change in households' income.

Findinds from Focus Group Discussion

In order to investigate the impact apart from the field survey, a focus group discussion has been done at the Gandachara sub-division of Dhalai during October 2022. The survey team has visited Gandachara sub-division and taken the focus group discussion at Purba kalajhari village under the Gandachara sub-division of the Dhalai district.

Figure 5.4: First Focus Group Discussion at the Entry Point of Purba Kalajhari Village, Gandachara

From this focus group discussion, following findings are given below on the basis of interaction with the beneficiary villagers belongs to Purba Kalajhari village and physical investigation of the village and its surrounding area in the Gandachara sub-division. These findings are divided into different sub-headings:

Socio-Economic Conditions

- The majority of the locals are subsistence farmers who are involved in various agricultural and horticultural pursuits, including jhoom cultivation.
- Some of them work as day labours, while others make their living by chopping bamboo and woods from the surrounding forest.
- The majority of the locals have no access to water supply for drinking water; they still rely on unsafe sources of drinking water.
- Most of them have, on average, 2–3 goats, 5–6 poultry and 1–2 pigs
- The majority of the locals have bank accounts, around half of them have gas connection and everyone has electricity connection in their houses.
- The locals mostly rely on informal sources of credit for borrowing.

Infrastructure

- Poor road connectivity, even no ambulance is available for emergency situations. The situation is more severe during the rainy season.
- Transportation vehicles are scarce. On market days, only a handful of vehicles are available. During emergency, the villagers rely on private vehicles, which are very costly. Sometimes they cannot afford it.
- Amount provided by the Govt. for PM Avas Yojna are not sufficient to build a pakka house as the locals have to incur a huge cost to transport raw materials due to poor road connectivity.
- Some of them are reported to involve in horticulture such as the production of bananas and battle nuts; nevertheless, they are unable to bring their products to market due to poor connectivity.

Agriculture

- Farmers are mostly practicing paddy cultivation in compliance with SRI system.

- Farmers have received paddy seeds under NFSM from Agriculture Department.
- Farmers are using their traditional knowledge for doing agricultural activities.
- Farmers are needed to be acknowledged regarding different schemes launched by government for the benefit of farmers.
- Farmers are needed to be facilitated the fertilizers by the government department of agriculture because the farmers in that area are not able to get it.
- Organic farming techniques are used by the farmers in that area because the farmers are unable to purchase required fertilizers for agricultural production.
- The farmers are facing lack of inputs and agro-machineries for doing agricultural activities in village.
- Farmers are needed to be acknowledged regarding new types of technology for doing agricultural activities with the support of scientists from ICAR, Officers from Agriculture Department and other resource persons.
- Farmers are mostly marginal as their land is below one hectare (6 kani) for doing their agricultural activities.
- Farmers are mostly used their own labour force for doing agriculture and the women labours are also involved in agricultural activities.
- Farmers all are not getting the money at amount of Rs. 6000 under PMKISAN yearly.
- Beneficiary farmers in that area are not benefited under the KCC scheme.
- Farmers are mostly used their agricultural output paddy for their self-consumption purpose.
- Beside paddy, farmers are also associated with other vegetables productions but not it at huge quantity because of circumstances relating with environment that can remove partially with the help of proper plan.
- The initiative taken by the govt. to distribute patta land to the villagers for the purposes of living on it and farming is a positive step toward inclusive growth. However, the majority of them reported that they have not received any kind of legal paperwork,

and some of them even do not know which specific piece of land they have been given.

- Majority of them got agricultural seeds from the govt. but they use those seeds for food rather than agriculture.
- The production of principal crops is not adequate to meet their food requirements throughout the year, and they rely on public distribution system in meeting those needs.
- The locals are found not very much aware about the process of rubber plantation. The government provided seedlings of rubber trees to some of them. However, they are unable to start because they do not have sufficient funds for the initial investment.
- Mango, banana and battle nuts are the important horticultural crops in the study area.

Marketing

- Farmers are not able to sell their agricultural productions at market price owing to lack of market facilities with better condition.
- Farmers are basically not going to city for selling their product due to lack of infrastructural facilities like road, vehicle and other facilities.
- Lack of rural mart in village and farmers failed to sell their agricultural products at market price.

Figure 5.5: Second Focus Group Discussion at the Entry Point of Purba Kalajhari Village, Gandachara

CHAPTER 6

Major Findings, Conclusion and Suggestions

This chapter is devided into three sections. Section 6.1 shows the major findings of the study, Section 6.2 shows the conclusion and Section 6.3 shows the suggestions based on the findings and conclusions.

6.1 Major Findings

Chapter-wise major findings of the study are discussed in detail in the following.

From Chapter 4, it is observed that health infrastructure is poor in the TTAADC area as there are only two hospital and one health sub-centre which is not sufficient for the area of 7132.56 square km. However, the educational infrastructure is relatively better than health infrastructure.

From the primary survey, it is found that male percentage of population is much higher than the female percentage of population. The sex ratio among these selected 14 blocks of Tripura is found poor in B.C. Nagar block and Rajnagar block of South Tripura district. It is observed that 64.20 percentages of the sample households are Hindu, followed by 20.60 Christian households and remaining 15.20 percentage households are the believers of Buddhist religion. Buddhist believers are mainly found in Manu and Rupaichhari block.

From the primary survey, it is found that respondents' level of education is very poor. 37.80 per cent of them are illiterate, 28.60 per cent have only primary level of education. After secondary education, the enrolment rate in higher classes is found to be poor. As the survey data indicates, 4.40 per cent of the respondents have completed higher secondary level of education and a mere 0.40 per cent is found to have studied up to graduate level.

It is found that housing condition of the beneficiary farmers is poor. More than 76 per cent households are living in kaccha houses and only 16 per cent live in pucca houses and rest are in semi-pucca houses. Most of the houses have only two rooms and they are living in very small area of house and their average area of bastu is in only around one kani of land. Though most of them are living in kaccha house, but their sanitation condition is improved. It is found that 68.6 per cent households are using semi-pucca sanitation facilities and only 17 per cent households have kaccha sanitation facilities.

It is observed that out of the 500 sample households, 29.2 per cent of the households are living under the above poverty line (APL) category, 35.2 per cent are living under the below poverty line (BPL) category and only 19 per cent are Ad-hoc families. The rest of the households belong to either Antyodaya (15.6 per cent) or Arnapurna (1 per cent) category.

Majority (79.2 per cent) of the sample households having the access to supply water for their drinking and only 11.4 per cent of the households collect their drinking water from tube wells.It is worth mentioning that 5.6 per cent of the total sample households still depend on unsafe sources of drinking water such as pond. 1.6 per cent of the respondents have reported that they rely on other sources like hand pump, use of motor in house etc. for their drinking water.

It is important to note that houses of all households are electrified and 86.4 per cent households have Ujjala gas connection. It is observed that out of the total sample households, 75.2 per cent have reported to possess television, 97.6 per cent possess smart phone and 69.8 per cent of the households have reported to possess bicycle.

Most of the beneficiary farmers are marginal farmers (29 per cent) and they have only up to one kani of land. 26.2 per cent farmers have only 1–2 kani of own land,19 per cent respondents have 2–3 kani of own agricultural land, 12.6 per cent have 3–4 kani own agricultural land and very few (only 0.60 per cent) have own land of above five kani agricultural land.

Most of the farmers have livestock for their both own consumption as well as additional supportive income for the family. It is observed that poultry, piggery, cow, goat, duck and broiler are the common livestock almost in all blocks. Rearing of Buffalo and sheep are very rare in the study area.

It is found that out of the total production of rice, the maximum 45 per cent rice is produced by the small farmers, which is under the production limit of 1000–2000 Kg. The next highest 31 per cent rice is produced by the marginal farmers which are under the lowest production limit of (up to 1000 Kg.) which is followed by the production limit of 2000–3000 Kg. (22 per cent) and only 1.80 per cent production belongs to the production group of above 3000 Kg.

It is found that out of the total sample beneficiaries only small percentage beneficiaries are doing horticultural practices and mainly they are doing rubber plantation, banana and betel nut. It is observed that only 14.40 per cent households have rubber plantation, 1.80 per cent households have betel nut and only 0.40 per cent households are doing banana. It is observed that a sizable amount of production and income is found from the rubber plantation. A total of 47159 kg of rubber production (rubber sheet) comes out annually from 72 beneficiaries and they earned total revenue Rs. 59,62,050.00 per annum. A total of 168 kg betel nut is produced annually by nine sample beneficiaries and they have earned revenue of Rs. 56,400.00 per annum.

It is found that most of the beneficiary farmers earn up to Rs. 10000 income and between Rs. 10000–20000 income groups from their agriculture. 29.4 per cent sample beneficiary farmers earn up to Rs. 10000 income by selling their agricultural product and 29.6 per cent sample beneficiary farmers earn Rs. 10000–20000 income, 17.6 per cent farmers earn Rs. 20000–30000 income and 13.4 per cent farmers earn Rs. 30000–40000 income by selling their agricultural products. Only very negligible percentage farmers earn more than Rs. 50000 income by selling their agricultural products.

It is found that monthly average household expenditure on food is Rs. 3186.55, which is followed by average expenditure on gas (Rs. 784.25), average educational expenditure (Rs. 568.60), average mobile expenditure (Rs. 391.35), average electricity expenditure (Rs. 245.24) etc.

The socio-economic status of B.C. Nagar block is best compare to other selected blocks which is followed Jirania block (0.625) which is followed by Matabari block (0.605), Jampuijala block (0.575), Kalyanpur block (0.504) etc. However, the worst socio-economic condition is found poor in Mandai block (0.330) of West Tripura district. The socio-economic condition is also poor in Rupaichhari block (0.349) which is ranked 13th, Ambassa is ranked 12th and Manu is ranked 11th.

Chapter 4 is focused on the development of agriculture and horticultural production in Tripura. The major findings of this chapter are mentioned in the following.

Out of the total operational holdings in Tripura, 87.95 percent holding belong to 'marginal' farmers, holding less than one hectare of land, and they operate 52.80 percent of the total operated area.

Rice is the principal staple food in Tripura and is cultivated in 54.54 percent of the total cropped area. It is grown in both hilly and valley regions of the state. Jhum or shifting cultivation is practiced in the hill region and settled farming in the plains.

Maize is the second most important food grain grown in Tripura. It is used both for direct consumption and as well as feed ingredient for pig and poultry farming of the state. The area under maize production has increased from 2150 hectares in 2005–06 to 14635 hectares in 2019–20 with a growth rate of 18.68 percent.

The total production of oilseeds in Tripura is found to increase significantly along with increase in area. Groundnut, sesamum and rape/mustard are the major important oilseed crops grown in Tripura. The area under groundnut cultivation is found to increase from 379 hectares in 2005–06 to 2367 hectares in 2019–20. The highest oilseed production has been recorded in 2019–20.

The suitable agro climatic conditions of Tripura also favour the cultivation of different types of non-foodgrain crops like jute, mesta, cotton and sugarcane in the state. It is observed that there is a gradual decline in the area coverage of jute while production is showing an increasing trend.

Cotton is another important fibre crop being cultivated in Tripura. It is found that there is a continuous decline in both area and production of this crop. The decline in area under cotton cultivation seems due to switching over to other remunerative short duration crops like maize, sesamum etc.

Sugarcane is another important agricultural crop grown in Tripura but over the years its production has declined along with decline in area.

The good agro climatic conditions, deep fertile soils, subtropical humid climate with abundance of rainfall offer tremendous scope for the development of horticulture in Tripura. Among the important horticultural crops, pineapple grown in Tripura is widely acclaimed as the best in the country.

There is huge potential of growing fruits and plantation crops like litchi, mango, pineapple, orange, guava, jackfruit, banana, lemon, cashew nut, coconut and areca nut commercially, which may cater to the needs of other North Eastern States and neighbouring country like Bangladesh as well. Recent development in Indo-Bangla relationship has also opened up new avenues for export possibilities.

The trend of production of mango is found to increase along with increase in area. Among the different tropical and sub-tropical fruits, pineapple grown in Tripura is widely known for its excellent quality. Since 2018 pineapple is being exported to many other countries.

Orange is another important fruit which is significant in terms of increase in area and production. Jackfruit is another important fruit grown in Tripura. The agro-climatic conditions, fertile and acidic soil with abundant rainfall favour the cultivation of jackfruits in Tripura. It is one of the major commercial fruit crops in Tripura and has high local demand. However, the area under jackfruit cultivation is found to decline from 8645 hectares in 2005–06 to 5487 hectares in 2019–20 with a negative growth of 2.11 percent.

Cashew nut is a commercially important plantation crop being cultivated in Tripura, which offers considerable scope for enhancing the state economy by generating more income and employment potential. The state has nearly 5,000 registered cashew nut growers, out of which 3,000 are from Rajnagar alone.

There are a large number of indigenous fruits such as mosambi, berry, palm, jamun, bael etc. being cultivated in Tripura.

Tripura occupies a pivotal position in India's rubber map in terms of relative shares in area, production as well as potential area identified for natural rubber cultivation.

Chapter 5 is discussed about the impact of agricultural and horticultural schemes on the tribal livelihoods. The major findings of this chapter are given in the following.

The Govt. of India has launched the several agricultural and horticultural schemes through out the nation to improve the agricultural scenario of the nation as well as to improve the economic condition. But only few of these schemes are successfully implemented especially in Tripura. PM Kishan is most important scheme in Tripura and which is successfully implemented in the state. Pradhan Mantri Krishi Sinchayee Yojana (PMKSY) is another successful scheme implemented in Tripura and through this scheme irrigation has been developed in the state.

Rashtriya Krishi Vikas Yojana (RKVY) scheme is also another important scheme through which the agro-infrastructure has been developed in the state. The farmers are benefited from this scheme; however there is a huge gap between allocation of fund and release of fund. National Food Security Mission is also another important scheme implemented in Tripura.

From the field survey, it is found that the farmers are received the benefit mainly from three schemes viz; PM Kishan, RKVY and NFSM. It is observed that maximum average benefit of the RKVY scheme is received by the beneficiary households from Matabari block, followed by Killa block, B.C. Nagar block, Taliamura, Kalyanpur etc. whereas the minimum average amount of money is received by the beneficiary households from the Nalchar block.

In case of NFSM scheme, the beneficiaries from Kalyanpur block of Khowai district have received the highest amount of benefit which is followed by Teliamura block, Rupaichhari block, B.C. Nagar block, Jirania block etc.

It is observed that average growth of change in agricultural income is highest in Mandai block (97.24 per cent).

It is also observed that the average income from agriculture after getting the benefit is comparatively higher than before getting the benefit.

The minimum growth of change in household's agricultural income in Nalchar block (4.41 per cent) whereas the highest growth change in household's income 365.78 per cent is found in Mandai block of West Tripura district.

It is observed that mean value of households' annual income is highest in the Matabari block (Rs. 221771.30).

The highest annual income is found in one beneficiary household belongs to B.C. Nagar block (Rs. 723900.00) of South Tripura district whereas the minimum annual income is found in one beneficiary household belongs to Nalchar block (Rs. 21600.00) of Sepahijala district.

All beneficiaries are facing the problem inadequate availability and also low quality of seed/planting materials. The beneficiary farmers are also facing the problem of inadequate farm power and poor quality of machinery. Due to MGNREGA activities sometimes labour are not available for the farming activities. 62.40 per cent respondents are facing the problem of inadequate infrastructure during post-harvesting period.

The beneficiary farmers are responded that there is non-existence of cold chain system, storage facility and unavailability of agro-processing industries. All of them are responded that packaging cost is very high due to shortage of packing materials.

All beneficiaries are responded that inadequate water is a major problem to the tribal beneficiaries as mostly they belong to tilla and hilly land.

All beneficiaries are responded that inadequate water is a major problem to the tribal beneficiaries as mostly they belong to tilla and hilly land. All beneficiary farmers are responded that transportation such as poor road connectivity, lack of vehicles and due to the high transport charges are major problems in tribal area.

All beneficiaries are responded that they are not getting adequate financial facilities. Sometimes it is available at very higher rate of interest. There is also lack of commodity pledge loan facilities.

All farmers are facing the problem of inadequate market information even if it is very limited information. They are facing the middleman and also higher commission. There is a problem of minimum support price as well as lack of competitive price. Due to digital illiteracy they are unable to access online trading facilities. They are also admitted that there is also lack of grading and quality testing facilities in their area. Though young family member can operate smart phone but, they don't have an idea about online trading of the product.

Cent per cent respondents are admitted that they don't know about all govt. schemes. They are not aware how to get the benefit through these schemes. They are responded that no capacity building programme has been done in their area.

Cent per cent respondents are admitted that they don't know about eligibility criteria of getting subsidy. In case of agricultural credit, they are facing the problem of getting the subsidy payment after making entire cost components.

Cent per cent beneficiaries are facing the irrigation problem.

6.2 Conclusions

From the findings it is concluded that the tribal farmers in Tripura are mostly marginal farmers and they depend on the agriculture and horticulture for their livelihoods. They are producing mainly foodgrains such as rice, maize, oilseeds etc. Apart from this they are also producing non-foodgrains items such as jute, mesta, cotton etc. Apart from the agricultural products they are also producing horticultural products such as rubber, pineapple, jackfruits, banana, orange and these are also commercially viable.

PM Kishan, RKVY and NFSM are the most successful schemes implemented in Tripura and tribal beneficiaries are getting more benefits from these schemes. There a high potential to develop the agro-infrastructure if the overtime gap between allocation of fund and release of fund reduces. The more release of fund under this scheme would develop the storage facilities and market facilities such as more mandi can be constructed and as a result farmers can be benefited.

Finally, it is also concluded that agricultural schemes have positive impact on change in agricultural income of the beneficiary households in the study area. The impact is also positive and significant on change in households' income. Though there are some problems faced by the beneficiary farmers such as irrigation, agricultural credit, agro-infrastructure and marketing, but that can be removed if the appropriate necessary actions are taken by the concerned department. The necessary suggestions are given in the following in order to improve its betterment; so that sustainable development goals 1 and 2 can be achieved.

6.3 Suggestions

On the basis of findings and conclusions following suggestions can be given in order to improve the sustainable agricultural development and also to improve the socio-economic condition of the beneficiary farmers in the state of Tripura.

- As there is a gap between allocation of fund and release of fund is found in case of RKVY scheme, it is recommended that more fund should be released for that scheme; so that agro-infra-structure can be constructed in Tripura.
- Proper monitoring is needed from the government official how to increase the lease of funds.
- Marketing is a major issue to the beneficiary farmers in Tripura. No Kishan mandi is found in the study area. As a result of this farmers are facing serious marketing issue. In order to solve the problem of the farmers Kishan mandi should be constructed. The fund can be taken from different sponsoring agency like NABARD, APEDA etc.
- There is lack of sufficient of warehouse and storage facilities in Tripura. The small and marginal farmers unable sotre it after post harvesting. As a result they are bound to immediate after post-harvesting at the lower price to the middleman. The problem can be solved with proper initiatives by the concerned department. Some sponsoring agencies like APEDA, NABARD etc. are providing support to construct the warehouse and cold storage.
- Irrigation is a major problem in tribal cultivated land. Water conservation (rain water) is need in the tilla land and that can be done under the MGNREGA. Installation of standalone solar agricultural pums can be constructed in Tripura under PM-KUSUM scheme. This is useful for bothdeep irrigation and water conservation also.
- To improve the marketing issue Kishan Mandi can be constructed at the block level; so that farmer can sale their product to kishan mandi directly not to the middleman.
- Food processing industries can be constructed in the state especially for horticultural product in order to promote youth employment under MSME. So, that partially SDG 8 can be fulfilled.

- Awareness about the govt. schemes is needed to familiarize the several govt. schemes. An official initiative or capacity building programme at the block level is required in this regard and makes them aware what types of benefits are available and how to get these benefits through these schemes. A bi-annual awareness programme should be conducted at the block level to make all farmers aware. To make it more effective and functional, it should be completely apolitical.
- Soil testing for fertility of land, quality of seed testing should be a mandatory task before cultivation of land. In this regard, a necessary step should be taken towards this direction with the help of Indian Council of Agricultural Research, Lembuchhera.

In Table 6.1, problem-wise suggestions are given at a glance.

Table 6.1: Issues Faced by the Farmers and Suggestions at a Glance

Sl.	*Issues Faced*	*Suggestions*
1.	**Input-based Issues** • Inadequate availability of seeds and planting materials. • Problem of getting seed/planting materials in proper time as it is mostly imported from other states. • Low quality of seeds.	• Construction of warehousing and storage facilities within the state can solve this problem to meet the farmer's input demand in proper time. • Seed village project can be a right step towards this direction with the help of NABARD. • Proper monitoring for distribution of seeds and fertilizers is needed in order to get the better outcome. • To test fertility of land and to test quality of seed, a necessary step should be taken towards this direction with the help of Indian Council of Agricultural Research, Lembuchhera.
2.	**Infrastructure Issues** • Irrigation is a major problem especially to the tribal land.	• Water conservation (rain water) is need in the tilla land and that can be done under the MGNREGA. • Installation of standalone solar agri-cultural pums can be constructed in Tripura under PM-KUSUM scheme. This is useful for both deep irrigation and water conservation also.

Sl.	*Issues Faced*	*Suggestions*
3.	**Marketing Issues** • Inadequate facilities of Kishan mandi • Inadequate facilities of agro-based industry • Isuues of packaging and branding	• Construction of warehousing and storage facilities within the state for stroge of agricultural/hortural during post-harvesting period with help of Funding Agency such as APEDA, NABARD. • Kishan Mandi can be constructed at the block level; so that farmer can sale their product to kishan mandi directly. • Food processing industries can be constructed in the state especially for horticultural product in order to promote youth employment under MSME. So, that partially SDG 8 can be fulfilled. • Well packaging and branding can improve the product more market oriented. • Organic certification is needed especially for horticultural products.

A model is given through schematic presentation in order to develop agriculture and horticulture in the state. This model is formulated with my scholars for the betterment of this sector so that farmers' income can be increased. The model is presented in the following.

'Das, Bhowmik and Hoque Development Model' for Agriculture/Horticulture

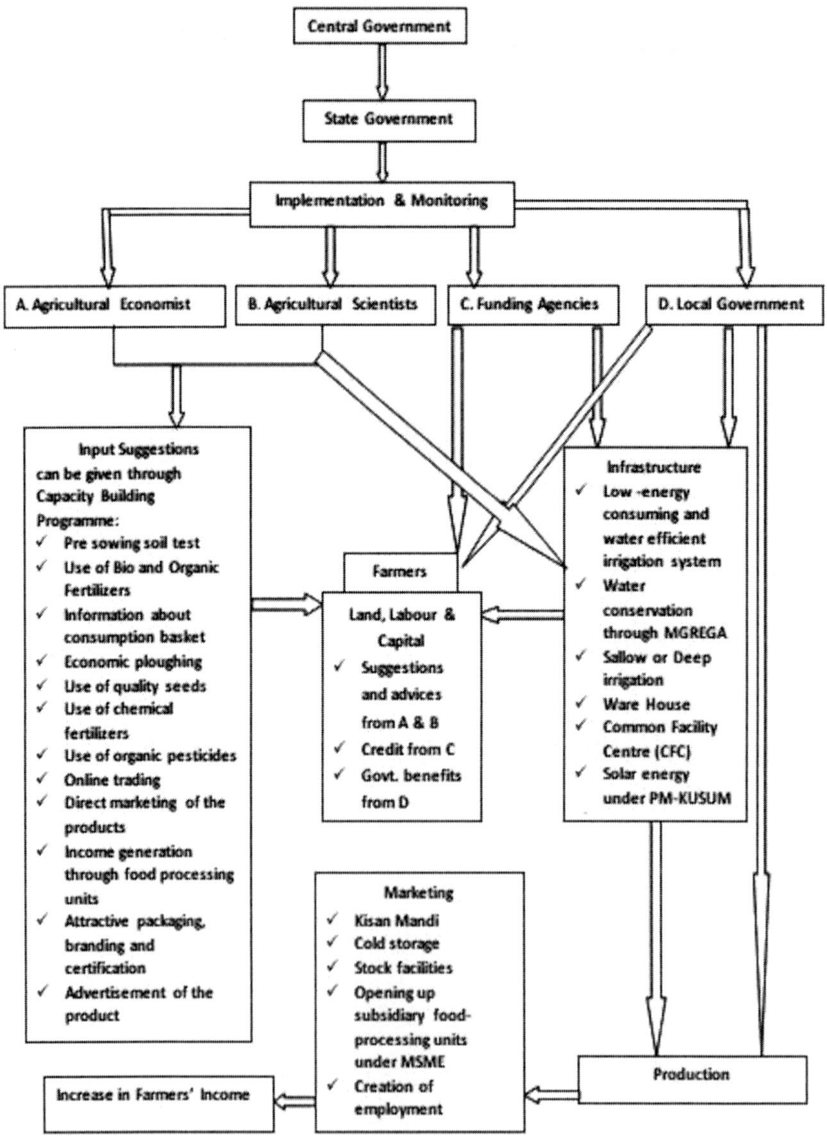

Bibliography

[1] Aditya, K.S., Khan, T. and Kishore, A. (2018). "Adoption of Crop Insurance and Impact: Insights from India", *Agricultural Economics Research Review*, Vol. 31(2), pp. 163.

[2] Agarwal, B. (1998). "Disinherited peasants, disadvantaged workers; a gender perspective on land and livelihood", *Economic and Political Weekly*, Vol. 33(13), pp. A2–A14.

[3] Agrawal, G. (2014). "Impact Assessment of National Food Security Mission (implemented in Madhya Pradesh)", *Atal Bihari Vajpayee Institute of Good Governance and Policy Analysis*, Bhopal.

[4] Amarender, A.A. (2018). "Impact Study of Paramparagath Krishi Vikas Yojana (An organic agriculture scheme of Government of India)", *National Institute of Agricultural Extension Management (MANAGE)*, Hyderabad, pp. 81.

[5] American Psychological Association (APA) (2007). Task Force on Socioeconomic Status. Report of the APA Task Force on Socioeconomic Status, Washington, DC: https://www.apa.org/pi/ses/resources/class/measuring-status

[6] Aurora, G.S. (1964). "Economy of a Tribal Economy", The Economic Weekly, September 26, pp. 1557–1560.
http://www.epw.in/system/files/pdf/1964_16/39/economy_of_a_tribal_village.pdf Accessed on 26.08.2017.

[7] Awotide, B.A. Karimov, A.A. and Diagne, A. (2016). "Agricultural Technology Adoption, Commercialization And Smallholder Rice Farmers' Welfare In Rural Nigeria", *Agricultural and Food Economics, Springer*, Vol. 4, No. 3, pp. 1–24.

[8] Ayaz, S. and Hussain, Z. (2011). "Impact of Institutional Credit on Production Efficiency of Farming Sector—A Case Study of District Faisalabad", *Pakistan Economic and Social Review*, Vol. 49(2), winter, pp. 149–162.

[9] Bansal, A. (2018). "A Study on Employability Skills of MBA Students: Employers and Students Perspective", *Gurukul Business Review (GBR)*, Vol. 14, Spring, pp. 47–51.

[10] Behera, D.K. (2015). "Agricultural Development and Inclusive Growth in India: A Case Study of Gujrat", *International Journal of Food, Agriculture and Veterinary Sciences*, Vol. 5 (1), January–April, pp. 41–52.

[11] Bofah, E.A. and Hannula, M.S. (2017). "Home resources as a measure of socio-economic status in Ghana", *Large-scale Assessments in Education, An IEA-ETS Research Institute Journal,* Vol. 5(1), Springer, https://doi.org/10.1186/s40536-017-0039-5

[12] Bolt Richard (2004). "Accelerating Agriculture and Rural Development for Inclusive Growth: Policy Implications for Developing Asia", ERD Policy Brief No 29, Asian Development Bank, Manila.

[13] Chakravorty, B. and Bedi, A.S. (2017). "Skills Training and Employment Outcomes in Rural Bihar", IZA – Institute of Labor Economics, Discussion Paper Series, IZA DP No. 10902, July, pp. 1–29.

[14] Chatterjee, R. and Deb, A.K. (2017). "Effect of Government Programmes on Entrepreneurship: A Study on NE India with Special Reference to Tripura", *EPRA International Journal of Economic and Business Review,* Volume 5, Issue 8, August, pp. 47–58.

[15] Chattopadhayay, K.S. and Roy, D. (2011). "Impact Study of the National Horticulture Mission Scheme in West Bengal", *Study No. 166,* Agro-Economic Research Centre, Visva-Bharati, Santiniketan.

[16] Chaturvedi, A.M. (2018). "Evaluation of Rashtriya Krishi Vikas Yojana", *Final Report,* AMC Research Group, New Delhi and Directorate of Programme Implementation & Evaluation, Government of Meghalaya.

[17] Chavda, M.D. and Trivedi, B.S. (2015). "Impact of Age on Skills Development in Different Groups of Students", *International Journal of Information and Education Technology,* Vol. 5, No. 1, January, pp. 55–59.

[18] Choudhury, J. and Ghosh, R. (2016). Tribal Development in Tripura: An Assessment of Tribal Sub-Plan, Tribal Research and Cultural Institute, Government of Tripura.

[19] Clements, K.W. and Si, J. (2017). "Engel's Law, Diet Diversity, and the Quality of Food Consumption", *American Journal of Agricultural Economics,* Vol. 100(1), September, pp. 1–22.

[20] Das, S. (2022). "Impact of Globalization to Sustainable Development Goals: A Study of the State Tripura" in "Globalization, Income Distribution and Sustainable Development: A theoretical and empirical investigation" by Ramesh Chandra Das (edited), Emerald Publishing Limited, New Delhi. https://doi.org/10.1108/9781801178709

[21] Das, S. (2021). "Determining Optimum Size of Government Intervention for Sustainable Development of Agricultural Farming in India" in "Optimum Size of Government Intervention Emerging Economies and Their Challenges" by Ramesh Chandra Das (edited), Routledge India, New Delhi, https://doi.org/10.4324/9781003026495

[22] Dev, S.M. and Venkatanarayana, M. (2011). "Youth Employment and Unemployment in India", *Indira Gandhi Institute of Development Research,* Mumbai, April, WP-2011–009, pp. 1–30.

[23] Dung, K.D. and Pattanaik, B. (2013). "Lives and livelihood of Tribals in Naxalite affected Villages: A study in Sundargarh District of Odisha", *Asian Journal of Social Sciences & Humanities,* Vol. 2(4), pp. 94–107.

[24] Gozgor, G. (2019). Effects of The Agricultural Commodity And The Food Price Volatility on Economic Integration: An Empirical Assessment, Empirical Economics, Springer, Vol. 56, pp. 173–202.

[25] Hamsini, H.P. and Rashmi, R. (2019). "A Study on Effectiveness of the Crop Insurance in Karnataka with Special Reference Chikmagalur District", *Indian Journal of Finance and Banking,* Vol. 3(2), pp. 1–4.

[26] Hoda, A. and Terway, P. (2015). "Credit Policy for Agriculture in India—An Evaluation", Working Paper 302, *Indian Council for Research on International Economic Relations (ICRIER).*

[27] Jayakumar, A. and P. Palaniyammal (2016). Socio-economic Status of Scheduled Tribes in Kalrayan Hills, *International Journal of Research Granthaalayah,* Vol. 4, Issue 3, March.

[28] Kalamkar, S.S., Swain, M. and Bhaiya, S. (2015). "Impact Evaluation of Rashtriya Krishi Vikas Yojana (RKVY) in Gujarat", *Agro-Economic Research Centre,* Sardar Patel University, Vallabh Vidyanagar, Gujarat.

[29] Kalyani, K.S., Krishnamurthy, V., Rao, C.C. and Kumari, N.A. (2011). "Role Performance of Tribal Women–A Study in Agency Area of East Godavari District of Andra Pradesh", *Journal of Dairying, Foods and Home Sciences,* Vol. 30(3), pp. 221–224.

[30] Kaur, J. and Dogra, M. (2018). "Skill Development in Punjab: A Critique Study of Initiative, Challenges and Way Forward", *Amity Journal of Entrepreneurship,* Volume 3, Issue 1, pp. 24–34.

[31] Kc. Deepti and Samik Adhikary (2015). "Socio-economic and Gender Analysis of Tribal Populations in India", Working Paper, January, IFMR, Andhra Pradesh.

[32] Kshirsagar, K.G. (2008). "Impact of Organic Farming on Economics of Sugarcane Cultivation in Maharashtra", Gokhale Institute of Politics and Economics, Pune, Maharashtra.

[33] Kumar, B.B. (1998). The Tribal Societies in India, Osons Publications, New Delhi.

[34] Kumar, A., Singh, K.M. and Sinha, S. (2010). "Institutional Credit to Agriculture Sector in India: Status, Performance and Determinants", *Agricultural Economics Research Review,* Vol. 23, July–December, pp. 253–264.

[35] Kumar, N.S. (2009). "Impact Assessment of Agriculture Interventions in Tribal Areas in Madhya Pradesh", *Final Report,* Catalyst Management Services, Bhopal.

[36] Kumar, P. (2013). "Impact Study of the National Horticulture Mission Scheme: A Consolidated Report", Agricultural Development and Rural Transformation Centre, Institute for Social and Economic Change, Bangalore.

[37] Lavanya, A., Raju, G., Suresh, J. and Devi, K.S. (2015). "Impact of RKVY Programme on Income Distribution Pattern of Piggery Beneficiaries", *Indian Journal of Veterinary and Animal Science Research,* Vol. 44(2), March–April, pp. 93–101.

[38] Manjunatha, A.V., Ramappa, K.B., Maruthi, I. and Kumar, P. (2017). Impact Evaluation of National Horticulture Mission (NHM) and Horticulture Mission for North East and Himalayan States (HMNEH), ADRT Centre, Institute for Social and Economic Change, Bengaluru, Karnataka.

[39] MART (2011). "Livelihood Agri Business and Market Studies for North-East Rural Livelihood Project", Final Report Tripura (April 2011), MART, Noida, pp. 1–151.

[40] Ministry of Development of North-Eastern Region, Govt. of India, 2011. "North East Rural Livelihood Project" http://www.mdoner.gov.in/sites/default/filesAccessed on 20.08.2017.

[41] Nag, N., Srivastava, J.P. and Behera, B.S (2015). "Impact of Participatory Seed Production Programme on Knowledge Level of Paddy Seed Producers under Rastriya Krishi Vikas Yojona (RKVY) on Junagarh Block of Kalahandi District (Odisha)", *International Journal of Agricultural Science and Research*, Vol. 5(6), December, pp. 239–246.

[42] Panda, N.K. (2006). Policies Programmes and Strategies for Tribal Development, Kalpaz Publications, Delhi.

[43] Pandey, R. (2009). "Forest resource utilization by tribal community of Jaunsar, Uttarakhand, Indian Forester, Vol. 135(5), pp. 652–662.

[44] Patil, B.O. and Hosamani, S.B. (2018). "Impact of National Horticulture Mission (NHM) Scheme on Horticulture Development in Karnataka", *Journal of Pharmacognosy and Phytochemistry*, Special Issue 4, pp. 389–394.

[45] Patnaik, G. (2014). "Impact Evaluation of National Mission on Micro Irrigation (NMMI)", Global Agri System and Department of Agriculture and Cooperation, Government of India.

[46] Pinder, C. and Wood, D (2013). "Socio-economic Impact of Commercial Agriculture on Rural Poor and other Vulnerable Groups",

Working Document, Department for International Development, Zambia.

[47] Ragasa, C. Babu, S.C. and Ulimwengu, C. (2014). Institutional Reforms and Agricultural Policy Process: Lessons from Democratic Republic of Congo, Agriculture and Food Economics, Springer, Vol. 3, No. 4, pp. 1–21.

[48] Ramesh, G.B., Lokesha, H. and Wali, V.B (2017). "NHM Scheme Impact on Beneficiaries of Horticultural Farmers in Karnataka—An Economic Analysis", *International Journal of Pure and Applied Bioscience*, Vol. 5(6), pp. 990–995.

[49] Reddy, M.G and Kumar, Anil (2010). "Political Economy of Tribal Development: A Case Study of Andhra Pradesh", Working Paper Series No. 85, February, Centre for Economic and Social Studies, Hyderabad. http://www.cess.ac.in/cesshome/wp/wp_85.pdfAccessed on 26.08.2017.

[50] Roy, A., Singh, N.U., Dkhar, D.S., Mohanty, A.K., Singh, S.B. and Tripathi, A.K (2015). "Food Security in North-East Region of India—A State-wise Analysis", *Agricultural Economics Research Review*, Vol. 28, pp. 259–266.

[51] Roy, R. (2014). "Food Consumption Pattern in Rural India in the Reform Period: Trend, Composition and Implication for Nutritional Security", *Journal of Economic and Social Development*, Vol. X (2), December, pp. 1–22, ISSN 0973-886X.

[52] Saheb, M. Shaik Basa and Babu C. Giri (2013). Research Study Report on "Impact of Skill Development Programmes of Jan Shikshan Sansthan's on the Neo-literates in the States of Andhra Pradesh, Tamil Nadu, Karnataka and Kerala" Noble Social and Educational Society, Tirupati, http://planningcommission.nic.in/reports/sereport/ser/ser_impact0609.pdfAccessed on 26.08.2017.

[53] Sahoo L.K. (2011). "Socio-Economic Profile of Tribal Populations in Mayurbhanj and Keonjhar Districts", Orissa Review, May, pp. 63–68.

[54] SenAmartya (1993). "Capability and Well-Being" in "The Quality of Life" by M. Nussbaum and A. Sen (ed.), Oxford Clarendon Press, New York.

[55] Sen, Amartya (2000). "Social Exclusion: Concept, Application and Scrutiny", Working Paper, Social Development Paper No. 1, June, Asian Development Bank, Bangkok.

[56] Sharma Rajeev and Indervir Singh (2010). "Inclusive Growth and Sustainable Development of Agriculture: An Examination of Major Indian States", in "Economic and Environmental Sustainability of the Asian Region", Sucha Singh Gill LS (ed.), Routledge India, New Delhi, pp. 101–123.

[57] Sharma, H.O (2016). "Impact of Pradhan Mantri Krishi Sinchai Yojana (Watershed Development) on Land Use and Cropping Pattern in Madhya Pradesh", *Study No. 116*, Agro-Economic Research Centre, Jawaharlal Nehru Krishi Vishwa Vidyalaya, Jabalpur (M.P.).

[58] Sharma, V.P. (2018). "Tribal forest interfaces and conservation", National Institute of Rural Development, Hyderabad, Unpublished Article, pp. 1–8, accessed from https://nomadit.co.uk/conference/iuaes2014/paper/19286

[59] Shavers, V.L. (2007). Measurement of socio-economic status in health disparities research. Journal of the National Medical Association, 99, pp. 1013–1023.

[60] Simtowe, F. Asfaw, S. and Abate, T. (2016), Determinants of Agricultural Technology Adaptation Under Partial Population Awareness: The Case of Pigeonpea In Malawi, Agriculture and Food Economics, Springer, Vol. 4, No. 7, pp. 1–21.

[61] Sindhi Swaleha (2012). "Prospects and Challenges in Empowerment of Tribal Women", *Journal of Humanities and Social Sciences,* Vol. 6, Issue 1, pp. 46–54.

[62] Singh, I.P. and Grover, D.K. (2011). "Economic Viability of Organic Farming: An Empirical Experience of Wheat Cultivation in Punjab", *Agricultural Economics Research Review*, Vol. 24, July–December, pp. 275–281.

[63] Sivagnanam, K.V. (2012). "Impact Study of the National Horticulture Mission (NHM) Scheme in Kerala", *Research Study No: 150*, Agro-Economic Research Centre, University of Madras, Chennai.

[64] Thangjam, D., Chouhan, J.K., Singh, R.J., Singh, R. and Hemochandra, L. (2020). "Performance of Agricultural Livelihood Security of the Farmers: Tribal Sub Plan Executed by Central Agriculture University, Imphal in Meghalaya", *International Research Journal of Extension Education*, Vol. 20(2 & 3), pp. 114–118.

[65] Tuteja, U. (2011). "Impact of the National Horticulture Mission (NHM) Scheme in Haryana" *Research Study No. 2011/03*, Agricultural Economics Research Centre, University of Delhi.

[66] Vamsi, K., Prasad, R., Suresh, J., Ekambaram, B. and Ravi, A. (2019). "Impact of RKVY project on income distribution pattern of beneficiaries of sheep rearers in Chittoor district of Andhra Pradesh", *The Pharma Innovation Journal*, Vol. 8(7), pp. 42–46.

Appendix

Socio-Economic Impact Study with Concurrent Evaluation on Agriculture/ Horticulture based Schemes

Section-I: General Information

Beneficiary Name:

Schedule No: Date:

Q1.1) *Personal Profile:*

Head of Family:		Household No.:	
Village:		Block:	
Sub-division:		District:	
Education:		Religion:	
Ration card:	APL/BPL/ Arnapurna/ Ad-Hoc./ Antyodaya	Community:	
Language:		Married:	
E-mail:		Mobile No:	

Q1.2) *Family Profile:*

Sl. No.	*Name*	*Sex*	*Age*	*Relation*	*Qualification*	*Main occupation (Mention hours per day in parenthesis)*	*Secondary occupation (Mention hours per day in parenthesis)*	*Total Income (Monthly)*
1.								
2.								
3.								
4.								
5.								
6.								
7.								

Qualification = Illiterate-1, Primary = 2, Middle = 3, Matriculation/Secondary = 4, Higher Secondary = 5, Degree/Diploma = 6, Above Degree = 7. Main occupation = Agriculture & allied activities = 1, Service (Salary and Pension) = 2, Self-business = 3, Unemployed = 4, others __________) = 5

SECTION-II: Social Information

Q2.1) *Housing Type:*
[Tick √]

Kaccha	Pucca	Semi pucca	Tong ghar/Cottage	Others

Q2.2) *Household's Housing Details:*

Housing Type[a]		Electrification[b]	
Numbers of rooms		Gas Connection[c]	
Area of the house (in sq. ft.)		Sanitation type[d]	
Area of the Bastu (in Kani)		Drinking Water[e]	
Area of the pond (in Kani)		Purification of Water[f]	

Note: a: Kaccha-1, Pucca-2, Semi Pucca (tin wall)-3, Semi Pucca (tin roof)-4, Other-5. b: Electricity = E, Solar = S, Generator = G, Kerosene = K, Inverter = I, Others = O c: Ujjawala gas connection - 1, Lan connection-2, General coonection-3, Bio Gas-4. d: Kaccha-1, Pucca-2, Semi Pucca (tin wall)-3, Semi Pucca (tin roof)-4, Other-5. e: Tube well-1, Water supply-2, Bore wells-3, Tank-4, Pond-5, Other-5. f: General Filter-1, Electric Filter-2, Boiled water, None of these-3, Don't filter-4

Q2.3) *Household Assets:*

Category	*Number*	*Price (Rs.)*	*Category*	*Number*	*Price (Rs.)*
T.V			Sound system		
Laptop			Inverter/Battery		
Computer			Smart mobile		
Refrigerator			Four wheeler		
Air Conditioner			Three wheeler		
Air Cooler			Motor bike		
Washing Machine			Bicycle		

Q2.4) *Distance of Drinking water source (in meter) from house:*

....

Q2.5) *Health Problems:*

Member (Sl.)	*Any Diseases Illness, Injury in 6 Months?*	*No. of Days Suffer*	*Treatment in**	*Cost of Treatment*			
				Doctor's Fee	*Medicine*	*Test*	*Others (if any)*

*Treatment in = 1-Private Hospital, 2-Govt. Hospital

SECTION-III: Economic Information

Q 3.1) *Live Stock and Income Details:*

Category	*Broiler*	*Poultry*	*Duck*	*Piggery*	*Cow*	*Buffalo*	*Goat*	*Sheep*	*Others*
Number									
Value Rs.									

Q 3.2) *Live Stock/Other Resource Monthly Production, Sales Details:*

Cat.[A]	*Monthly Produce (in Kg.)*	*Own Consumption (in Kg.)*	*Monthly Sales (in Kg.)*	*Sales type*[B]	*Price/Kg.*	*Transport Cost*	*Net Income*

A = 1-Broiler, 2-Poultry, 3-Duck, 4-Pig, 5-Cow, 6-Buffalo, 7-Goat, 8-Sheep, 9-Others[B] [Sales Type = Retail-1, Whole sale-2]

Q3.3) *Details Cost of Production for Live Stock Management:*

Farm[A]	*Farm 1):*			*Farm 2:*		
Inputs	*Physical Units*	*Required Expenditure*		*Physical Units*	*Required Expenditure*	
		Own	*From other*		*Own*	*From other*
Breed						
Feed						
Medicine						
Manpower (Self + Hired)						
Machinery[B]						
Land						
Farming House						
Transport						
Others..........						

A = 1-Broiler, 2-Poultry, 3-Duck, 4-Pig, 5-Cow, 6-Buffalo, 7-Goat, 8-Sheep, 9-Others B = (1-Pump Machine, 2-Fan, 3- Water Sprayer, 4-light, 5-Others ______)

Q3.4) *Landed Property Details (in kani) and Production:*

Land Category	*Area of Cultivated land (plain)*			*Area of Cultivated tilla land*		
	Own	*Lease in*	*lease out*	*Own*	*Lease in*	*lease out*
Land Size (in kani)						
Physical units (kg.)						
Price/Value (Rs.)						

Q3.5) *Agricultural Annual Production, Sales Details:*

Cat.[A]	*Cultivated Area (Kani)*	*Production (Kg.)*	*Own Consumption (in Kg.)*	*Sales (in Kg.)*	*Sales type*[B]	*Price/Kg.*	*Transport Cost*	*Net Income*

A = 1-Paddy, 2-pumkin, 3- Corn, 4-Potato, 5-Chilli, 6-Bringal, 7-Tomato, 8-Cucumber, 9-Bottle gourd, 10-Ginger, 11-Garlic, 12-Onion, 13-Leafy vegetables, 14-Guri Kachu, 15-Winter Melon, 16-Rubber, 17-Others[B] [Sales Type = Retail-1, Whole sale-2]

Q3.6) *Agricultural Production Details (in Physical Unit):*

Cat[A]	*Period*	*Amount (kg.)*	*Machinery*[B]	*Labour*		*Seed (kg.)*	*Fertilizer (kg.)*	*Pesticides*	*Type of Irrigation*[C]
				Self	*Hired*				
	Summer (April–October)								
	Winter (Oct./Nov.-Mar/April)								

A = 1-Paddy, 2-pumkin, 3-Corn, 4-Potato, 5-Chilli, 6-Bringal, 7-Tomato, 8-Cucumber, 9-Bottle gourd, 10-Ginger, 11-Garlic, 12-Onion, 13-Leafy vegetables, 14-Guri Kachu, 15-Winter Melon, 16-Rubber, 17-Others[B] 1 = Tractor, 2 = Power Tiller 3 = Water Sprayer, 4 = Others ________)[C] Rain -1, Pond – 2, [River] – 3, Canal - 4, Shallow – 5, Deep well – 6,

Q3.7) *Agriculture Production Details (Monetary Unit):*

Cat [A]	*Period*	*Amount (Rs.)*	*Machinery*	*Labour*		*Seed (বীজ)*	*Fertilizer (সার)*	*Pesticides কীটনাশক*	*Irrigation (সেচ)*
				Self	*Hired*				
	Summer (April–October)								
	Winter (Oct./Nov.- Mar/April)								

(A = 1-Paddy, 2-pumkin, 3- Corn, 4-Potato, 5-Chilli, 6-Bringal, 7-Tomato, 8-Cucumber, 9-Bottle gourd, 10-Ginger, 11-Garlic, 12-Onion, 13-Leafy vegetables, 14-Guri Kachu, 15- Winter Melon, 16-Rubber, 17-Others

Q 3.8) *Subsidy in Agriculture:*

Seed	*Fertilizer*	*Irrigation*	*Machinery*	*Monetary (in Rs)*	*Other*

Q3.9) *Annual Horticultural/Floricultural Production, Sales Details:*

Cat.[A]	*Cultivated Area (Kani)*	*Production (Kg.)*	*Own Consumption (Kg)*	*Sales (in Kg.)*	*Sales type*[B]	*Price/Kg.*	*Transport Cost*	*Net Income*

(A: 1-Banana, 2-BetelNut, 3-Coconut, 4-Green Coconut, 5-Guava, 6-Jackfruit, 7-Lemon, 8-Lichi, 9-Mango, 10-Mosambi, 11-Mushroom, 12-Pineapple, 13-Papaya, 14-Sugar cane, 15-Rajnigandha, 16- Chrysanthemum, 17-Dahlia, 18-Gerbera, 19-Lilium, 20-Marigold, 21-Orchid, 22-Petunia, 23- Rose, 24-Other B [Sale Type = Retail-1, Whole sale-2]

Q 3.10) *Horticultural/Floricultural Production Details (in Physical Unit):*

Cat[A].	*Period*	*Amount (kg.)*	*Machinery*[B]	*Labour*		*Seed (kg.)*	*Fertilizer (kg.)*	*Pesticides*	*Types of Irrigation*[C]
				Self	*Hired*				
	Summer (April–October)								
	Winter (Oct./Nov.- Mar/April)								

[A] 1-Banana, 2-Betel Nut, 3-Coconut, 4-Green Coconut, 5-Guava, 6-Jackfruit, 7-Lemon, 8-Lichi, 9-Mango, 10-Mosambi, 11-Mushroom, 12-Pineapple, 13-Papaya, 14-Sugar cane, 15-Rajnigandha, 16- Chrysanthemum, 17-Dahlia, 18-Gerbera, 19-Lilium, 20- Marigold, 21-Orchid, 22-Petunia, 23- Rose, 24-Other.

[B] 1 = Tractor, 2 = Power Tiller 3 = Water Sprayer, 4 = Others.

[C] Rain -1, Pond – 2, River – 3, Canal – 4, Shallow – 5, Deep well – 6,

Q 3.11) *Horticultural/Floricultural Production Details:*

Cat[A]	*Period*	*Amount (Rs.)*	*Machinery*	*Labour*		*Seed*	*Fertilizer*	*Pesticides*	*Irrigation*
				Self	*Hired*				
	Summer (April–October)								
	WinterOct./Nov- Mar/April)								

A: 1-Banana, 2-Betel Nut, 3-Coconut, 4-Green Coconut, 5-Guava, 6-Jackfruit, 7-Lemon, 8-Lichi, 9-Mango, 10-Mosambi, 11-Mushroom, 12-Pineapple, 13-Papaya, 14-Sugar cane, 15-Rajnigandha, 16- Chrysanthemum, 17-Dahlia, 18-Gerbera, 19-Lilium, 20-Marigold, 21-Orchid, 22-Petunia, 23-Rose, 24-Other.

Q 3.12) *Subsidy in Horticultural/Floricultural Production:*

Plant	*Fertilizer*	*Medicine*	*Machinery*	*Monetary (in Rs)*	*Other*

Q 3.13) ***Are your family engaged with Jhum cultivation? If yes move next If yes.....***

Code[A]	*Cultivated Area (Kani)*	*Annual Production K.G*	*Own consumption (K.G)*	*Monthly Sale K.G*	*Price/Kg.*	*Sale Type[B]*	*Transport cost*	*Net income*

(A: 1-Paddy, 2-pumkin, 3-Corn, 4-Potato, 5-Chilli, 6-Bringal, 7-Tomato, 8-Cucumber, 9-Bottle gourd, 10-Ginger, 11-Garlic, 12-Onion, 13-Leafy vegetables, 14-Guri Kachu, 15-Winter Melon, 16-Others B [Sales Type = Retail-1, Whole sale-2]

Q 3.14) *Jhum Production Details (in Physical Unit):*

Cat[A]	*Period*	*Amount (kg.)*	*Machinery*[B]	*Labour*		*Seed (kg.)*	*Fertilizer (kg.)*	*Pesticides*	*Type of Irrigation*[C]
				Self	*Hired*				
	Summer April–October)								
	Winter(Oct./Nov.- Mar/April)								

A:1-Paddy, 2-pumkin, 3-Corn, 4-Potato, 5-Chilli, 6-Bringal, 7-Tomato, 8-Cucumber, 9-Bottle gourd, 10-Ginger, 11-Garlic, 12-Onion, 13-Leafy vegetables, 14-Guri Kachu, 15-Winter Melon, 16- Others B:1 = Tractor, 2 = Power Tiller 3 = Water Sprayer, 4 = Others ______)

C: Rain -1, Pond – 2, River – 3, Canal - 4, Shallow – 5, Deep well – 6,

Q3.15) *Jhum Production Details (Monetary Unit):*

Cat [A]	*Period*	*Amount (Rs.)*	*Machinery*	*Labour*		*Seed*	*Fertilizer*	*Pesticides*	*Irrigation*
				Self	*Hired*				
	Summer (April–October)								
	Winter (Oct./Nov.- Mar/April)								

(A = 1-Paddy, 2-pumkin 3- Corn, 4-Potato, 5-Chilli, 6-Bringal, 7-Tomato, 8-Cucumber, 9-Bottle gourd, 10-Ginger, 11-Garlic, 12-Onion, 13-Leafy vegetables, 14-Guri Kachu, 15- Winter Melon, 16-Others

Q3.16) *Subsidy in Jhum Cultivation:*

Seed	*Fertilizer*	*Irrigation*	*Machinery*	*Monetary (in Rs)*	*Other*

Q3.17) *Monthly Family Expenditure Details:*

Type of Exp.	*Physical unit*	*Monetary unit(Rs.)*	*Type of Exp.*	*Physical unit*	*Monetary unit(Rs.)*
Education			Cosmetics		
Health			Mobile bill		
Electrification (in meter)			Cable/DTH		
Gas			News paper		
Kerosene			Transport		
Fuel for bike/car			Miscellaneous		

Q3.18) *Weekly Food Consumption/Expenditure:*

Item	*Physical Unit*	*Price*	*Item*	*Physical Unit*	*Price*	*Item*	*Physical Unit*	*Price*
Rice			Milk			Fish		
Wheat			Biscuit			Egg		
Muri/Chira			Health drink			Meat		
Pulses			Sugar			Dry Fish		
Cooking Oil			Tea Leaf			Fruits		
Spices			Vegetables			Miscellaneous		

Q 3.19) *Monthly Expenditure for any other habits:*

Category	*Alcohol*	*Tobacco*	*Pan*	*Bidi*	*Gutkha*	*Khaini*
Quantity						
Expenditure						

Q 3.20) *Bank Account Details:*

Available Facilities	*SBI*	*UBI*	*UCO*	*Bandhan*	*Grameen*	*Others*
Savings Account						
Current Account						
Jandhan Account						
ATM Card						
Fixed deposit						
Loan taken from						
Govt. Money deposited						
Pradhan Mantri Bima Yojona						
Salary Account						
Pension Account						

SECTION -IV: Impact of Agriculture/Horticulture based Schemes

Q4.1) *Awareness and Benefits from the Different Agriculture/Horticulture based Schemes*

Schemes	*Awareness [Tick √]*	*Period of Benefits*	*Benefits (in Physical unit)*	*Benefits (in Monetary unit)*
National Agriculture Market (eNAM)				
National Mission for Sustainable Agriculture (NMSA)				
Pradhan Mantri Krishi Sinchai Yojana (PMKSY)				
Paramparagat Krishi Vikas Yojana (PKVY)				
Pradhan Mantri Fasal Bima Yojana (PMFBY)				
Gramin Bhandaran Yojna				
Commercial Horticulture Scheme under NHB				
Cold Storage Scheme under NHB				
Technology Development Transfer Scheme under NHB				

Market Information Service Scheme for Horticulture Crops under NHB				
Horticulture Promotion Service under NHB				
Recognition of Horticulture Nurseries under NHB				
Cultivation of Medical Plants under AYUSH Mission				
Coconut Development Board Schemes for SC/ST and women				
Rashtriya Krishi Vikas Yojona (RKVY)				
Horticulture Mission for North East & Himalayan States (HMNEH)				
National Horticulture Mission (NHM)				
State Horticulture Mission (SHM)				
National Agriculture Insurance Scheme				

Q4.2) *Cropping pattern of Agriculture/Horticulture crops before and after availing benefits*

Crops/Plants	*Area (in Kani)*		*Production (in Kg.)*		*Prevailing average market price*	*Annual Net Income (Rs.)*	
	Before Intervention	*After Intervention*	*Before Intervention*	*After Intervention*		*Before Intervention*	*After Intervention*

Q4.4) *Components Covered under Scheme* ....

Area coverage/expansion -

Please specify the month .... *Year* ....

Crops/ Plants	*Investment*		*Rate of Interest*	*Borrowing Institutions if any*	*Final Survival rate (%)*	*Reasons for low survival*[A]	*Source of planting material*[B]	*Cost of Planting material*	*Subsidy Received if any*	*Quality of planting material supplied*[C]	*Farmer's View on production*[D]
	Own	*Borrowed*									

[A] Unsuitable soil = 1; Bad quality of plants/seeds = 2; Lack of water/failure of rains = 3; Untimely supply of inputs = 4; Pestsand diseases = 5; lack of monitoring and supervision = 6; Others (Specify)..............7.

[B] Private Nursery = 1; Public Nursery = 2; NGO nursery = 3; Hort. Dept. = 4; Imported material = 5; Others (Specify) = ...5.

[C] Very good = 1; Good = 2; Average = 3; Below average = 4.

[D] High = 1; Moderate = 2; Average = 3; Low = 4; No change = 5

4.4.1. Are you satisfied with this component (Yes = **1**; No = **2**)	If **Yes**, how do you rate the programme? (Very good = **1**; Good = **2**; Satisfactory = **3**; Average = **4**; Not satisfied = **5**)
4.4.2. Have you tested your soil? (Yes = **1**; No = **2**)	If **Yes**, are you practicing the recommendation? (Fully = **1**; Partially = **2**; Not at all = **3**)
4.4.3. Do you think that any other crops to be included under this component? (Yes = **1**; No = **2**)	If Yes, Please, specify the crop/s (eg. Crop 1, crop2):

Q4.5) *Rejuvenation of Horticulture: Please specify the month...................... Year............................*

Crop	*Rejuvenated Area (Kani)*	*No. of plants/Kani*	*Final Survival rate (%) A*	*Reasons for low survival B*	*Source of planting material C*	*Quality of planting material supplied D*	*Total Production MT)*	*Unit E*	*Net Income (Rs.)*	*Income increased due to this F*

[A] 100% = **1**; 75 to 90% = **2**; 50 to 75% = **3**; less than 50% = **4**.

[B] Unsuitable soil = **1**; Bad quality of plants/seeds = **2**; Lack of water/failure of rains = **3**; Untimely supply of inputs = **4**; Pests and diseases = **5**; lack of monitoring and supervision = **6**.

[C] Private Nursery = **1**; Public Nursery = **2**; NGO nursery = **3**; Hort. Dept. = **4**; Imported material = **5**; Others (Specify)............ = **5**.

[D] Very good = **1**; Good = **2**; Average = **3**; Below average = **4**.

[E] Numbers = **1**; Kgs = **2**; Quintals = **3**; Tons = **4**; Others (Specify) = **5**.

[F] Yes = **1**; No = **2**; No change = **3**.

4.5.1. What are the reasons for plant loss in old (Senile) plantations? (Poor Management = **1**; Water Problem = **2**; Pesticides = **3**; Natural calamities = **4**; Change in variety = **5**; Increase yield = **6**; To remove old plantation = **7**; Quality of fruit was not good = **8**; Disease management = **9**; Shifting to HD/UHD = **10**; Others (Specify) .... = **11**)	
4.5.2. Who has carried out the rejuvenation/Replacement of Senile Plantations? (Individual Farmers = **1**; Farmer organizations = **2**; Self Help Groups = **3**; NGOs = **4**; Grower Organizations = **5**; Commodity organizations = **6**; Others (Specify)......................... = **7**)	

4.5.3. Have you tested your soil? (Yes = **1**; No = **2**)	If **Yes**, are you practicing the recommendation? (Fully = **1**; Partially = **2**; Not at all = **3**)	

Q4.6) *Nurseries – Please specify the month .... Year ....*

Crops/ Plants	*Investment*		*Rate of Interest*	*Borrowing Institutions if any*	*Final Survival rate (%)*	*Reasons for low survival*[A]	*Source of planting material*[B]	*Cost of Planting material*	*Subsidy Received if any*	*Quality of planting material supplied C*	*Farmer's View on production*[D]
	Own	*Borrowed*									

[A] Unsuitable soil = **1**; Bad quality of plants/seeds = **2**; Lack of water/failure of rains = **3**; Untimely supply of inputs = **4**; Pests and diseases = **5**; lack of monitoring and supervision = **6**; Others (Specify).............7.

[B] Private Nursery = **1**; Public Nursery = **2**; NGO nursery = **3**; Hort. Dept. = **4**; Imported material = **5**; Others (Specify) = ...5.

[C] Very good = **1**; Good = **2**; Average = **3**; Below average = **4**.

[D] High = **1**; Moderate = **2**; Average = **3**; Low = **4**; No change = **5**

4.6.1 Details of use of nursery material. (Own use = 1; Farmers = 2; Govt. department = 3; Self Help groups = 4; Producer organizations = 5; Private = 6; Others (Specify) .... = 7)			
4.6.2. Have you tested your soil? (Yes = 1; No = 2)		If **Yes,** are you practicing the recommendation? (Fully = 1; Partially = 2; Not at all = 3)	

Q4.7) *Water Resources: Details of water resources intervention– Please specify the month................Year.............*

Type of water resource [A]	*Dimension (Length * breath * depth = cubic mts)*	*Total Investment (Rs.)*			*Subsidy (Rs.)*	*Unit (Liters = 1; Cu.mts = 2)*	*Actual irrigated Area (Ha)*	*Type of water lifting device Used* [C]	*Source of water for storage* [D]	*Usefulness of the interventionE*	*No. of farmers benefitted in the case of community tanks*
			Borrowed								
		Own investment	*Source codeB*	*Borrowed Amount.*							

[A] Community Tanks = 1; Community Tanks Renovated = 2; Individual Farm Ponds = 3; Individual Reservoirs/pond with RCC lining = 4; Individual Reservoirs/pond with plastic lining = 5; Solar Pump sets = 6; Bore well Recharge Structures = 7; Digging of Tubewells/Borewells = 8; Infiltration Ponds = 9; Storage tanks = 10.

[B] Institutional = 1; Non-institutional = 2.

[C] Diesel engine = 1; Electrical pump = 2; Sluice = 3; Others (Specify) = 4.

[D] Rain = 1; Bore well = 2; Rain + Bore well = 3; Others (Specify) = 4.

[E] Very useful = 1; Partially useful = 2; Structure damaged = 3.

Q 4.8) ***Market Infrastructure - Please specify the month.............................. year ....***

Intervention A	*Beneficiary type B*	*Own investment*	*Borrowed investment*		*Subsidy (Rs.)*	*Commodity Handled*	*Unit*[C]	*Volume Handled*	*Total Turnover*	*Net Income (Rs.)*
			Amount	*Source*						

[A] Terminal market = **1**; Whole sale markets = **2**; Rural Markets/ Apnimandies/Direct markets = **3**; Retail Markets/outlets = **4**; Static/Mobile Vending cart/platform with cool chamber = **5**; Others (Specify) = 6

[B] Farmer = **1**; Trader = **2**; APMC = **3**; Others (Specify) = **4**

[C] Institutional = **1**; Non-institutional = **2**.

[D] Tons = **1**; Kgs = **2**; Quintal = **3**.

Q 4.9) *Horticulture Mechanization- Please specify the month............................... year .... wage rate.........*

Intervention A	*Manual/Power[B]*	*Investment on Machine*			*Whether got the machineries or cash equivalent[C]*	*If cash, was it transferred directly to bank account?[D]*	*Current status of equipment[E]*	*Performance of the equipment[F]*	*No. of Hours used monthly*	
		Own amount	*Borrowed amount*	*Source*					*Own use*	*Hired*

[A] Tractor = **1**; Power Tiller = **2**; Tree pruners = **3**; Fruit harvesters = **4**; Fruit graders = **5**; Track trolley = **6**; Nursery media filling = 7; Pruning/budding/grafting tools = **8**; Plant protection equipment = 9; Others(Specify).......... = **10**.

[B] Power operated = 1; Manual operated = 2

[C&D] Yes = 1; No = 2

[E&F] Good = 1; Satisfactory = 2; Poor = 3

Q 4.10) *Sources of Annual Net Income*

Sl.	*Particulars*	*Annual Net Income (Rs.)*	
		Before Intervention	*After Intervention*
1.	Agriculture		
2.	Horticultural		
3.	Livestock		
4.	Salary/Pension		
5.	Self-Business		
6.	Agricultural Wages		
7.	Others (specify) …………..		

Q 4.11) *What are the Perceptions?*

Perceptions	*Response (Y/N)*	*Perceptions*	*Response (Y/N)*
Availability of Quality seeds and planting material		Increase in Employment	
Increase in Area		Capacity Building Improved	
Increase Income		Marketing Facilities improved	

Q 4.12) *Constraints faced by the Beneficiaries:*

1.	Seeds/Planting Materials	Yes = 1 No = 2	7.	Market	Yes = 1 No = 2
	Inadequate availability of planting materials			Inadequate market information	
	Low quality of planting material			Limited market Information	
2.	Farm Power			Higher commission charges	
	Inadequate availability of farm power			Middlemen (brokers/village merchants) Problem	

	Poor quality of implements/machinery available in the market	
	Shortage of labour for farming operations	
3.	Post-Harvest Infrastructure	
	Inadequate post-harvest facilities	
	Cold chain system is virtually non- existent	
	Absence of agro-processing industry	
	Shortage of packing Material	
	High prices of packing Material	
	Inadequate modern packing material	
	Inadequate storage facility	
	Lack of pre-cooling facility	
4.	Climatic Constraints	
	Floods	
	High Rainfall	
	Persistent Drought	
	Inadequate water for area expansion	
5.	Transport	

	Higher marketing costs	
	Delay in Payment	
	Do not consider farmer consent while selling of produce	
	Quote lower price than actual price	
	Lack of MSP	
	Lack of competitive price	
	Lack of transparency in transactions	
	Lack of storage facility	
	Lack of online trading facility	
	Lack of grading and quality testing facility	
8.	Govt. Schemes	
	Information about programme details are not easily available	
9.	Capacity Building	
	Capacity building/ technical advice was not provided	
10.	Subsidy	
	Eligibility or criteria for availing the subsidy not known	
	Procedure for the subsidy very tedious	

	Poor rural road connectivity			Number of documents required for availing subsidy are too many	
	Lack of transport vehicles			Subsidy paid after making entire cost of the benefit/ component	
	High transport charges			Considerable time lag between the purchase and receiving the subsidy amount	
	Lack of refrigerated vans			Difficulty faced while availing subsidy at level- at which level	
6.	Banks/Credit linkage		11.	Any other specify	
	Relatively high interest rate for loans			Irrigation and others integrated inputs	
	Inadequate financial facility				
	Lack of commodity pledge loan facility				

Q4.13) *Do you have own business? Yes/No*

Q4.14) *If yes: Name of Business Firm:*

Name of the Product:

Category	*Own Sources*	*Other Sources*
Landed Property (in area)		
Landed Property (in monetary units)		
Capital Invested		
Labour Engaged (Monthly in physical units)		
Labour Engaged (Monthly in monetary units)		
Raw materials required (Monthly in physical units)		
Raw materials required (Monthly in monetary units)		
Monthly Cost for Production (in monetary units)		
Required Machinery (In physical units)		
Required Machinery (In monetary units)		

Q 4.15) *Monthly Cost for Business:*

Item	*Expenditure*	*Item*	*Expenditure*
Rent of Land/house		Interest Payment	
Labour		Electrification	
Machinery		Raw Materials	
EMI Payment of Loan		Miscellaneous	

Q 4.16) *Impact of Benefit in Business:*

Category	*Before*	*After*
Capital Invested (in Rs.)		
Getting Loan (in Rs.)		
Production (in Physical unit)		
Production (in Monetary unit)		
Cost of Production		
Profit (without GST)		
Profit (After GST Payment)		

Q 4.17) *Performance of Business during last Five years:*

Year	*Investment*	*Production (in physical unit)*	*Sales (in Rs.)*	*Profit (in Rs.)*
2014				
2015				
2016				
2017				
2018				

Q 4.18) *Have you taken any loan? Yes/No If yes*

Sl.	*Name of the Source*	*Amount*	*Rate of Interest*	*Time*	*Purpose*	*Conditions for getting Loan*

Q 4.19) *Have you faced problem of Demonetization?* 1-Yes 2-No

Q 4.20) *If yes, what kind of problems have you faced?* 1-Yes 2-No

Q 4.21) *Have you faced problem of GST?* 1-Yes 2-No

Q 4.22) *If yes, what kind of problems have you faced?*

Date:

Place:

Investigator Name & Signature:

